COACHING

Cathy,

Thank you so much for your contribution to this book. Your reputation truly enriched this book's ability to get peoples interest, but more importantly, your article's rich, nuanced, content is outstanding. You really made me think a lot, and I'm very grateful. I can't wait to meet you.

Thanks,
Jim

COACHING
APPROACHES & PERSPECTIVES

JAKE CORNETT • JANE ELLISON • CAROLEE HAYES

JOELLEN KILLION • JANE A. G. KISE • JIM KNIGHT

WENDY M. REINKE • KARLA REISS • RANDY SPRICK

CATHY A. TOLL • LUCY WEST

JIM KNIGHT
EDITOR

CORWIN
PRESS
A SAGE Company

For information:

Corwin Press
A SAGE Company
2455 Teller Road
Thousand Oaks, California 91320
www.corwinpress.com

SAGE Ltd.
1 Oliver's Yard
55 City Road
London EC1Y 1SP
United Kingdom

SAGE India Pvt. Ltd.
B 1/I 1 Mohan Cooperative
    Industrial Area
Mathura Road, New Delhi 110 044
India

SAGE Asia-Pacific Pte. Ltd.
33 Pekin Street #02-01
Far East Square
Singapore 048763

Printed in the United States of America

Library of Congress Cataloging-in-Publication Data

Coaching: Approaches and perspectives/edited by Jim Knight.
    p. cm.
Includes bibliographical references and index.
ISBN 978-1-4129-6924-6 (cloth)
ISBN 978-1-4129-6925-3 (pbk.)
    1. Mentoring in education. 2. Teachers—Inservice training. 3. First-year teachers—Inservice training. I. Knight, Jim. II. Title.

LB1731.4.C63 2009
371.102—dc22   2008025676

This book is printed on acid-free paper.

08   09   10   11   12   10   9   8   7   6   5   4   3   2   1

Acquisitions Editor:	Dan Alpert
Associate Editor:	Megan Bedell
Editorial Assistant:	Tatiana Richards
Production Editor:	Melanie Birdsall
Copy Editor:	Tina Hardy
Typesetter:	C&M Digitals (P) Ltd.
Proofreader:	Cheryl Rivard
Indexer:	Jean Casalegno
Cover Designer:	Lisa Riley

Contents

About the Editor

**Jim Knight** is the Director of the Kansas Coaching Project at the University of Kansas Center for Research on Learning. He has spent more than a decade studying instructional coaching, writing two books on the topic: *Instructional Coaching: A Partnership Approach to Improving Instruction,* published by Corwin Press, and *Coaching Classroom Management,* written with Randy Sprick, Wendy Reinke, and Tricia McKale Skyles. Jim's articles on instructional coaching have been included in publications such as the *Journal of Staff Development, Principal Leadership, The School Administrator,* and *Teachers Teaching Teachers.* Jim directs several research projects and leads the coaching institutes and the Annual Instructional Coaching Conference offered by the Kansas Coaching Project. He is frequently asked to guide professional learning for instructional coaches and can be reached at jimknight@mac.com.

About the Contributors

Jake Cornett is a project manager at the University of Kansas Center for Research on Learning. In his current position he coordinates a Naturalistic Inquiry investigation of literacy coaching across Florida. Jake is an active researcher in the areas of professional learning and educational coaching. Jake also works with the Schoolwide Application Model (SAM Schools) structural reform model being implemented in several Washington, DC, public schools. Jake has worked on several small-scale design studies over the past few years within the Kansas Coaching Project. His professional interests are in the areas of coaching, professional development, and school reform system evaluation.

Jane Ellison, EdD, is the codirector for the Center for Cognitive Coaching and Kaleidoscope Associates in Highlands Ranch, Colorado, with Carolee Hayes. Jane has worked for almost 10 years in Douglas County schools as the Director of Elementary Education. She was a principal for many years in Tinley Park, Illinois, and Parker, Colorado. Today, Jane travels throughout the United States and internationally to expand the influence of Cognitive Coaching in educational systems. Her most recent publication is *Effective School Leadership: Developing Principals Through Cognitive Coaching*.

Carolee Hayes, MA, is the codirector for the Center for Cognitive Coaching and Kaleidoscope Associates in Highlands Ranch, Colorado, with Jane Ellison. Carolee has worked for almost 10 years in Douglas County schools as the Director of Staff Development. She was a teacher and staff developer in Jefferson County schools before moving to Douglas County. Today, Carolee travels throughout the United States and internationally to expand the influence of Cognitive Coaching in educational systems. Her most recent publication is *Effective School Leadership: Developing Principals Through Cognitive Coaching*.

Joellen Killion is the Deputy Executive Director for the National Staff Development Council. In her work with NSDC, Joellen focuses on improving professional learning for all educators. She is a frequent contributor to the *Journal of Staff Development* and her books focus on key topics in professional learning. Joellen has extensive experience in professional development. At NSDC, she has led initiatives to examine the link between professional development and student learning. She has extensive experience in professional development planning, design, implementation, and evaluation at both the school and system levels and focuses now on NSDC's initiatives to support school-based staff developers.

Jane A. G. Kise, EdD, is an educational consultant, specializing in team building, coaching, and professional development. She is currently President of the Association for Psychological Type International. She is also the author or coauthor of more than 20 books, including her series from Corwin Press: *Differentiated Coaching: A Framework for Helping Teachers Change, Differentiation Through Personality Types,* and *Differentiated School Leadership.* She holds an MBA in finance and a doctorate in Educational Leadership. Kise's clients include Minneapolis public schools, The Bush Foundation, and the Minnesota Department of Education.

Wendy M. Reinke, PhD, is an assistant professor in the School Psychology program at the University of Missouri-Columbia and codirector of the Missouri Prevention Center. She earned her doctoral degree from the University of Oregon and completed a Prevention Science fellowship at Johns Hopkins Bloomberg School of Public Health. Her research interests include teacher consultation, school and family-centered interventions for children with disruptive behavior problems, and classroom management. She has published widely and presents regularly at national conferences on these topics. She is the developer of the Classroom Check-Up and coauthor of *Coaching Classroom Management: Strategies and Tools for Administrators and Coaches.*

Karla Reiss is the author of *Leadership Coaching for Educators: Bringing Out the Best in School Administrators* and recipient of the National Staff Development Council Book of the Year Award, 2007. She is the founder of The Change Place, a coaching, consulting firm, and the developer of the POWERful Coaching for Powerful Results™ training program, a professional coach training program based on International Coach Federation's Professional Coaching Core Competencies. As a former coordinator of professional development and school improvement school administrator for a regional education center, Karla has worked with more than 50 school districts, planning teams, and individuals. Karla holds a school district administrator license and a master's degree in elementary and special education. She is a graduate of the Institute for Professional Empowerment Coaching and had additional coach training at the College of Executive Coaching.

Randall Sprick, PhD, is the author of the *Safe and Civil School Series*, a collection of books and inservice training materials widely used in school-wide and classroom discipline. His most recent publications include *Interventions: Evidence-Based Behavioral Strategies for Individual Students*, *Coaching Classroom Management: Strategies and Tools for Administrators and Coaches*, and *Discipline in the Secondary Classroom, Second Edition*. He is the lead author on the widely used books *CHAMPs: A Proactive and Positive Approach to Classroom Management* and *The Teacher's Encyclopedia of Behavior Management: 100 Problems/500Plans*. Throughout his career, Randy has received numerous awards and honors such as from The Council for Exceptional Children (CEC) Lifetime Achievement Award.

Cathy A. Toll is the founder and lead consultant of Toll and Associates. In this capacity, she is committed to serving the needs of literacy coaches and those who support them. She has published widely for literacy leaders, including four books for literacy coaches. Prior to her leadership of Toll and Associates, Cathy worked as a teacher at the elementary, middle, high school, and university levels, a reading specialist, a curriculum coordinator, a principal, director of literacy research and development, grant director, and consultant. Cathy's current research is focused on developing a model of teacher professional growth with which she hopes to help school districts and policymakers rethink the entire nature of "professional development." Cathy recently returned to her home state of Wisconsin, where she lives in Madison and bicycles whenever she can.

Lucy West's particular expertise is effective-effort-based instruction, and her thoughtful approaches to professional learning that foster and sustain it have earned her recognition and professional partnerships internationally. Ms. West is the author of *Content-Focused Coaching: Transforming Mathematics Lessons* and began her career as a classroom teacher and served NYC schools in a variety of roles including assistant principal, director of mathematics, and deputy superintendent. As principal investigator in a National Science Foundation Teacher Enhancement grant, she created an extensive differentiated menu of professional learning opportunities for teachers, coaches, and administrators. Through her company, Metamorphosis Teaching Learning Communities, she now serves districts nationwide and weaves the threads of professional learning communities, content coaching, and lesson study into a coherent professional learning tapestry for her clients.

Acknowledgments

This book exists only because of the generous contributions made by many people, most importantly, of course, the authors who shared their ideas in these pages. I am doubly grateful to those who contributed their royalties to the ongoing work at the Kansas Coaching Project at the University of Kansas Center for Research on Learning—thanks to them, more than 75% of the royalties of this book will be used for the ongoing study of coaching.

Carol Hatton and Jake Cornett, at the Kansas Coaching Project, worked tirelessly to help put together the final manuscript of this publication. My colleagues at the Center for Research on Learning made my workplace the ideal setting for the development and study of new ideas, and the coaches on Pathways to Success give me more good ideas than anyone else. Our acquisitions editor at Corwin Press, Dan Alpert, was always gracious, supportive, helpful, and above all, patient.

Finally, I acknowledge, as always, my children, Geoff, Cameron, David, Ben, Emily, and Isaiah—your hearts and imagination give me hope for the future; my parents—your unwavering support gives me motivation to do well; and my wife Jenny—your love always shows me that true love does exist.

—Jim Knight

CONTRIBUTOR ACKNOWLEDGMENTS

Jake Cornett: I would like to acknowledge Jim Knight and Don Deshler for their encouragement, guidance, and advising. Jim is owed special thanks for providing me the opportunity to write this chapter while acting as my writing coach, critic, editor, and coauthor. Jim and Don provide me with constant mentorship, coaching, and a plethora of opportunities for professional learning. I would also like to acknowledge Gary Adams and Jenny Edwards for reviewing the chapter and providing invaluable feedback.

My friends and family have been a wonderful support system; thank you for acting interested even when you were bored to tears. Last and most important, Ramsey Cox; without her unending support I would have never been able to complete this task.

Jane Ellison and Carolee Hayes: We would like to acknowledge Art Costa and Bob Garmston for their brilliant work in developing Cognitive Coaching. They have provided the world with a rich means for developing children and adults as self-directed learners. We are grateful to them for the opportunity to sustain their work. We also are indebted to the Training Associates for the Center for Cognitive Coaching, who represent the work so well throughout the world and support all of our community in lifelong learning.

Joellen Killion: I want to particularly acknowledge three people. Stephanie Hirsh, NSDC Executive Director, and Hayes Mizell, NSDC's Distinguished Senior Fellow, developed a vision for NSDC's support of school-based coaches and teacher leaders that resulted in numerous resources to support coaches and to recognize the significant role they have in improving teaching and student learning. I want to thank Cindy Harrison, who has been a partner in the exploration and study of coaching and is coauthor of *Taking the Lead: New Roles for Teacher Leaders and School-Based Staff Developers.* Cindy plays a significant role in NSDC's coaching cadre by designing and supporting other members of NSDC's coaching, cadre and in providing professional development for coaches across the country.

Jane A. G. Kise: I am deeply indebted to three people who informed and enriched my differentiated coaching practices: Sandra Hirsh, who passed on to me her knowledge and passion for using personality type to make constructive use of differences; Beth Russell, who opened her schools to me and partnered with me in creating professional learning experiences for teachers; and Bruce Kramer, who advised my research and continues to offer wisdom and structure to my ongoing research efforts.

Wendy M. Reinke: I would like to thank the many teachers who collaborated with me in the development of the Classroom Check-Up. I have learned so much from them and the students in their classrooms. I must also thank Jim Knight and Randy Sprick for their support and mentorship. Last, I thank my loving partner Keith and our darling daughter. They inspire me to strive for the best each and every day.

Karla Reiss: I am grateful to many people who have supported me in the development of my work in the area of leadership coaching. I have learned coaching skills, tools, and processes from highly skilled coaches who are as passionate about coaching and its potential for personal and professional change as I am.

Many thanks to Bruce Schneider, founder of the Institute for Professional Empowerment Coaching, for an amazing learning opportunity; to Cheryl Richardson, author and my first coach, for supporting me in creating a brand-new life and designing meaningful work; and to Michael Keany, Director of the Long Island School Leadership Center, for helping me launch my first leadership coaching project. I also wish to thank Susan Sparks, Executive Director, Front Range BOCES, for supporting my training program in the Denver area.

I must thank each and every coaching client who has so courageously embarked on a leadership coaching journey with me. Although I cannot reveal their names to protect our confidentiality, I have been so touched by their bravery to face change and do the hard work that accompanies it.

My family and friends have been a wonderful support system and I appreciate their patience. I especially thank Ed Kletzky, my life partner and business development associate for The Change Place, who has encouraged me every step of the way.

Randy Sprick: I wish to acknowledge Siegfried Engelmann, Wes Becker, and Doug Carnine for teaching me how to be an instructional coach during the early years of Project Follow Through. One of many important lessons I learned is that an effective coach must spend time in the classrooms, not in meetings and the office. I also learned that often teachers need assistance with both behavior and curriculum. These years of coaching provided invaluable experience to my own professional development.

I would also like to acknowledge Don Deshler, Jean Schumaker, and their colleagues at the Center for Research on Learning at the University of Kansas. Their professionalism and generosity help the coauthors of this chapter develop a classroom management coaching model that incorporates the best of what we know about instruction, behavior, and treating people with dignity and respect.

Cathy A. Toll: I wish to acknowledge literacy coaches throughout the United States for all that they have taught me. As well, I acknowledge the Professional Learning Group, consisting of Kathy Egawa, Sunday Cummins, Janet Files, and, until recently, Diane DeFord, with whom I have had the pleasure of puzzling over many issues related to teacher professional learning.

Lucy West: Thank you Sandra Nye and Jake Cornett for your invaluable help and support in the preparation of this chapter. Thanks also to Fritz Staub for his theory, which is the foundation for Content-Focused Coaching, and to Anthony Alvarado for providing profound and influential leadership under which so many educators, including myself, blossomed into leaders.

PUBLISHER'S ACKNOWLEDGMENTS

Corwin Press gratefully acknowledges the contributions of the following reviewers:

Candace Bixler, Educational Specialist
Education Service Center Region XIII, Austin, TX

Beverly Colombo, Director of Programs and Development
Strategic Learning Center, Lawrence, KS

Kathi Crowe, Reading Consultant
Kentucky Department of Education, Lexington, KY

Beth Lasky, Professor
Department of Special Education
California State University, Northridge, CA

Belinda B. Mitchell, Special Education Doctoral Fellow
The University of Kansas, Lawrence, KS

Leslie Novosel, Reading Specialist/Instructional Coach
Doctoral Student, The University of Kansas, Lawrence, KS

Lisa Sligh, Educational Consultant
Davidsonville, MD

Helen Waldron, Dean of Academic Affairs
The Forman School, Litchfield, CT

Tiffany Wiencken, Instruction Coach Facilitator
Beaverton School District, Beaverton, OR

Dennis Wilson, Superintendent
Labette County, USD 506, Altamont, KS

Introduction

Jim Knight

In the past decade, there has been an explosion of interest in the form of professional learning loosely described as coaching. The magnitude of this explosion can be measured by comparing conference programs from the nation's leading professional learning organization, the National Staff Development Council (NSDC). In the 1997 NSDC conference program, the word *coach* (or variations such as *coaching, coaches*) occurs 19 times. Ten years later, in the 2007 program, the word *coach* or variations is used 193 times. People are talking and learning about coaching, and school districts and states are implementing coaching on a grand scale.

WHY HAS INTEREST IN COACHING GROWN SO DRAMATICALLY?

Up until recently, one of the most common forms of professional learning in schools was traditional one-shot workshops offered on professional development days. Unfortunately, traditional one-shot professional development sessions are not effective for fostering professional learning. When there is no follow-up to workshops, the best educational leaders can hope for is about 10% implementation (Bush, 1984). What's more, traditional one-shot training sessions involve complex interactions that can actually decrease teachers' interest in growth and development and increase a culture in schools that is hostile to professional learning (Knight, 2000).

After the No Child Left Behind Act of 2001 became law on January 8, 2002, educational leaders' questions about the effectiveness of traditional professional development became more frequent, and many came to see that moving schools forward requires a variety of approaches to professional learning. One of the most promising approaches appeared to be coaching.

What coaching offers is authentic learning that provides differentiated support for professional learning. Coaching is not a quick fix; it is an approach that offers time and support for teachers to reflect, converse about, explore, and practice new ways of thinking about and doing this remarkably important and complex act, called *teaching*. Perhaps most importantly, coaching puts teachers' needs at the heart of professional learning by individualizing their learning and by positioning teachers as professionals.

WHAT IS COACHING?

Although many schools and districts have been quick to recognize the potential effectiveness of coaching, leaders have understandably been less clear on what kind of coaching they are actually adopting. Today, schools employ instructional coaches, or cognitive coaches, or leadership coaches, or differentiated coaches, or reading or literacy coaches, or data coaches, or math coaches, or content coaches, to name a few. As my friend and colleague Candace Bixler (personal communication, March 16, 2008), a leader of professional developers in Austin, Texas, has commented, "What we are doing right now in education is like bringing together successful coaches from varied sports, basketball, gymnastics, football, tennis, and swimming, to develop a winning team when we haven't even determined the sport or the playing field." With so many different approaches, leaders are excused if they are just a little confused about what coaching is and what coaching offers their school, teachers, and students.

This book has been created to, we hope, undo some of the confusion. The authors are among the leaders in the field of coaching, and their mandate has been to present an overview of their ideas about a particular approach to coaching or their thoughts on what coaching is and what it can be. The book does not and could not paint a complete picture. The chapters have been written by authors who have published at least one book that more fully describes the ideas they summarize, and so the overviews and think-pieces cannot fully capture the theory and practice of each approach. However, this book is a starting point. We hope the book helps readers better understand coaching's potential so that they will be able to make better decisions about what kind of coaching best fits their schools', teachers', and students' needs.

WHAT IS IN THIS BOOK?

Each chapter in this book can be read by itself or in the sequence in which it occurs. Readers shouldn't hesitate to jump around to find the chapters that are most useful, reading the chapters in the sequence that works best for them. The following is a brief summary of the purpose and ideas of each chapter.

Chapter 1. Coaches' Roles, Responsibilities, and Reach

Joellen Killion

Joellen Killion opens this book by answering a very simple question: What roles do coaches hold in schools? In her chapter, "Coaches' Roles, Responsibilities, and Reach," Joellen draws on decades of experience, first as a coach herself, then as an author, consultant, and leader at the NSDC, to describe 10 roles in which coaches might serve. Additionally, Joellen makes an important distinction between what she refers to as "coaching heavy" and "coaching light."

Chapter 2. Instructional Coaching

Jim Knight

The model for instructional coaching described here was designed by my colleagues and me at the University of Kansas Center for Research on Learning to support teachers as they implement proven practices. The chapter describes the partnership principles behind this approach, the components of the instructional coaching process, "The Big Four" framework coaches can use to identify starting points with teachers, and success factors that seem to be especially important for any coaching program.

Chapter 3. Literacy Coaching

Cathy A. Toll

Cathy A. Toll, whose name is synonymous with literacy coaching, "discusses literacy coaching," as she says, "in order to provide a common perspective on the phenomenon." Cathy asserts that schools need to adopt a "fresh approach to literacy coaching," positioning coaches as partners who listen and learn from teachers before they offer assistance. Additionally, she describes the extent of literacy coaching across the United States, the research base in support of literacy coaching, and the effects that literacy coaching can have on teachers, students, and schools. Finally, Cathy describes inaccuracies in the representations of literacy coaching and offers suggestions for future investigations of the field.

Chapter 4. Cognitive Coaching

Jane Ellison and Carolee Hayes

Jane Ellison and Carolee Hayes, codirectors of the Center for Cognitive Coaching, provide a concise, packed, overview of Cognitive Coaching[SM]. Their chapter distinguishes Cognitive Coaching from other coaching models and provides a brief summary of the research that has been conducted on Cognitive Coaching. The authors describe Cognitive

Coaching as an approach that focuses on, as they say, "reflection, complex thinking, and transformational learning," and one where thinking is seen as driving practice. Jane and Carolee define Cognitive Coaching, the theoretical framework for this approach, and the three coaching maps that guide the interactions between Cognitive Coaches and others they are coaching.

Chapter 5. Coaching Classroom Management

Wendy M. Reinke, Randy Sprick, and Jim Knight

Wendy M. Reinke, Randy Sprick, and I have developed the Coaching Classroom Management approach, summarized here, so that coaches can assist teachers as they create positive learning communities where students are engaged and learning. This chapter provides an overview of powerful teaching practices, classroom variables, data collection techniques, and communication tools that coaches can employ to decrease disruptions and increase student engagement, on-task behavior, and most important, student achievement.

Chapter 6. Content Coaching: Transforming the Teaching Profession

Lucy West

"The *essence* of content coaching," Lucy West writes, "is simple: to improve learning, teachers must focus on relevant, important, rich content." In her chapter, which primarily focuses on mathematics instruction, Lucy explains that content coaching is an iterative process between coaches and teachers, based on specific learning principles, during which the coach works from an "inquiry stance." Consequently, during content coaching, the art of questioning is especially important. Lucy defines the work of content coaching as lesson design, enactment (teaching the lesson), and diagnosis and enhancement of student learning. She also summarizes many tools of content coaches.

Chapter 7. Differentiated Coaching

Jane A. G. Kise

Jane A. G. Kise suggests that teacher resistance may not arise because of teachers' actions but because coaches fail to differentiate their coaching approach to the unique learning style of individual teachers. In her chapter, Jane, the leading expert on coaching and personality styles, explains how the use of a personality type framework, such as the Myers-Briggs Type

Indicator®, can help coaches unpack the unique needs of teachers. Her chapter summarizes specific steps coaches can take to better understand the most effective way to influence each teacher to change.

Chapter 8. Leadership Coaching

Karla Reiss

Karla Reiss makes the important assertion that coaching is not just for teachers. In her chapter, Karla, who draws on the coaching processes and tools described by the International Coaching Federation, suggests that all leaders in schools can benefit from coaching. She paints a picture of a typical leadership coaching session, debunks several coaching myths, and explains why she believes school administrators should adopt a coaching style of leadership.

Chapter 9. Research on Coaching

Jake Cornett and Jim Knight

In this chapter, my colleague Jake Cornett and I tackle the thorny question: What does the research say about coaching? To write this article, we reviewed 235 articles, dissertations, books, and presentations to gain a clearer understanding of what research has to say about the effectiveness of coaching as a methodology for improving teaching practice, increasing teacher efficacy, and improving student achievement. We hope the chapter will provide a point of departure for more rigorous study of the fields of coaching.

HOW SHOULD THE BOOK BE READ?

I have written short introductions for each chapter, so that readers will have an advanced understanding of the particular approach or perspective on coaching described in the chapter, some insight into how the particular approach came to be developed, and how it is distinguished from others described in the book.

I recognize how convenient it would be if readers could hold a simple chart explaining the similarities and differences among the approaches described in this book as they move through these pages. However, I have chosen not to reduce the complexity of each chapter by putting it into such a chart. To be fair to the authors, I feel it is more appropriate to leave all readers free to identify their own connections among the chapters, to uncover the similarities and differences, and to draw their own conclusions. Each chapter summarizes years of work conducted by a leader in the field of coaching. I hope your experience reading this book will be as stimulating and helpful as mine was while working with each of these leaders to create this book you hold in your hands.

REFERENCES

Bush, R. N. (1984). *Effective staff developments in making our schools more effective.* San Francisco: Far West Laboratories.

Knight, J. (2000, April). *Another damn thing we've got to do: Teacher perceptions of professional development.* Paper presented at the meeting of the American Educational Research Association, New Orleans, LA.

No Child Left Behind Act of 2001, Pub. L. No. 107-110 (2002).

1

Coaches' Roles, Responsibilities, and Reach

Joellen Killion

INTRODUCTION

Joellen Killion has been involved in coaching, as a coach, author, professional developer, and consultant, for more years than she wishes to admit. Her work in coaching began in 1976 when she worked as a coach in a large suburban high school. Joellen started out charged to use Madeline Hunter's instructional model as a way to help teachers, mostly teachers who were "in trouble." Back then, Joellen says, "my office was in a closet next to the boiler room because the principal believed that no teacher would want to be seen speaking to me, because that would have a meaning. And the meaning would be that that they were in trouble." Much has changed since her first experiences coaching.

Despite this challenging beginning, Joellen always "believed very strongly that the power of teachers helping teachers was a significant way to make a difference in a building." When she moved into a central office role, Joellen continued to spend time in teachers' classrooms, working with teachers on instruction. Eventually, in 1986, her district partnered with the University of Colorado, employing teachers in

(Continued)

(Continued)

full-time positions to work as "clinical professors." These pioneering coaches spent a half a day a week in a new teacher's classroom supporting that new teacher's development, while also conducting professional development in the district and at the university. This university-school district partnership continues successfully to this day.

When the literacy movement began, Joellen found herself sharing what she had learned about coaching and professional development (Joellen is the deputy executive director of the NSDC) with coaches around the nation.

Joellen explored coaching models, including peer coaching and Cognitive Coaching^SM (described in more detail in Chapter 4). Additionally, she broadened her understanding of what coaching is and its potential through her examination of The Learning Network, where she came to understand instructional dialogue. She studied teacher reflection and metacognition as processes that advanced teacher development. Finally, she learned more about coaching school and district leaders through The Brande Foundation's Life Coaching Program, developed by David Ellis. Through this program, NSDC developed a cadre of leadership coaches who provided coaching to superintendents and principals in schools across the country.

As a professional developer, consultant, and author for NSDC, Joellen has guided coaches and coaching leaders to build capacity for content knowledge, pedagogy, and the coaching process. At NSDC, she coordinates NSDC's highly successful Coaching Academies, working with a cadre of skillful coach developers. Additionally, she and her colleagues at NSDC are working with state departments of education and state NSDC affiliates to further the development of coaching locally, working on policy and coaching practice. Finally, Joellen supports NSDC's summer conference for teacher leaders, including coaches and the administrators who support them. She coauthored with Cindy Harrison *Taking the Lead: New Roles for Teacher Leaders and School-Based Staff Developers* (Killion & Harrison, 2006).

In Joellen's chapter, the most important message may be that coaches take on numerous roles—she describes 10—and coaches can have many important responsibilities. As Joellen has said in conversation with me, "We really need to broaden the lens through which we see coaching. I guess in some cases people will say, well, that is not really coaching. And I'll say okay, use whatever word you want to use to describe it, but the notion is that we are all focused on helping teachers think deeply about their practice. And we are doing it because we want to make sure that every student is successful." Certainly this is an important message to consider as we embark on reading this book about different approaches and perspectives on coaching.

Improving student academic success is hard work and the challenge grows each day. School and district leaders have initiated reforms that range from curriculum alignment; common assessment; new curricular programs; increased expectations for students, teachers, and principals; and improved instruction. Each of these initiatives has the potential to add value to the educational system. The potential impact of these and other reform initiatives increases exponentially if school-based implementation support is added into the mix.

Implementation support provides crucial school- and classroom-based support that facilitates the use of, rather than knowledge about, the reform efforts. Increasingly schools and districts are employing coaches to assume some of the responsibilities related to implementation support. Coaches are master teachers who participate in explicit professional development about coaching to become skillful. In professional development, they examine their fundamental beliefs about student learning, teaching, and coaching; acquire deep knowledge about adult development and change; and acquire skillfulness with a broad range of strategies to use in their new role. Called by many different titles, teacher leaders in this role are primarily school-based professional development specialists who work with individuals and teams to design and facilitate appropriate learning experiences, provide feedback and support, and assist with implementation challenges. Their work centers on refining and honing teaching, and their indicator of success is student academic success.

This chapter focuses on the work coaches do when they interact with individuals and teams. First, it describes the variation in coaches' work by identifying the 10 most common forms of assistance coaches provide to teachers and some of the challenges coaches face in each role. Second, it examines variables that influence coaches' decisions regarding the support they provide teachers. Last, this chapter explores the concepts of coaching heavy and coaching light—ways to think about the intensity and impact of coaching and how the roles and coaches' beliefs influence their decisions about how they allocate their time and services to support teachers.

TEN ROLES OF COACHES

In our book, *Taking the Lead: New Roles for Teacher Leaders and School-Based Coaches,* my colleague Cindy Harrison and I (Killion & Harrison, 2006) describe 10 different roles coaches fill in their work. Some coaches serve in all 10 roles. Others have a narrower focus and may serve in only a few roles. By narrowing the range of roles, coaches focus their work more intensely on those roles that have the greatest potential for impact on teaching and student learning. However, determining which roles have the greatest leverage on improving teaching and learning depends on several factors. This section first describes the roles and second, examines factors that influence the allocation of time and effort to each role.

Without a clear framework for their day, coaches find that their time is fragmented. When coaches' work is so expansive, the potential exists that coaches will take on too many roles and, as a result, dilute the impact of their work.

The roles described here constitute a range of support coaches provide teachers. Each role requires a specific set of knowledge and skills. Each role has a distinctive set of challenges. Each meets a specific teacher need.

Data Coach

A data coach assists individual teachers or teams of teachers in examining student achievement data and in using these data to design instruction that addresses student learning needs. School improvement planning teams usually begin the data analysis process in a school by analyzing state and district achievement data to identify school improvement goals. Coaches take this work a step further. Their data work concentrates on facilitating teachers' understanding of grade-level, team, and classroom data, helping teachers use these data to make instructional and curricular decisions. Through fine analysis guided by coaches, teachers determine which students will benefit from moving on, reteaching, additional practice, or extension. Coaches assist teachers in using a wide variety of classroom data to monitor progress on academic goals. One of the most significant challenges coaches have as data coaches is creating a safe, blame-free environment for ruthless analysis of data.

Resource Provider

Teachers turn to their coach for resources that are not immediately available to them. Sometimes, the request for resources includes accessing supplies, leveled books, and additional resources for students to use in the classroom that would meet the needs of students with different learning preferences, academic ability, or interest. Sometimes, the requests for resources are teacher resources such as lesson or unit plans, assignments, or references to help teachers develop instructional plans. Occasionally, the resource requests are for services outside the school or district such as a guest speaker. Teachers expect coaches to be knowledgeable about what is available within the school and district and even within the community. This resourcefulness does not go unnoticed. Their challenge as resource providers, many coaches find, is that this role constitutes a good deal of their time.

Mentor

Coaches serve the needs of new teachers or new-to-the-school teachers. When working with this particular client group, coaches may find that they are engaging in all 10 of the roles simultaneously. The role of mentor is distinguished as a distinct role for coaches because the teacher client is unique and requires coaches to have specific knowledge about stages of teacher development and coaching skills specific to novice teachers. As a mentor, the coach's primary responsibility is acclimatizing the new teacher to the school's professional norms, practices, and policies. With support, the new-to-the-school teacher or novice teacher more quickly feels comfortable and adjusts to the expectations and routines of the school. Mentors frequently provide other support particular to new teachers that includes the roles of curriculum specialist, instructional specialist, and classroom supporter. A challenge coaches encounter as mentors is balancing support with building professional capacity. The struggle between dependence and independence looms in coaches' daily interactions with novice teachers. Coaches balance providing advice with developing novice teachers' capacity to make decisions.

Curriculum Specialist

The coach serving as a curriculum specialist focuses on the *what* of teaching rather than the *how*. A coach in this role helps a teacher understand and use the district's adopted curriculum, know how to break concepts into attributes, use the pacing guide, and understand the scope of concepts taught. In this role, coaches might find that they are deepening teachers' understanding of the concepts they teach. Teachers, with the support of their coach, use a deep understanding of the curriculum to engage in planning the sequence of concepts within instructional units that have both rigor and relevance. Teachers with support of their coaches develop a clear understanding of what successful learning looks like to guide the development of student assessments. Assessments of student learning align with the curriculum and developmental and academic needs of students, engage students in critical and creative thinking, and provide students multiple ways to demonstrate their learning. Coaches responsible for supporting teachers in grades beyond their teaching experience or content area may feel inadequate and, as a result, may find it challenging to provide schoolwide support to *all* teachers.

Instructional Specialist

Once teachers know *what* to teach and what successful learning looks like, they turn their attention to *how* to teach it. Coaches help teachers choose appropriate instructional methodologies and differentiate instruction to meet students' different learning preferences and academic readiness levels. Matching instructional approaches with curriculum requires that teachers have a broad repertoire of strategies as well as assessment methodology to reach all students. Coaches also support teachers in creating safe and productive learning environments that enhance learning for all students, including English-language learners, special needs learners, and gifted students. Coaches help teachers think about how to manage grouping within their classrooms, integrate resource staff when appropriate, hold students responsible for their learning, and establish classroom routines that facilitate students' independence and responsibility. A significant challenge that coaches in this role face is that they may not know enough about instructional methodology to reach *all* students.

Classroom Supporter

This is often called the *big* role for coaches. Typically, when people talk about coaching, they hold an image of this role in which the coach works side by side with the teacher inside the teacher's classroom engaged in modeling effective teaching practices, coteaching, and/or observing and giving feedback. What is unique to this role is the location of the coaches' work. They work inside the classroom with one or more teachers while teaching and student learning are occurring. No other role takes place in the same way. All others are done outside the classroom or in the classroom when students are elsewhere. Yet for some coaches, this role constitutes only a small portion of their work. This role requires a broad range of skills including coplanning, coteaching, observing, crafting feedback, and engaging in thoughtful, reflective conversation about teaching and learning. In this role, coaches may face resistance from teachers because of the intrusiveness required to fulfill the role.

Learning Facilitator

Learning facilitators organize, coordinate, support, design, or facilitate learning among adults within the school. Some might call this role *professional development*; however, coaching *is* professional development. A learning facilitator enhances or enriches teachers' instructional repertoire, deepens teachers' content knowledge, and expands their understanding of how students learn. In this role, coaches may lead a book study, coordinate action research teams, hold a workshop on new instructional strategies, engage a team in lesson study, facilitate a faculty meeting in which teachers examine student work using the Tuning Protocol or Critical Friends Process, or engage a department in scoring common assessments. In each of these roles, the coach starts with student achievement data. From these data, working together coaches and teachers determine the teacher learning needs. Then coaches create their instructional plan driven by explicit outcomes for teachers and procedures that are respectful and appropriate for the adult learners and the content. Meeting the diverse learning needs of *all* teachers is a challenge coaches in this role face, yet by employing more collaborative, team-based designs for professional learning, coaches build communities of learners who learn with and from one another.

School Leader

As school leaders, coaches contribute to schoolwide reform initiatives. Those in the role of coach have a difficult time avoiding this role. They are perceived as leaders both by their peers and by the school's administrators. In this role, coaches lead reform within their schools and classrooms. Coaches advocate for school and district initiatives and assist teachers in fully implementing the reform behaviors. Coaches may lead task forces, facilitate school improvement teams, chair schoolwide committees, and represent their school on districtwide committees. Coaches lead most importantly with their attitude and integrity. They model salient behaviors of education professionals and work to create a healthy, collaborative community of learners among adults in their schools. Yet coaches walk a delicate line between administration and teachers. They are neither really. Coaches have no supervisory responsibilities and so their allegiance rests most often with teachers. Occasionally, however, they are asked to engage in administrative responsibilities that confuse their identity within a school.

Catalyst for Change

Beyond serving as school leader, coaches frequently initiate change. In the role of catalyst for change, coaches demonstrate dissatisfaction with the status quo and question routines with inquiry. By making observations, stating their point of view, and inquiring into practice, coaches erode stagnant practice and unchallenged routines to spark analysis, reflection, and appropriate change. In this role, a coach is not about change for change sake, but rather for continuous improvement and fine-tuning to meet clearly articulated goals. In his landmark research of schools in Georgia, Carl Glickman (1993) notes that schools that had the greatest improvements in student achievement were those in which the staff expressed dissatisfaction with their work, and that schools with limited improvement in student achievement had staff who were satisfied with their work. Coaches have the capacity to question and instill curiosity and doubt, thereby generating dissonance essential to promote change. As one coach reported, finding the delicate balance between sufficient dissonance and disruptive dissonance is tricky. She said it is hard to know if she goes too far until she arrives there.

Learner

The last of the 10 roles of coaches is that of learner. As a learner, a coach engages in his or her own continuous development, searching for ideas, resources, and strategies to strengthen coaching practices, and to reflect on his or her work as a coach. Coaches, as learners, attend conferences and workshops on topics related to their school's reform efforts and coaching skills. They read widely both in education and outside. Together with other coaches, they network and problem solve in their own community of practice. They write to develop deep understanding of their experiences and to identify both their strengths and their areas for improvement. Their journals or logs serve as a source of reflective analysis about their work as a coach. Using the data from their logs, they ask whether they have engaged in the most appropriate roles with a particular group of teachers and if they are balancing their time among their many roles and responsibilities. Coaches as learners model learning for their peers by talking about what they are learning and reading, their mistakes, their insights, and their discoveries. They talk too about how they learn and explore multiple learning approaches. Their challenge in this role, coaches report, is devoting time to their own learning.

BALANCING THE ROLES

While most coaches recognize these roles as the work they do, they also wonder how to balance the roles. This curiosity represents a significant programmatic issue that many coaching programs fail to address in the earliest stages. Sadly, too many coaching programs have been launched with an insufficient program framework designed to maximize the impact of coaching on teaching and student learning. Multiple factors influence the balance among the roles. They include coaches' job descriptions, their role expectations, the goals of the coaching program, the goals of a school's improvement plan, the context in which they work, the time of the school year, the experience of the coach, and the experience of the teacher. The influence of some of these factors may seem obvious; others may not. Knowing how to allocate time during the workday is difficult when any of these factors are fuzzy.

Job Descriptions and Role Expectations

When asking the question about balancing the roles, coaches first look to their clear job descriptions and role expectations. Some job descriptions make coaches' work explicit. In the School District of Philadelphia, for example, the school growth teachers have three explicit roles—mentor, data coach, and learning facilitator. Literacy and numeracy coaches fill the roles of instructional and curriculum specialist and classroom supporter and work in tandem with school growth teachers. Working as a team, these resource personnel provide comprehensive support to teachers. In Fairfax County (Virginia) public schools, cluster-based instructional coaches are responsible for improving reading and math achievement, closing the achievement gap, and creating a culture of collaboration. Their primary roles are data coach, instructional specialist, curriculum specialist, classroom supporter, and learning facilitator. Because they spend 60% of their time working with teams of teachers and 40% with individuals, they are able to focus on more roles. In Walla Walla (Washington) public schools, coaches are responsible for increasing math and literacy achievement. They do this mostly in the roles of data coach, classroom supporter, curriculum specialist, instructional specialist, and learning facilitator.

Role expectations are defined in the performance standards for the role of coach. Many school districts with coaches attempt to use teacher performance standards when evaluating coaches. This does a disservice to coaches. Their new role as a coach has new expectations, new responsibilities, and therefore requires new standards of performance. Missing even more frequently than job descriptions in coaching programs are performance standards specifically for the role of coaches. When the job description and performance standards give clear direction and focus, coaches and their supervisors can make decisions about how coaches allocate their time.

Goals

The goals of the coaching program are another source of information that helps coaches know how to structure their workday. Some coaching programs have unspecific goals such as *supporting teachers.* Other goals are clearer such as *improving reading and math achievement in the lowest-performing schools by 15%* or *creating a collaborative culture in which teachers work together to improve teaching and student learning.* The clearer the goals of the coaching program, the easier it is for coaches to prioritize the many requests they receive for services and to say *no* to what isn't related to the goal and *yes* to what is.

Both district and school personnel have a responsibility to make the goals of the coaching program clear. Primary responsibility for this decision rests with the individuals or team overseeing coaching in a school or district. These individuals or team usually include those responsible both for financing coaching and for supervising coaches. The bottom line is this: the clearer the program's goals and coaches' role expectations, often defined in a set of performance standards, the easier it is for a coach to know how to allocate time and which services to provide during that time.

Context

Another factor influencing coaches' work is the context in which they work. Several considerations arise in this arena. Time of the school year, experience of the coach and teachers, the role of the principal, and the culture of the school are a few influencing factors.

Time of the School Year

The sequence of the school year influences how coaches allocate time. Early in the year, coaches may spend more time on data coaching, facilitating learning, and providing resources. As the year evolves and the beginning-of-the-year routines are in place, teachers and coaches can turn their attention to instruction and curriculum. Coaches facilitate meetings of teacher teams to plan instruction, analyze classroom data, and monitor implementation of the approved curriculum. In individual, team, and schoolwide meetings, coaches guide decision making about adjustments in their pace and instruction to meet student learning needs. Coaches share in new strategies, resources, or information to help teachers address topics and problems related to their classrooms. In these meetings, coaches serve as curriculum specialists, instructional specialists, classroom supporters, and learning facilitators. As the year moves on, attention turns to schoolwide initiatives, changing the status quo, and becoming a community of adult learners. In these situations, the coach serves as school leader, catalyst for change, and learner.

New to a School

If a coach is new to a school or the school is new to coaching, coaches strive first to establish a trusting, safe relationship with their colleagues. Some roles are more conducive to this. Resource provider is one. In this role, coaches demonstrate their resourcefulness, their commitment to help, and their ability to meet the needs of teachers without an expectation for change. They provide materials and resources teachers may request or find helpful. They do it in a timely manner. They provide resources that are tailored to the requestor. They keep their promises. Yet in this role, there is little intrusiveness in classroom practices or even expectation that the resources will be used appropriately. Once relationships are established and the coach has proven his or her trustworthiness, then conversations begin about how to use the resources and their impact on teaching and student learning.

Coaches' Experience Level

If a coach is new to coaching, he or she may tread lightly until relationships are developed. Novice coaches, especially those with thorough preparation for their new role, want to be useful, yet not intrusive. So, they wait patiently until someone extends an invitation for assistance. Coaches sometimes call this "getting used" and they speak of it with great pride. Once teachers recognize that the coach brings a wealth of knowledge and skills, the floodgate of requests for assistance opens. Most novice coaches want to be accepted and to demonstrate the value they add to the school. As a result, they may *overpromise* and *underdeliver,* a dangerous situation for a coach. Novice coaches feel more comfortable in roles that open doors, build their own competence and their acceptance in this new role of coach, and demonstrate their skills as a coach. The two roles they take on most often are resource provider and the model teaching aspect of classroom supporter.

As coaches grow more competent, confident, and even courageous in their work, they are willing to take on the roles that are more complex, require more focus on teaching and learning, and hold a greater expectation for change in teacher behavior. Some of these roles are data coach; classroom supporter, specifically, observing and giving feedback; school leader; and catalyst for change. Coaches, when they have established their commitment to teacher and student success, have more leeway and permission to step into classrooms and interact about teaching practices and the impact of those practices on student learning.

Experience Level of Teachers

Teachers' years of experience may influence how coaches allocate time among the roles. When teachers are less experienced, coaches (a) may serve as mentors helping teachers feel comfortable; (b) have the right resources including curriculum guides, student texts, classroom supplies, and handbooks; (c) know procedures for situations, such as discipline; and (d) provide emotional and work-related support, especially to teachers who are new to the profession. Discussion and support may focus on classroom routines, behavior management systems, and curriculum expectations. As the year proceeds, coaches assist with lesson and unit planning, common assessments, and using data. These responsibilities include the roles of curriculum specialist, instructional specialist, and data coach.

Among more veteran teachers, coaches may experience some resistance. However, most experienced teachers are open to any support available to help them improve their instructional practices. They describe more precisely what help they want, how that help is best delivered, and whether the help is useful. They tend to want assistance and to define the parameters of that assistance. While more experienced teachers may benefit from observation and feedback or coteaching, they may want resources instead of the instructional support from which they might benefit most. Skillful coaches are flexible and know how to provide a variety of services to accomplish similar outcomes.

Role of the Principal

How principals view coaching influences the roles coaches fill. When principals view themselves as the sole instructional leader in the school, coaches may assume roles that have less impact on teaching and student learning because they are respectfully deferring to principals. If principals abdicate their responsibility for instructional leadership to coaches, coaches have little hope of making a difference because teachers will believe that continuous improvement is unimportant. When principals engage coaches as coinstructional leaders, coaches will approach their work with heightened responsibility for students' academic success.

Principals are essential to the success of coaches within a school. Principals' actions as instructional leaders help coaches focus their daily work with teachers on teaching and learning by

- creating structures and schedules that allow teachers to interact with coaches individually and in teams;

- meeting frequently with coaches to review their work plans and the impact of their work;
- being visible in classrooms and monitoring curriculum implementation;
- protecting coaches' time from interruptions that distract their attention from the most crucial work with teachers;
- examining with coaches data about their work;
- holding coaches accountable for meeting their role expectations;
- upholding the parameters of the school's or district's coaching program; and
- interacting with teachers about the importance of coaching to support continuous improvement.

School Culture

A school's culture—the invisible yet powerful structure of a school—influences how a coach allocates time in each role. Culture includes the school's history with deep change. The relationship and trust among teachers and the relationship between the teachers and the principal are contributors to a school's culture. How a school faculty communicates, whether openly and honestly in meetings and other forums or secretly in the parking lot, influences a coach's potential for impact. The longevity and stability of the school's administration and the staff contribute to the culture. How a staff solves problems, whether it shares or hordes resources, and how it handles conflict are other factors.

In essence, culture exists on a continuum. There are schools with healthy cultures and a few, unfortunately, with weak or divisive cultures. There are many along the continuum. A coach is better able to influence improvements in teaching and student learning in a school with a healthy culture. The same work in a school with an unhealthy culture may be futile. Coaches assess the culture, check perceptions, and adjust their work depending on the culture in which they work. This topic alone is sufficient for its own book. What we know is that some coaching roles work better in one school than in another school. The factor is frequently the culture of the school, not the coach.

ASSESSING ROLE ALLOCATION

In *Taking the Lead: New Roles for Teachers and School-Based Coaches* (Killion & Harrison, 2006), the authors make this statement: "When school-based coaches appear to be everywhere doing everything all the time within a school, it is possible that that image is accurate" (p. 30). This may be the image, yet the question now is this: "Is this effective?" Perhaps not. Assessing the allocation of time among the roles helps coaches hone their skills and their impact.

To assess the allocation of time among the roles, coaches consult data. They analyze their logs and solicit feedback from teachers and their supervisor. As a part of the evaluation of the National Staff Development Council's Coaches Academy, funded by the Wachovia Foundation's Teachers and Teaching Initiative, coaches logged the nature of their interactions with teacher clients. Logs such as these provide useful information to the coach primarily to assess his or her decisions related to services provided. They can provide data for conversations with supervisors that allow the coach and supervisor together to draw inferences about the relationship between the work provided and its impact.

The interaction log chart of a coach whose primary responsibility is to provide curriculum and instructional support appears in Table 1.1. This chart confirms that the coach allocated more of his time to interactions that align with those roles. The large percentage of time devoted to planning, curriculum, and instructional assistance are consistent with the roles of instructional and curriculum specialists.

Table 1.2 shows the aggregated interactions for one elementary coach for five months: September, October, November, January, and February.

This table indicates that the coach used seven different types of interactions. She devoted considerable time to assistance with classroom management. The coach focused on data more in September than in any other months. Less demonstration teaching occurred in September than in any other month. January and February included substantial time focused on planning. More team facilitation occurred in January than in any other month. The chart does not provide information on whether the allocation of support is appropriate; however, by using these data as a base, coaches

Table 1.1   Coach and Client Interactions: 2006–2007 Summary for a Coach Responsible for Curriculum and Instructional Support

Type of Interaction	Percentage of Total Interactions by Type					
	Sept.	Oct.	Nov.	Dec.	Jan.	Feb.
Classroom management assist	11	10	5	0	24	9
Curricular assist	25	10	8	80	9	19
Instruct assist	6	37	22	0	20	39
Planning assist	44	39	31	7	24	18
Resource assist	13	2	21	0	17	8
Data related	0	0	0	3	5	1
Facilitate groups	0	0	0	0	0	0
Teach/model/demo	0	0	7	10	0	2
Workshop/training	0	0	0	0	0	2
Other	0	2	5	0	1	3

SOURCE: Adapted from Taylor (2007), p. 34.

Table 1.2   Coach and Client Interactions: 2006–2007 Summary 1 School, K–5, 23 Clients

Type of Interaction	*Percentage of Total Interactions by Type*				
	Sept.	*Oct.*	*Nov.*	*Jan.*	*Feb.*
Classroom management assist	30	55	56	17	27
Curricular assist	10	3	0	9	2
Instruct assist	8	9	6	2	7
Planning assist	0	9	5	49	42
Resource assist	4	0	6	4	2
Data related	44	0	17	0	7
Facilitate groups	0	9	0	11	0
Teach/model/demo	4	15	9	8	13
Workshop/training	0	0	2	0	0
Other	0	0	0	0	0

SOURCE: Adapted from Taylor (2007), p. 37.

Table 1.3   Coach and Client Interactions: 2006–2007 Summary for a Coach Returning to Teaching

Type of Interaction	*Percentage of Total Interactions by Type*					
	Sept.	*Oct.*	*Nov.*	*Dec.*	*Jan.*	*Feb.*
Classroom management assist	1	7	6	3	4	14
Curricular assist	24	20	11	10	15	19
Instruct assist	10	11	16	17	8	17
Planning assist	10	1	5	12	21	7
Resource assist	24	15	15	20	8	14
Data related	0	10	9	0	7	6
Facilitate groups	13	4	6	7	3	6
Teach/model/demo	0	3	2	0	14	9
Workshop/training	9	3	0	0	7	0
Other	7	25	31	31	14	8

SOURCE: Adapted from Taylor (2007), p. 36.

and their supervisors can engage in inquiry about whether the allocation is appropriate for this school.

By comparison, Table 1.3 is an aggregated interaction log for a coach who is returning to the classroom next year. The principal expressed dissatisfaction with the skill level of the coach. It is interesting to notice the differences between Table 1.2 and Table 1.3 and how the two coaches spent their time.

The most notable differences between Tables 1.2 and 1.3 are evident in percentage of "Other" interactions and in the number of different kinds of interactions. This comparison raises a question about whether streamlining or narrowing the coaches' responsibilities allows coaches to develop greater competence in a few roles rather than to work with fewer skills in many roles.

Examining data about how coaches allocate their time in terms of services and teacher clients helps both the coach and the coach's supervisor analyze the coach's work. Some questions coaches may use in their reflective analysis about these data are as follows:

- To whom am I providing services?
- Is the distribution of time to individuals or groups appropriate at this point in time (recognizing that there may be a teacher, a grade level, team, or department that needs more intensive services for some length of time)?
- What kinds of services do teachers request most often?
- How might I work teacher X toward more strategic use of my time?
- How does the nature of services provided change from month to month and during the course of a year?
- Are the changes appropriate? Do I want to play a more active role in directing the changes?
- How have my interactions with teachers changed as I have gained experience/trust/expertise?
- Is there a "typical" interaction curve from inductee to competent experience professional (e.g., are there different types of interactions with new vs. experienced teachers)? Are there activities/interactions I would like to use more?
- What skills do I need to work on (e.g., strategies or services that are not requested—why not? Is it because they don't know I can do this for them, or is it that I haven't had good success with it, or is it that I'm simply not good at it?)? (Killion & Harrison, 2006, Tool 17.8)

COACHING HEAVY AND COACHING LIGHT

As coaches and their supervisors analyze coaches' work with the intention to strengthen both the work and its impact, they examine how coaches allocate their time among the 10 roles. As is visible in Tables 1.1–1.3, coaches who have specific role expectations devote more time to those clearly defined roles. Table 1.3 suggests a potential problem that might arise when coaches do not have clear role expectations. They might not spend enough time in any one role to develop and refine the skills of coaching. They may not know how to assess teachers' needs and then prioritize their work to align with those needs. Or, they may regard all of their work as equally important. Without strong supervision and adequate skills, coaches fall into traps that may lead to ineffectiveness. For the promise of coaching to have the greatest impact on teaching and student learning, it is essential that coaches make choices about how to allocate their time that are driven by a clear intention to have the greatest impact on the results they seek from coaching—improving student learning.

From my perspective, the hope of coaching rests with coaches providing teachers foundational support that can make a significant impact on teacher practice and student learning. The Tennessee Value-Added studies conducted by William Sanders and his colleagues (Sanders, Saxton, & Horn, 1997) and others (Resnick, 2004; Rowan, Correnti, & Miller, 2002) demonstrate that the quality of teaching and the policies related to "teacher hiring, placement, and training make a difference for academic achievement" (Resnick, 2004, p. 4). If the goal of a coaching program is to improve student academic performance, then coaches who focus their services on strengthening the quality of teaching and learning will likely make a greater contribution to achieving that goal. If any of the providers of the coaching program—the school, the district, or the coach—are unclear about the intended results of coaching, then coaches will struggle to keep a laserlike focus on doing what matters.

I assert that there are two kinds of coaching—coaching *light* and coaching *heavy*. The difference essentially is in the coaches' perspective, beliefs, role decisions, and goals, rather than in what coaches do. The difference is magnified in the results achieved. It is possible to have two coaches working side by side, one coaching light and the other coaching heavy, and have their overt behaviors strongly resemble each other. As a result, the distinction between coaching light and coaching heavy is not easy to see in practice. It is, rather, evident in how coaches talk about their work, their motivation, their purpose, and the results they achieve.

Coaching light results in coaches being accepted, appreciated, and even liked by their peers. When coaches' work is driven by the goal of being appreciated, coaches tend to say "yes" to services that they believe will ingratiate them with staff members, particularly those who may exhibit some reluctance to working with a coach. Coaches who coach light are valued, although they may not be needed.

Coaching light occurs when coaches want to build and maintain relationships *more* than they want to improve teaching and learning. From this perspective, coaches act to increase their perceived value to teachers by providing resources *and* avoiding challenging conversations. They may provide demonstration lessons, curriculum materials, or facilitate learning without holding an expectation that the learning will be applied in classrooms. While each of these services has value and contributes to improving teaching and learning, they can also be acts of avoidance. When budget cuts are inevitable, coaching programs or even coaches who focus mostly on coaching light may find themselves on the "cut list" because while they are valued, they may not be needed.

From the perspective of the teacher, coaching light feels supportive. Teachers appreciate the resources and ideas, yet they simultaneously wonder if it wouldn't be better if the coach were working directly with students. Teachers feel as if they have an advocate in the coach, someone who understands the complexity of their work and who will empathize with them. They may request resources or support from the coach that they might ask from a classroom aide, if they had one. Teachers acknowledge that they have received strategies and ideas from the coach that are useful and that they may even try some in their classrooms. Coaches who lack confidence and courage may tread lightly in their interactions with teachers and limit the focus of their interactions to praise or to questions that merely ask teachers to recall or describe their actions.

To build relationships and establish their credibility, coaches may compromise their influence by engaging in tasks that have limited potential for impact on teaching and learning. This is coaching light. Identifying examples of coaching light is not easy since the key distinguishing factor is the coaches' intention and results. Some coaching services that tend toward the light side include testing students, gathering leveled books for teachers to use, doing repeated demonstration lessons, finding Web sites for students to use, or sharing with teachers professional publications or information about workshops or conferences. Coaching light might include providing feedback to teachers that focuses on their behavior rather than on student learning.

Coaches may be saying, "Yes, but the services you describe as coaching *light* have the potential to build trusting relationships, establish my credibility, convey to teachers that we are serious when we say, 'We are here to help you.'" I agree that coaching light achieves these goals; however, I also believe that there are other ways to build trusting, professionally respectful relationships and establish credibility grounded in tackling the difficult issues by addressing what has previously been "undiscussable" in schools—the relationship between teaching and student learning.

Coaching heavy, on the other hand, includes high-stakes interactions between coaches and teachers, such as curriculum analysis, data analysis, instruction, assessment, and personal and professional beliefs and how they influence practice. It is driven by a coach's deep commitment to improve teaching and learning, even if that commitment means risking being liked. Coaching heavy focuses on planning powerful instruction, implementing and analyzing frequent formative assessments, holding high expectations for teachers' performance, and delivering a rigorous curriculum. Coaching heavy requires coaches to say "no" to trivial requests for support and to turn their attention to those high-leverage services that have the greatest potential for improving teaching and learning.

Coaching heavy requires coaches to work with *all* teachers in a school, not just those who volunteer for coaching services. Coaching heavy requires coaches to seek and use data about their work and regularly analyze their decisions about time allocation, services, and impact. When coaching heavy, coaches work outside their comfort zone and stretch their coaching skills, content knowledge, leadership skills, relationship skills, and instructional skills. They are increasingly aware of the beliefs that drive their actions and reexamine them frequently. Coaching heavy is not being heavy-handed, but rather having significant impact.

From a teacher's perspective, just as coaching light feels light, coaching heavy feels heavy—in the sense that each coach shares equally with teachers the collective responsibility and commitment for the success of every student. To teachers, coaching heavy causes them to feel on edge, questioning their actions and decisions. This does not mean that teachers feel fear, anxiety, or dread. Rather, teachers feel a heightened sense of professionalism, excitement, increased efficacy, and satisfaction with teaching. Coaching heavy holds all adults responsible for student success and engages them as members of collaborative learning teams to learn, plan, reflect, analyze, and revise their daily teaching practices based on student learning results.

Coaching heavy occurs when coaches ask thought-provoking questions, uncover assumptions, have fierce or difficult conversations, and engage teachers in dialogue about their beliefs and goals rather than their knowledge and skills. For example, rather than talking about what a teacher decides to do in a lesson, the coach asks the teacher to describe his of her belief about teaching, student learning, and student capacity to learn. These differences are not just subtle shifts in the way questions are worded, but rather are tied directly to the coach's desire to engage teachers in examining their mental models and how those beliefs drive their decisions and resulting behaviors. For example, rather than asking, "What did you think about when the students were unable to respond to your questions?" the coach asks, "What do you believe is the role of teacher questions in the learning process? What intentions do you hold when asking questions in your lessons?" The purpose of interaction at the belief and goal level rather than at the knowledge and skills level is to facilitate teachers' exploration of who they are as teachers as much or more than what they do as teachers. It is at this level where deep reform can occur.

I presented the concept of coaching heavy and coaching light to coaches in Walla Walla public schools. This conversation was as enlightening as the conversations with coaches in Fairfax County public schools. Where I have visualized coaching heavy and light as two ends of a seesaw with the light end in the air and the heavy end on the ground, they see an image that is more of a spiral with each revolution focusing more narrowly on the target—student learning. Coaches, they said, use a blend of coaching heavy and light and with each turn they narrow their focus.

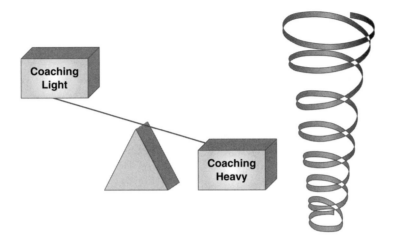

The views of these coaches helped me clarify my own understanding of these concepts. My perspective shifted as a result of listening to their thinking. I recognize that coaches may use both coaching heavy and light in their repertoire of strategies. Yet I believe that beyond a few introductory weeks of coaching light, coaches must shift to coaching heavy and stay there. In this way, coaches increase the potential to significantly impact teaching practices and student learning. I will grant coaches a short period of time at the beginning of a new coaching program—when they are new to a school or when coaching is new to the school—to coach light. During this time, coaches assess the culture, context, and conditions in which they work. However, the shift to coaching heavy cannot wait long because students cannot wait for the best teaching possible.

When I talked with a team of coaches in Fairfax County public schools about the concepts of coaching heavy and coaching light, I expressed my uncertainty about using the words *heavy* and *light*. I worry, I said, that *heavy* connotes that coaching heavy focuses on corrective action or conveys a supervisory or evaluative orientation to coaching. This is not coaching heavy. Rather, the orientation is one of laserlike focus on the work of improving teaching and student learning. Like a laser, a coach focuses intense energy into a small space. That small space is the interaction that occurs between teachers and students. Coaching heavy is not heavy-handed or directive, but rather focused like a laser, a narrow ban of intense energy.

These insightful coaches suggested another way to describe coaching heavy and coaching light. They suggested coaching *shallow* and coaching *deep*. I have thought about their metaphor and share it with my own embellishments. In shallow water, both the coach and teacher feel safe. They can touch bottom. They have a limited perspective of what it means to swim because they can still stand.

In deep water, however, both the coach and the teacher, unless they are competent swimmers, are outside their comfort zone. Depending on their skills, both the coach and the teacher may experience anxiety or even fear. Coaches can provide flotation devices to reduce teachers' anxiety if necessary, yet coaches must be competent swimmers and be ready to rescue a teacher who may struggle, tire, or need to refine his or her strokes. When coaches and teachers need a break from the intensity of navigating deep water, they can resort to the shallow water to rest and renew. Coaches help teachers improve the strength and accuracy of their strokes so they become as competent and confident in deep water as they are in shallow water. Eventually, nonswimmers develop a view of themselves as master of both elementary and advanced swim strokes, and when they demonstrate that they have become swimmers, they navigate easily and eagerly and even for distances. Coaching heavy builds teachers' competence, capabilities, and courage to accomplish goals beyond what they may think possible.

Coaching heavy demands that coaches shift their drivers from being liked and appreciated to making a difference. To know which orientation to coaching they are using, coaches examine their goals and the beliefs they hold about who they are as a coach, the role of coaching in the school, and about change. These beliefs drive who they are as coaches.

Coaching heavy requires that coaches move to the edge of or beyond their comfort zone and perhaps their competence to encourage teachers to move beyond theirs as well. For some coaches, this notion produces tremendous anxiety. When coaches opt to stay in their own or in teachers' comfort zones too long, they limit the impact of their work and even waste their precious time and the resource of coaching. When coaches decide to stay in their comfort zone, their practice conveys their belief that the primary goal of coaching is to help teachers feel good or to make coaches feel valued. It is by operating outside their comfort zone, moving from coaching light to coaching heavy, that coaches improve teaching and student learning.

Some beliefs that may interfere with a coach's ability to accept responsibility to coach heavy are identified in Table 1.4, along with possible side effects.

CONCLUSION

Coaches' work is complex and challenging. What coaches do each day influences what teachers do, and that, in turn, influences what students know and do. When coaches choose to allocate their time to services that hold the greatest potential for deep change in teaching and student learning within their schools, students, teachers, and principals will benefit. The benefits might include the following:

- Every student succeeds as a result of high-quality teaching.
- Every teacher succeeds as a result of coaching *heavy*.

Table 1.4   Beliefs and Possible Side Effects

Belief	Side Effects
1. Being accepted gives me more leverage to work with teachers.	Working on being accepted may delay conversations on what matters most—teaching and learning.
2. Being viewed as credible is essential to being a coach.	Credibility emerges from the alignment between one's actions and one's words. Acting on what matters immediately builds credibility.
3. The work of coaches is to support teachers.	Saying that a coach's role is to support teachers misleads teachers. A coach's primary responsibility is to improve student learning.
4. Teachers are resistant to change.	As professionals, teachers seek continuous improvement. Teachers are motivated to change when they see proven results in terms of student success. When that success can be evident in their own classrooms, they become change enthusiasts.
5. Coaches can't impose on teachers since they have no supervisory responsibilities.	Coaches can't afford not to impose on what teachers believe and how that impacts their actions. Their work is too important, and without conversations about beliefs, deep change is unlikely.
6. Helping teachers to know *about* or learn *how* to implement new instructional strategies is a coach's primary responsibility.	Coaches' primary responsibility is student learning often mediated by teachers' application of effective practices rather than knowing *about* or knowing *how* to use those practices.
7. Coaches are not responsible for what teachers do.	Coaches are responsible for helping teachers explore the beliefs that drive their actions. In dialogue, through reflective questioning, and by presenting data, coaches can influence what a teacher thinks and does.

- No teacher ever faces an instructional challenge alone.
- Every school community engages in ongoing, ruthless analysis of data, and continuous cycles of improvement that allow its members to measure results in a matter of weeks, not months or years.

Coaches support teachers as they work together to grapple with problems of practice and to make smarter, collaborative decisions that are enriched by the shared practice of the entire community. When coaches choose roles and allocate their time and services to those that have the greatest potential for impacting teaching and student learning, the value of coaching and coaches will be unquestioned, even when budgets are tight and other competing priorities emerge.

REFERENCES

Glickman, C. (1993). *Renewing America's schools.* San Francisco: Jossey-Bass.

Killion, J., & Harrison, C. (2006). *Taking the lead: New roles for teachers and school-based coaches.* Oxford, OH: National Staff Development Council.

Resnick, L. (Ed.). (2004, Summer). Teachers matter: Evidence of valued-added assessments. *Research Points, 2*(2), 1–4.

Rowan, B., Correnti, R., & Miller, R. (2002). What large-scale research tells us about teacher effects on student achievement: "Insights from the prospects" study of elementary schools. *Teachers College Record, 104*(8), 1525–1567.

Sanders, W., Saxton, A., & Horn, B. (1997). The Tennessee value-added assessment system: A quantitative outcomes-based approach to educational assessment. In J. Millman (Ed.), *Grading teachers, grading schools: Is achievement a valid measure?* Thousand Oaks, CA: Corwin Press.

Taylor, M. (2007). *National Staff Development Council's Coaches Academy Annual Report.* Littleton, CO: MJT Associates, Inc.

2

Instructional Coaching

Jim Knight

INTRODUCTION

When I began my career as a researcher at the University of Kansas Center for Research on Learning, I never intended to study instructional coaching. I simply wanted to identify what professional developers had to do so that teachers would adopt scientifically proven practices and implement them effectively.

This goal grew out of my early experiences as a teacher. Working with college students who were at risk for failure in Toronto, Canada, I myself was lucky enough to work with an incredible coach, Dee LaFrance, who stood side by side with me in the classroom and helped me learn to teach using a variety of scientifically proven teaching practices, taken from the Strategic Instruction Model. With Dee's empowering assistance, I learned how to teach in ways that really made a difference for my students (Knight, 1992).

After seeing my students succeed, naturally I wanted to share my successes, and I began to provide professional development workshops on the model. Although most of the people attending my sessions listened respectfully, I quickly realized that they were not actually planning to implement the practices I was sharing. Thus began a 15-year journey during which I have tried to identify best practices for sharing proven practices with teachers. More and more I find myself advocating for the kinds of actions that Dee first did when she helped me start out as a teacher.

In 1992, I moved to the University of Kansas and began a number of formal and informal studies of professional development. My colleagues and I ultimately won a Federal GEARUP grant in 1999 to provide support to students in Topeka,

(Continued)

(Continued)

Kansas. Our GEARUP project, Pathways to Success, put onsite professional development at the heart of our efforts to help more students succeed in Topeka. Over time we won two other GEARUP grants and several school-improvement grants that allowed us to develop and deepen our understanding of effective onsite professional development.

During the past decade, my colleagues and I have fine-tuned this approach to professional learning, which we first referred to as "learning consulting," then "instructional collaborating," and eventually "instructional coaching." We have learned that to support quality implementation of teaching practices there are several practices coaches should use. This approach, which started out with two coaches, has come to be adopted by school districts and state organizations in more than 30 states in just 3 years since we first offered our coaching workshops and conferences at the University of Kansas Center for Research on Learning.

This chapter provides an overview of the specific components of instructional coaching that grew out of our ongoing study of onsite professional development. The chapter also describes the framework we use to identify where to start with teachers—The Big Four—and several factors that we have found to be important when it comes to the success of coaching programs. The research we conducted to develop this model is described in Chapter 9.

Instructional coaching, more completely described in *Instructional Coaching: A Partnership Approach to Improving Instruction* (Knight, 2007), provides intensive, differentiated support to teachers so that they are able to implement proven practices. Like other coaches using other models described in this book, instructional coaches (ICs) have excellent communication skills and a deep respect for teachers' professionalism. Additionally, ICs have a thorough knowledge of the teaching practices they share with teachers. Unlike some other approaches, instructional coaches also frequently provide model lessons, observe teachers, and simplify explanations of the teaching practices they share with teachers.

This chapter provides an overview of the specific components of instructional coaching that grew out of our ongoing study of onsite professional development. The chapter also describes the framework we use to identify where to start with teachers—The Big Four—and several factors that we have found to be important when it comes to the success of coaching programs.

WHAT IS INSTRUCTIONAL COACHING?

ICs partner with teachers to help them incorporate research-based instructional practices into their teaching. They are skilled communicators, or relationship builders, with a repertoire of excellent communication skills that enable them to empathize, listen, and build trusting relationships. ICs also encourage and support teachers' reflection about their classroom practices. Thus, they must be skilled at unpacking their collaborating teachers' professional goals so that they can help them create a plan for realizing those goals, all with a focus on improving instruction.

Instructional coaches deeply understand many scientifically proven instructional practices. ICs focus on a broad range of instructional issues, which might include classroom management, content enhancement, specific teaching practices, formative assessment, or other teaching practices, such as the Strategic Instruction Model, reading in the content areas, Marzano's strategies, or other proven ways to improve instruction (Marzano et al., 2001). ICs help teachers choose appropriate approaches to teaching for the different kinds of learning students are experiencing. They frequently model practices in the classroom, observe teachers, and engage in supportive, dialogical conversations with them about what they observed. An instructional coach, in other words, partners with teachers so they can choose and implement research-based interventions to help students learn more effectively.

WHAT IS THE PARTNERSHIP PHILOSOPHY?

One of the most important aspects of instructional coaching, as I define it, is the theory behind the approach. Theory provides a foundation for all aspects of our professional and personal life. When we undertake any task, we operate from a set of taken-for-granted rules or principles of how to be effective, and these tacit rules represent the *theory* for that particular task. Theory is the gravity that holds together any systematic approach, including instructional coaching.

I describe the theoretical framework for instructional coaching as a partnership approach, seeing coaching as a partnership between coaches and teachers. This approach is articulated in seven principles, which are derived from research and theoretical writing in a variety of fields, including adult education (Friere, 1970; Knowles, 1988), cultural anthropology (Eisler, 1998, 2000), leadership (Block, 1993, 2001; Greenleaf, 2001), organizational theory (Senge, 1990), and epistemology (Bernstein, 1983; Feyerabend, 1988; Kuhn, 1970). The principles were also validated in a study of two approaches to professional development (a partnership approach and a traditional approach) (Knight, 1999).

The Partnership Principles

ICs use the partnership principles as touchstones for reflecting on the work they have done in the past and for planning the work they will do in the future. More information on the partnership approach is available in *Partnership Learning: Scientifically Proven Strategies for Fostering Dialogue During Workshops and Presentations* (Knight, 2009b). The seven partnership principles follow.

1. Equality: Instructional Coaches and Teachers Are Equal Partners

Partnership involves relationships between equals. Thus, instructional coaches recognize collaborating teachers as equal partners, and they truly believe that each teacher's thoughts and beliefs are valuable. ICs listen to teachers with the intent to learn, to really understand, and then respond, rather than with the intent to persuade.

2. Choice: Teachers Should Have Choice Regarding What and How They Learn

In a partnership, one individual does not make decisions for another. Because partners are equal, they make their own individual choices and make decisions collaboratively. For ICs, this means that teacher choice is implicit in every communication of content and, to the greatest extent possible, the process used to learn the content. ICs don't see it as their job to make teachers think like them; they see their goal as meeting people where they are and offering choices.

3. Voice: Professional Learning Should Empower and Respect the Voices of Teachers

All individuals in a partnership have opportunities to express their point of view. Indeed, a primary benefit of a partnership is that each individual has access to many perspectives rather than the one perspective of a leader. ICs who act on this principle encourage teachers to express their opinions about content being learned. ICs see coaching as a process that helps teachers find their voice, not a process determined to make teachers think a certain way.

4. Dialogue: Professional Learning Should Enable Authentic Dialogue

To arrive at mutually acceptable decisions, partners engage in dialogue. In a partnership, one individual does not impose, dominate, or control. Partners engage in conversation, learning together as they explore ideas. For ICs, this means that they listen more than they talk. ICs avoid manipulation, engage participants in conversation about content, and think and learn with participants.

5. Reflection: Reflection Is an Integral Part of Professional Learning

If we are creating a learning partnership, if our partners are equal with us, if they are free to speak their own minds and free to make real, meaningful choices, it follows that one of the most important choices our collaborating partners will make is how to make sense of whatever we are proposing they learn. Partners don't dictate to each other what to believe; they respect their partners' professionalism and provide them with enough information so that they can make their own decisions. Thus, ICs encourage collaborating teachers to consider ideas before adopting them. Indeed, ICs recognize that reflective thinkers, by definition, have to be free to choose or reject ideas, or else they simply are not thinkers at all.

6. Praxis: Teachers Should Apply Their Learning to Their Real-Life Practice as They Are Learning

Partnership should enable individuals to have more meaningful experiences. In partnership relationships, meaning arises when people reflect on ideas and then put those actions into practice. A requirement for partnership is that each individual is free to reconstruct and use content the way he or she considers it most useful. For ICs, this means that in partnership with collaborating teachers, they focus their attention on how to use ideas in the classroom as those ideas are being learned.

7. Reciprocity: Instructional Coaches Should Expect to Get as Much as They Give

In a partnership, all partners benefit from the success, learning, or experience of others—everyone is rewarded by what each individual contributes. For that reason, one of an IC's goals should be to learn along with collaborating teachers, such as learning about each teacher's classroom, the strengths and weaknesses of the teaching practices being learned when used in each teacher's classroom, various perspectives of the teaching strategy when seen through the eyes of teachers and students, and so on.

WHAT TEACHING PRACTICES DO INSTRUCTIONAL COACHES SHARE WITH TEACHERS? THE BIG FOUR

If instructional coaches are going to share proven teaching practices with teachers, they likely need a framework to help them identify where to start. ICs working with the University of Kansas Center for Research on Learning employ a framework we refer to as "The Big Four," which includes (1) classroom management, (2) content, (3) instruction, and

The Big Four

1. Classroom Management
2. Content
3. Instruction
4. Assessment for Learning

(4) assessment for learning. More information on The Big Four is available in *The Big Four: A Framework for Instructional Excellence* (Knight, 2009a), *Instructional Coaching: A Partnership Approach to Improving Instruction* (Knight, 2007), and *Coaching Classroom Management: A Toolkit for Coaches and Administrators* (Sprick, Knight, Reinke, & McKale, 2006).

1. Classroom Management

If a teacher's students are on task and learning, an IC and collaborating teachers can turn to a variety of other issues related to student learning. However, if student behavior is out of control, in our experience, the coach and collaborating teacher will struggle to make other practices work if they do not first address classroom management issues. More information about classroom management is available in the book *Coaching Classroom Management: A Toolkit for Coaches and Administrators* (Sprick et al., 2006). ICs can explore starting points for coaching by considering several questions that might help identify whether behavior is an issue that needs to be addressed immediately:

- Are students on task in class?
- Does the teacher make significantly more positive comments than negative comments (at least a 3:1 ratio)?
- Has the teacher developed clear expectations for all activities and transitions during the class?
- Has the teacher clearly communicated those expectations, and do the students understand them?
- Do students have frequent opportunities to respond during the class?

More difficult to identify, but no less important to ask, are the following questions:

- Does the teacher care about his or her students' welfare?
- Does the teacher respect his or her students?
- Does the teacher communicate high expectations?
- Does the teacher believe his or her students can achieve those expectations?

2. Content

Does the teacher understand the content, have a plan, and understand which information is most important? If a teacher's class is well managed, a second question is whether the teacher has a deep knowledge of the content. Teachers need to know which content is most important, and they also need to know how to explain that content clearly. Several questions might help a coach determine whether a teacher has mastery of his or her content. They include the following:

- Does the teacher have a complete, detailed plan for teaching the course?
- Has the teacher developed essential questions for all units?
- Do those questions align with the state standards?
- Can the teacher identify the 10 to 15 core questions that are answered by the course?
- Can the teacher identify the top 10 concepts in the course?
- Can the teacher clearly and simply explain the meaning of each of the top 10 concepts?

3. Instruction

Is the teacher using teaching practices that ensure that all students master content? If teachers hold a deep understanding of their content, and if they can manage their classroom, the next big question is whether they can teach their knowledge to their students. Effective instruction involves numerous teaching practices, the need for which may be surfaced by the following questions:

- Does the teacher properly prepare students at the start of the class?
- Does the teacher effectively model thinking and other processes for students?
- Does the teacher ask questions at an appropriate variety of levels?
- Does the teacher use cooperative learning and other activities to keep students engaged?
- Does the teacher provide constructive feedback that enables students to improve?
- Does the teacher use language, analogies, examples, and stories that make it easier for students to learn and remember content?
- Does the teacher effectively sum up lessons at the end of the class?

4. Formative Assessment

Do the teacher and students know if students are mastering content? If a teacher's students are on task, if the teacher has a deep knowledge of the content, knows what's most important and can communicate that knowledge using effective instructional practices, then the final question is whether the teacher and student know how well the students are learning. Several questions will help ICs explore a teacher's understanding of formative assessment:

- Does the teacher know the target or targets the students are aiming for in the class?
- Do the students know the target they are aiming for in the class?

- Does the teacher use formative assessments or checks for understanding to gauge how well students are learning?
- Are students involved in the development and use of formative assessments?
- Can a teacher look out into the classroom and know with some degree of accuracy how well each student is doing?

WHAT DO INSTRUCTIONAL COACHES DO? THE COMPONENTS OF INSTRUCTIONAL COACHING

Instructional coaching, as we define it, has very clear components that enable ICs to respond to the unique challenges of personal change. The eight components of this process (Enroll, Identify, Explain, Model, Observe, Explore, Refine, Reflect) are described as follows.

Enroll

How does an IC get people onboard? We propose five methods: (1) one-to-one interviews, (2) small-group presentations, (3) large-group presentations, (4) informal conversations, and (5) administrator referral.

1. One-to-One Interviews

Perhaps the most effective way for coaches to enroll teachers is through the use of one-to-one interviews. One-to-one interviews help ICs achieve at least three goals. First, they are a way to gather specific information about teacher and administrative challenges, student needs, and cultural norms specific to a school. Coaches can use this information to tailor coaching sessions and other professional learning to the unique needs of teachers and students. Second, interviews enable ICs to educate participants about the partnership philosophy, methods, and opportunities offered by instructional coaching. During interviews, ICs can explain their partnership approach to coaching, listen to teachers' concerns, and explain that as coaches they are there to help, not to evaluate. Finally, interviews provide an opportunity for ICs to develop one-to-one relationships with teachers.

How Should One-to-One Interviews Be Conducted? Interviews are most effective when they last at least 30 minutes, and more effective when they are 45 minutes to one hour long (generally, one planning period per interview). While a longer interview allows more time to learn about each person's particular burning issues, and provides more time to build a relationship, a great deal of information can be gathered from 15-minute interviews.

Whenever possible, interviews should be conducted one-to-one. In a group, people tend to comment in ways that are consistent with the cultural norms of their organization (Schein, 1992). One-to-one, on the other hand, allows people to speak much more candidly. Since effective instructional coaching may involve overcoming negative or even toxic cultural norms, creating a setting where teachers feel safe stepping outside their culture and speaking frankly is important.

During the Interviews. In most cases, your goals during an interview will be the same regardless of the amount of time available. We have found that it is most valuable to seek answers to at least four general questions:

1. What are the rewards you experience as a teacher?

2. What obstacles interfere with you achieving your professional goals?

3. What are your students' strengths and weaknesses?

4. What kinds of professional learning are most or least effective for you?

When you have more time to conduct interviews, you can broaden or focus the scope of your questions depending on the nature of the professional development session you are planning to lead. (A fairly extensive list of interview questions from which you might draw in structuring your interview can be found in Knight, 2007.)

How to Build Relationships During Interviews. Using interviews as a way to build an emotional connection with collaborating teachers can make it easier for coaches to communicate their message. By positioning themselves as listeners during the interviews, ICs have a chance to make many bids for emotional connection with participants (Gottman, 2001). During an interview, ICs can share stories, laugh and empathize, offer positive comments, discuss personal issues, and listen with great care. If done well, enrolling interviews provide ICs with many opportunities to listen with empathy, offer encouragement, and reveal themselves as real, caring people.

Asking Teachers to Commit: Contracting. As important as the interview process is for providing you with information about teachers, students, and your school, the most important outcome of the interview process is to obtain commitment from teachers to the coaching process. Many coaches in business and education refer to this as contracting. ICs must find time during the interview to tactfully explain how instructional coaching works and what benefits it might offer for the teacher being interviewed. An IC should search for appropriate times in the middle of the interview to explain aspects of instructional coaching in response to the teacher's comments.

The goal is to ensure that the teacher knows enough about coaching so that he or she can make an intelligent choice about whether to work with the coach. For that reason, ICs should see the interview as their first chance to demonstrate the respectful, partnering relationship that is at the heart of instructional coaching. At the end of the one-to-one interview, ICs should know whether a teacher is ready to collaborate with them, and in most cases the interview is an IC's best strategy for enrolling teachers. As Lucy West (whose chapter appears later in this book) has said, a coach's goal is to meet teachers where they are and offer them resources that uniquely respond to their particular needs.

2. Small-Group Presentations

In some cases, one-to-one interviews are not practical or necessary. One alternative to one-to-one interviews is small-group meetings. Usually an IC meets with the teachers during a team meeting, a grade-level meeting, or whatever small-group meeting is available.

During the get-together, an IC's goals are quite simple: (a) to explain the opportunities that exist for teachers' professional growth, (b) to clarify the partnership perspective that underlies the coaching relationship, (c) to explain other "nuts and bolts" issues related to instructional coaching, and, most important, (d) to sign up teachers who want to work with a coach.

The presentation during small-group meetings should be short, clear, and respectful. In many cases, this initial conversation is the IC's first opportunity to communicate an authentic respect and admiration for the important activity of teaching. If ICs honestly communicate their genuine respect for teachers, that may go a long way toward opening doors. On the other hand, if an IC appears to communicate a lack of respect for teachers, that may put the IC into a hole that will be very difficult to climb out of.

We suggest that ICs plan for about 20 minutes during small-group meetings. Following the informal presentation, ICs should answer any questions teachers raise. ICs can also provide a one-page summary of the teaching practices teachers can learn as a result of instructional coaching, such as classroom management, curriculum planning, teaching to mastery, or formative assessment.

At the close of the small-group presentation, after teachers have heard about the IC's partnership philosophy, the way the IC works, and the teaching practices that the IC can share, ICs should hand out a short form asking teachers to note whether they are interested in collaborating with their IC at this time. The form provides an opportunity for teachers to communicate their interest privately.

3. Large-Group Presentations

In some cases, ICs enroll teachers through a single presentation to a large group, possibly the entire staff. Such a presentation is usually held at the start of the school year, ideally before classes begin, or at the end of the year, to enroll teachers for the following year. A large-group presentation is a good idea when an IC wants to ensure that all teachers hear the same message. Large-group presentations are also effective when an IC is confident that teachers are interested in collaborating with them. As a general rule, the greater the resistance an IC expects to experience with teachers, the smaller the group should be, and when there is any concern that teachers will resist collaborating with ICs, one-to-one interviews are recommended.

ICs can enhance large-group presentations by employing partnership learning structures (Knight, 2009b), learning activities that foster dialogue in the middle of the presentation. For example, ICs might ask teachers to work in groups to identify the top needs of students and then match possible interventions to the identified needs.

At the end of the session, the IC asks participants to complete a form to indicate whether they are interested in collaborating with them. The form might be the same as the one proposed for the small-group session, or the IC might have participants complete a form throughout the presentation. When they employ this presentation tactic, ICs provide a brief explanation of a few teaching practices or interventions, and then they pause to provide time for the audience to write down their thoughts or comments about the practices or interventions that are described. In this way, the teachers have an opportunity to express their thoughts about what they are hearing, and ICs get a lot of helpful feedback. What is essential is that at the end of the session, teachers have a chance to write down whether they are ready to work with the coach, and the IC will have a list of people with whom to start coaching.

4. One-to-One Informal Conversations

Frequently, ICs enroll teachers through casual conversations around the school. ICs who are skilled at getting teachers to commit to collaboration usually are highly skilled relationship builders. An IC shouldn't feel compelled to get every teacher onboard immediately; a better tactic is to win over a few teachers with high-quality professional learning on an intervention that really makes a difference for students. In most cases, the IC should seek out a highly effective solution for a troubling problem a teacher is facing. If you respond to a real challenge a teacher is facing with a real solution, word will travel through the school, and teachers will commit to working with their coach.

5. Administrator Referral

When an IC and a principal work together in a school, inevitably there will be occasions when the principal or other administrators identify teachers who need to work with the IC. Principal referral can be a powerful way to accelerate the impact of coaching in a school, but it must be handled with care. If the partnership principles are ignored and struggling teachers are told they must work with a coach (or else!), the IC can be seen as a punishment, not a support, and teachers may come to resent the coach's help.

We suggest a different approach for principal referral, one consistent with the partnership principles. Rather than telling teachers they must work with coaches, we suggest principals focus on the teaching practice that must change, and offer the coach as one way the teacher can bring about the needed change. Thus, a principal might say, "John, when I observed your class, I noticed that 10 of your 24 students were off task during your lesson. You need to implement ways to keep those kids on task. Our instructional coach Tamika is great at time on task. You might want to talk with her about this, but if you can find another way, that's fine, too. What matters is that more kids are learning. I'll check back in a few weeks, and I expect to see a difference."

In this way, the principal can apply pressure on the teacher while at the same time leaving the IC as one option. Thus, the coach isn't a punishment forced on the teacher, but a lifeline, someone who provides a meaningful support for teachers doing this important and complex work in the classroom. When led to the coach in this way, many teachers are grateful for their coach's support and assistance. If other teachers are able to address the problem in the class in other ways, that is fine too, and it provides ICs with more time to work with teachers who want to work with their coach.

Identify

After enrolling teachers (either through interviews, one-to-one meetings, in small groups, in large groups, or through administrator referral), the IC will have a list of potential collaborating teachers. It is important that ICs reply promptly to every teacher expressing an interest in working with them. If the coach waits too long, the teachers may run out of time to collaborate, become focused on other priorities, or lose their desire to collaborate with the coach.

ICs shouldn't worry too much if their starting list of potential collaborating teachers is short. The list could include most of the school's teachers, but frequently it consists of fewer than 25% of the staff. The length of the list is not that important initially. What really matters is that the experiences of the first few teachers the IC collaborates with are successful because the first teachers will start the word-of-mouth process that should eventually lead to widespread implementation of the teaching practices provided by the coach.

The First Meeting

A lot can be accomplished during the first conversation after a teacher has enrolled in the coaching process. Both parties share the goal of identifying which of the teaching practices the coach has to offer might be most helpful to the teacher. On many occasions, the first conversation is all that is needed for the teacher and coach to identify the teaching practices to be implemented in the teacher's classroom. On other occasions, the first conversation, what some call a preconference, does not always provide enough data to identify where the coach and teacher start. In some cases, the collaborating teacher might not know where to start. Many ICs prefer to observe teachers before identifying a teaching practice. What counts is that the IC and teacher *together* identify a particular best practice that has the greatest chance of making a difference for students and naturally teachers' lives.

Explain

Once the IC and teacher have identified a proven practice to be implemented, the IC has to explain the teaching practice. This is not as easy as it seems. Many teachers' instructional manuals are more than 100 pages long, filled with fairly abstract language and concepts. Add to this the reality that the amount of time a coach and teacher might spend together can be quite short and, no doubt, will occur in a context of competing priorities. Clearly, coaches have their work cut out for them. Nonetheless, to be effective, an IC must translate research into practice. We suggest five tactics that enhance an IC's ability to do this.

1. Clarify

One of the most important and most frequently overlooked practices that ICs can employ is the simple task of reading, writing, and synthesizing what they plan to tell teachers. ICs need to read, reread, take notes, and reread the manuals and research articles that describe the instructional practices they are sharing. A simple overview of a manual is not sufficient. Coaches need to mark up their books, highlight key passages, write in the margins, and cover their manuals with sticky notes. They should have read these materials so frequently that they know the page numbers for key sections and recognize most pages in a manual the way one recognizes an old friend. During and after reading, ICs should write out their understanding of the materials they have read. This activity might take the form of writing outlines of documents, creating semantic maps or webs, or paraphrasing what has been read into simple language.

Five Tactics for Translating Research Into Practice

1. Clarify: Read, write, talk

2. Synthesize

3. Break it down

4. See it through teachers' (and students') eyes

5. Simplify

Once they have read and written about the materials they've been studying, ICs should seek out opportunities to explain, clarify, modify, and expand their understandings by communicating with others who are knowledgeable about the same interventions. Some ICs use e-mail or the telephone to share ideas with other ICs who are sharing the same practices. Others even contact the authors of the research articles and manuals to ask for their insights. In the best-case scenario, ICs set up informal or formal professional learning communities so they can meet with other ICs to discuss and deepen their knowledge of teaching practices.

2. Synthesize

After clarifying the meaning of research articles and manuals, ICs need to synthesize what they have learned and describe the essential features of the teaching practices they've studied. For some this is accomplished by writing one- to two-sentence statements that capture the essence of the interventions they are sharing with teachers. What matters is that coaches are able to identify and summarize what is most important about the teaching practices they are sharing.

ICs can develop short checklists that summarize the vital teaching behaviors that are essential components of the teaching practices they're sharing. Checklists can provide focus to conversations with teachers and shape the modeling and observing practices used to enable teachers to master successful teaching of new practices.

3. Break It Down

As a translator of teaching practices, ICs break down teaching practices into manageable components related to the specific teaching practices to be implemented. There is much coaches can do to make teacher manuals more accessible. Some literally tear apart manuals and divide them into easy-to-understand sections that they put into binders. ICs can also highlight important passages or put sticky notes beside especially important sections of a manual. When breaking down materials, ICs should ensure that teachers know exactly what needs to be done next. As personal productivity guru David Allen (2001) has observed, "It never fails to greatly improve both the productivity and the peace of mind of the user to determine what the next physical action is that will move something forward" (p. 237).

4. See It Through Teachers' (and Students') Eyes

ICs must plan their explanations by thinking carefully about what the new practice will look like in the classroom. In this way, ICs can address the practical concerns that teachers might have. For example, they might think through a number of classroom management issues, such as handing out papers, organizing grading assignments, or handling movement in the classroom. ICs might also discuss how to incorporate formative assessments into a lesson or explain what expectations should be taught when a certain teaching practice is introduced. Throughout the explanation, the IC should be intent on removing teachers' anxiety and making it easier for them to understand and eventually use a new teaching practice.

5. Simplify

ICs should not dumb down complex ideas and make them simplistic. As Bill Jensen said in his book *Simplicity: The New Competitive Advantage in a World of More, Better, Faster* (2000), we should not confuse "simplistic" with simplicity. Simplicity, Jensen explains, is "the art of making the complex clear" (p. 2). And "making the complex clear always helps people work smarter. Because it is a lot easier to figure out what's important and ignore what isn't" (p. i).

There are many things coaches can do to attain simpler explanations. Jensen (2000) proposes storytelling as a communication strategy that "easily creates common meaning and purpose for everyone" (p. 88). ICs can use stories to help teachers see what a teaching practice might look like in the classroom. Additionally, ICs should look for analogies, anecdotes, or simple explanations and comparisons that bring the materials to life.

Model: You Watch Me

ICs, as we define them, spend a great deal of their time in classrooms modeling lessons, watching teachers teach, and having conversations about what teachers saw when they watched the IC, or what the IC saw when he or she watched the teachers. Since some teachers find the business of observation somewhat intimidating, ICs try to keep the experience as informal as possible: "You watch me; I watch you."

The Observation Form

Before conducting a model lesson, an IC must ensure that the collaborating teachers are prepared to get the most out of it—that they know what to watch for and, in fact, are actually watching the model lesson. ICs can develop a shared understanding of the purpose of the model lesson by coconstructing with the teacher an observation form to help focus the attention of both the teacher and the IC. The observation form is a simple chart on which the IC, in partnership with the collaborating teacher, lists the critical teaching behaviors that a teacher should be watching for when watching a model lesson.

The observation form includes a column for listing these behaviors, one where teachers can put a check mark every time they observe a critical teaching behavior, and a column where they can include comments, questions, or thoughts about what they observe during a model lesson. By coconstructing the form with teachers prior to the model lesson, ICs can check for teachers' understanding of critical teaching behaviors. Later, by having teachers fill out the form during a model lesson, they can focus the teachers' attention on what matters most in the model. Of course, a coach and IC don't need a preconstructed form; they can simply create one on a sheet of paper.

Checklists of critical teaching behaviors can help coaches clarify and synthesize their understanding of teaching practices. However, we have found that giving a ready-made checklist to teachers is not as effective as coconstructing an observation form. Although the IC ensures that the coconstructed form includes most of the critical teaching behaviors on the original checklist, by involving the teacher in creating the form, a coach gets better buy-in to the form and can be more certain that the collaborating teacher understands all of the items listed on it. Also, teachers frequently suggest teaching behaviors for the form that the coach might not have considered but that are important. Thus, by involving teachers in the process as partners, we actually get a better product.

Giving a Model Lesson

Before providing model lessons, ICs must ensure that they have a deep understanding of the lesson they are modeling. Prior to the lesson, the IC and collaborating teacher also need to clarify their roles with respect to behavior management in the classroom. In some cases, teachers want to retain their role as manager of classroom behavior. In other situations, teachers are very comfortable with the IC taking primary responsibility for managing behavior during the model lesson. Both the teacher and IC must know how behavior will be managed. As every experienced teacher knows, students seem to have a sixth sense that makes them very sensitive to any vacuum in leadership with respect to classroom management, and if no one is in control, students can be off task in minutes, possibly seconds.

We have found that it is most effective for coaches to model only the specific practice that is described on an observation form, rather than model an entire lesson. During the model, the teacher observes the coach, using the observation form to focus his or her attention, checking off behaviors when the teacher sees them modeled by the coach. ICs need to be careful to include the teacher in the lesson and ensure that students know that they, the ICs, are just visitors in the teacher's classroom. Additionally, the coach should defer to the experience of the teacher throughout the lesson.

Observe: I Watch You

After the collaborating teacher has watched the coach provide a model lesson and then discussed his or her thoughts and questions about it with the IC, it is time for the IC to observe the teacher. While watching the teacher, the IC does the same as the teacher did while watching the model lesson: the IC watches for the critical teaching behaviors they identified using a copy of the coconstructed observation form that the teacher used to observe the coach when he or she did the model lesson. And, as the teacher did earlier, the IC watches the teacher carefully and checks off the form every time he or she sees the teacher perform one of the identified critical teaching behaviors.

Since teachers have already used the form to watch the IC's model lesson, they are usually quite comfortable with their IC using the form in the classroom. However, ICs need to be careful to stress the informality of the observation, which is why we emphasize the idea of simply saying, "You watch me, and I watch you." For some teachers, the very notion of "observation" is intimidating, and some ICs avoid using that term, choosing to say instead that they'll "visit" the classroom. If an IC is careful to watch for and record the many good aspects of the lesson that is observed, however, teachers will become much less reticent about inviting the IC to watch lessons.

As an observer, the IC should try to remove personal judgments from the activity of observing. Rather than seeing themselves as evaluating teachers, coaches should see themselves as a second set of eyes in the room, using the observation form or other data-gathering methods as tools for recording relevant data about how the lesson proceeds. While observing, the IC should especially attend to the collaborating teacher's efforts to use the critical teaching practices. Whenever the teacher uses one of the critical behaviors, the IC should check the appropriate column of the observation form, and write down specific data about how the teacher used the behavior. For example, if a critical teaching behavior is to explain expectations to students, the IC might jot down a quick summary of exactly what the teacher said when he or she clarified expectations.

What data the coach records during the observation vary, depending on what intervention teachers are learning to use. In many cases, the IC will need to use the observation form only to gather the necessary data. Other interventions require other kinds of data gathering. For example, ICs who are coaching teachers to increase the number of high-level questions used might simply write down each question posed by the teacher so that the coach and teacher can review them later. ICs who are coaching teachers with respect to "opportunities to respond" (the number of times students are invited to speak or interact during a lesson) might simply keep a tally of the number of opportunities to respond provided during a lesson. Thus, ICs may use the observation forms or other data-gathering methods depending on the teaching practice being learned.

While observing the lesson and gathering data, an IC has to be especially careful to note positive actions taking place in the class, such as effective interventional practices or positive student responses. While intuitively an IC might think that the most important part of observing a lesson is to find areas of weakness that need to be improved, in reality, the most important part of the observation may be to look for things the teacher does well. Seeing what needs to be improved is often quite easy; seeing, recording, and communicating what went well sometimes require extra effort.

ICs who are highly sensitive to the positive things that take place in the classroom can provide a great service to the teachers and the school. Too often the challenges of being an educator, and the emotional exhaustion that comes with trying to reach every child every day, make it difficult for teachers to fully comprehend the good they are doing. Furthermore, conversations in schools sometimes have a tendency to turn negative, perhaps as a defense mechanism for teachers who are frustrated that they cannot reach more students. Thus, ICs should consider it one of their goals to change the kind of conversations that take place in schools, one conversation at a time.

Explore: The Collaborative Exploration of Data

As soon as possible after observing a lesson, an IC should schedule a follow-up meeting with the collaborating teacher to discuss the data that were collected. This meeting, like other aspects of the instructional coaching process, is based on the mutual respect between professionals inherent in the partnership principles. The collaborative exploration of data taking place during this meeting is *not* an opportunity for the IC to share his or her "expert" opinion on what the teacher did right or wrong. More than anything else it is a learning conversation where both parties use data as a point of departure for dialogue.

This meeting is not an opportunity for top-down feedback. Top-down feedback, as Figure 2.1 suggests, occurs when one person, an expert, watches a novice and provides feedback until the novice masters a skill. This might be a great way to teach some skills, but it is problematic as a model for interaction between professionals who are peers.

The problem with top-down feedback is that it is based on the assumption that there is only one right way to see things, and that right way is the view held by the feedback giver. Kegan and Lahey (2001) explain the assumptions of this approach:

> The first [assumption] is that the perspective of the feedback giver (let's call him the supervisor)—what he sees and thinks, his feedback—is right, is correct. An accompanying assumption is that there is only one correct answer. When you put these two assumptions together, they amount to this: the supervisor has the one and only correct view of the situation. (We call this "the super vision assumption"; that is, the supervisor has *super* vision). (p. 128)

Figure 2.1   Top-Down Feedback

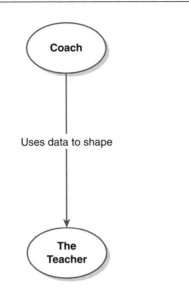

During top-down feedback, the feedback giver is prepared to "(1) say exactly what the person is doing wrong, (2) give the sense the criticism is meant to help, (3) suggest a solution, and (4) give a timely message" (Kegan & Lahey, 2001, p. 128). The person giving top-down feedback, in other words, working from the assumption that he or she is right, does all of the thinking for the person receiving the feedback. That is hardly the partnership approach, and the reason why Kegan and Lahey (2001) say, "many a relationship has been damaged and a work setting poisoned by *perfectly delivered* constructive feedback!" (p. 128).

An alternative to top-down feedback is the partnership approach or the collaborative exploration of data. As depicted in the Figure 2.2, during the partnership approach, the IC and teacher sit side by side as partners and review the data that the IC has gathered. The IC does not withhold his or her opinion, but offers it in a provisional way, communicating that he or she is open to other points of view.

A Language of Ongoing Regard

One important goal ICs should hold during the collaborative exploration of data is to communicate clearly the genuinely positive aspects of the lesson that was observed. I do not mean that they should be promoting thoughtless, vague, or empty happy words or phrases. A "language of ongoing regard" has specific characteristics. Kegan and Lahey (2001) stress that authentic, appreciative, or admiring feedback needs to be (a) direct, (b) specific, and (c) nonattributive. Most ICs recognize the importance of

Figure 2.2   Collaborative Exploration of Data

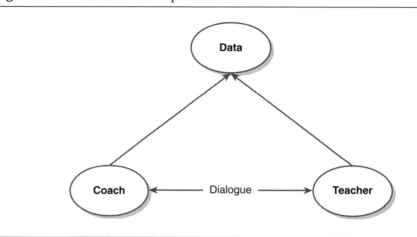

direct, specific feedback. Direct comments are spoken to a person in the first person, not about a person in the third person. Thus, it is preferable to tell someone directly, "I appreciate your help," rather than saying publicly, "I appreciate Jean's help." Specific comments clearly explain the details of what we are praising, rather than offering general statements. Thus, it is preferable to say, "You asked 42 questions today during your class," in contrast to "You asked a lot of questions today in your class."

The importance of making nonattributive comments may be less obvious. Kegan and Lahey (2001) explain that our positive comments about others are more effective when we describe our experience of others rather than the attributes of others. For example, it is less effective to say to someone, "You're very patient" (describing an attribute that we judge them to have), than it is to say, "You waited 10 seconds for Alison to give her answer, and when she got it right, she lit up like a Christmas tree." Kegan and Lahey (2001) explain why nonattribute feedback is more effective:

> It may seem odd to you that we're urging you not to make statements of this sort: "Carlos, I just want you to know how much I appreciate how generous you are" (or: "what a good sense of humor you have" or "that you always know the right thing to say"), or "Alice, you are so patient" (or, "so prompt," "so never-say-die," "always there when you are needed,"), and so on. . . . These seem like such nice things to say to someone. . . . The problem we see is this: the person, inevitably and quite properly, relates what you say to how she knows herself to be. You can tell Carlos he is generous, but he knows how generous he actually is. You can tell Alice she is very patient, but she knows her side of how patient she is being with you. (p. 99)

Learning how to give direct, specific, nonattributive feedback is a skill that every IC should develop and one that can be practiced and developed daily until it becomes a habit of thought. ICs can practice developing this "language of ongoing regard" at their workplace, but they can also practice it with their children, parents, spouse, or other people in their life. There is great benefit in practicing such feedback until it becomes a habitual way of communicating. Indeed, it seems strange that we often feel uncomfortable telling people directly and specifically why we appreciate them. Perhaps we're afraid our comments will seem insincere or like self-serving flattery. Nothing could be further from the truth. As Kegan and Lahey (2001) state, "Ongoing regard is not about praising, stroking, or positively defining a person to herself or to others. We say again: it is about enhancing the quality of a precious kind of information. It is about informing the person about *our* experience of him or her" (p. 101).

Dialogue

Frequently, during the collaborative exploration of data, the IC and teacher swiftly move toward identifying next steps that they both agree will have the most positive impact on teaching. On other occasions, however, the IC and teacher hold different opinions about the significance of the data or what the teachers' next steps should be. The best route for ICs to take here is not to withhold their perspective or push for their perspective. Partnership involves two equals sharing ideas, and this doesn't require one person to suppress or promote his or her ideas for another's. Rather, when the IC and the collaborating teacher see the data differently, the coach, acting on one of the partnership principles, can employ the tools of dialogue to foster an authentic learning conversation. When skillfully handled, a dialogue about differing perceptions of data can help both the IC and the teacher learn a great deal.

Refine

The components of coaching discussed in this chapter are the primary activities carried out by ICs. Usually, ICs use most or all of these components, but the sequence in which the components have been described is not always followed. Sometimes the IC opens the door to a teacher's classroom by offering to model a lesson. Sometimes coaching begins with the IC observing. Sometimes the IC provides several model lessons. Each coaching sequence must be tailored to the unique needs of each individual teacher.

During coaching, the IC provides as much support as necessary, but no more. In most cases, after a teacher has mastered a new teaching practice, the coach and teacher choose to move on to some other intervention. What matters is that the teacher and the IC keep learning together, working as partners to ensure that students receive excellent instruction.

Reflect

When an IC moves through the components of coaching with a teacher, both the teacher and the coach should be learning. The teacher is learning a new teaching practice. At the same time, the coach could be learning any number of new skills or insights related to working with students, providing model lessons, enrolling teachers in the instructional coaching process, building relationships, addressing teachers' core concerns, or any other aspect of instructional coaching. Every day provides numerous learning experiences for even the most experienced coaches.

To ensure that they do not forget what they learn along the way, many coaches keep journals, either on their computers or in handwritten notebooks, to record the important things they learn. ICs can also use a reflective practice developed by the U.S. Army—After-Action Review (AAR). According to *The U.S. Army Leadership Field Manual* (U.S. Army, 2004), "An AAR is a professional discussion of an event, focused on performance standards, that allow participants to discover for themselves what happened, why it happened, and how to sustain strengths and improve on weaknesses" (p. 6). Put another way, the AAR structures reflection on (a) what was supposed to happen, (b) what really happened, (c) why there's a difference between (a) and (b), and (c) what should be done differently next time.

WHAT FACTORS INCREASE THE SUCCESS OF COACHING PROGRAMS?

If ICs are going to be successful, they must work in a context that supports their focus on instruction. A few simple factors can make all the difference in the effectiveness of any coaching program.

Time

The simplest way to improve the effectiveness of a coaching program is to increase the amount of time coaches are actually coaching. This seems obvious, but the most frequent concern raised by the more than 2,000 instructional coaches we have worked with in the past four years was that they are asked to complete so many noninstructional tasks they have little time left to work with teachers. Because instructional coaches' job descriptions are often vague or nonexistent and because their schedules are more flexible than the schedules of others, they often are asked to do many clerical or noninstructional tasks. Paying ICs to copy and bind standards documents or shop for math lab furniture or serve as substitute teachers is a poor way to spend money and perhaps an even poorer way to improve teaching practices in schools.

In Cecil County, Maryland, ICs and administrators address this issue by drawing up a pie chart that depicts exactly how much time they agree coaches should spend on various tasks. Then, each week the coaches report to their principals how their time was spent. If necessary, this allows the coach and principal to adjust the time allocations so they can focus their efforts on improving instruction.

Proven Research-Based Interventions

If ICs are going to make a difference in the way teachers teach, they need to have scientifically proven practices to share. Hiring coaches but not ensuring that they have proven practices is a bit like trying to paint a beautiful painting without any art supplies. ICs need to have a repertoire of tools to help them assist teachers in addressing their most pressing concerns.

ICs working with the Center for Research on Learning learn how to use interventions that address The Big Four areas of behavior, content knowledge, instruction, and formative assessment. The coaches develop a deep understanding of scientifically proven practices they can share with teachers to help them improve in any or all of the four areas.

One way to address this concern is for the coach, principal, and other school leaders to come to a shared understanding of excellent instruction. Then, the team should identify what tools are necessary for all teachers to become excellent. Finally, the coach and team should identify how the coach can develop proficiency in those practices so that they can be shared with others in the school. Tools such as *The Big Four: A Framework for Instructional Excellence* (Knight, 2009a) or Charlotte Danielson's (1996) *Enhancing Professional Practice: A Framework for Teaching* can be very helpful when doing this task.

Professional Development for Instructional Coaches

Coaches need to understand the interventions they are sharing, and they need to understand how to productively employ the coaching process. Without their own professional development, ICs run the risk of being ineffective, wasting time and money, or even misinforming teachers. Therefore, the coaches need to participate in their own professional development to ensure that they know how to coach and what to share when they coach teachers.

Professional development for coaches should address at least two subjects. First, coaches should engage in various professional learning activities designed to improve their coaching practices. Specifically, ICs affiliated with our center learn how to employ powerful, proven practices to (a) enroll teachers in coaching, (b) identify appropriate interventions for teachers to learn, (c) model and gather data in the classroom, and (d) engage in dialogue about classroom and other data. Additionally, they improve their professional skills in areas such as communication, relationship building, change management, and leadership.

Second, professional development for coaches should deepen ICs' knowledge about the teaching practices they are sharing with teachers. Obviously, if coaches have a superficial knowledge of the information they share with teachers, they will not know what to emphasize when they discuss, model, or observe during professional learning with teachers. Indeed, coaches who do not deeply understand what they are sharing with teachers could misinform teachers and actually make things worse, not better, for students.

Protecting the Coaching Relationship

Many, perhaps most, teachers see their profession as an integral part of their self-identity. Consequently, if coaches or others are careless with their comments or suggestions about teachers' practices in the classroom, they run the risk of offending teachers, damaging relationships, or at the very least, not being heard. Because teaching is such a personal activity, coaches need to win teachers' trust. Trust is an essential component of an open coaching relationship.

To make it easier for coaches to maintain trusting partnerships with teachers, educational leaders must protect the coaching relationship. If leaders ask coaches to hold the dual role of administrator and coach, they put their coaches in a difficult situation. Administrators, by definition, are not peers. Usually people are more guarded when they talk with their bosses than when they talk with their peers. Coaches will find it easier to have open conversations about teaching practices if their collaborating teachers do not view them as bosses and, therefore, do not have to worry about how their comments might affect the way they will be evaluated.

Ensuring That Principals and Coaches Work Together

The IC can be and should be the right-hand person of the principal when it comes to instructional leadership in schools, but the principal must remain the instructional leader. No matter how much a coach knows, and no matter how effective a coach is, the principal's voice is ultimately the voice most important to teachers. For that reason, coaches must understand fully what their principal's vision is for school improvement, and principals need to understand fully the interventions that their coach has to offer teachers.

One way to ensure that principals get the most out of their ICs is to provide them with sufficient training. Principals who do not understand the importance of protecting the coaching relationship may act in ways that make it difficult for a coach to be successful. Also, a principal who is unaware of the tools that an IC can offer will be unable to suggest them to teachers who might benefit from learning them. District administrators around the country are addressing these issues by providing coaching professional development for principals. Another way to ensure that principals are on the same page as their coaches is for coaches and principals to meet frequently.

Hiring the Right Instructional Coaches

All the factors described here will not yield success if the wrong people are hired to be coaches. Indeed, the most critical factor related to the success or failure of a coaching program may be the skills and attributes of the IC.

Over the past 10 years, we have found that ICs must be excellent teachers, particularly because they will likely provide model lessons in other teachers' classrooms. They also need to be flexible since their job requires them to change their plans almost daily to meet the changing needs of teachers.

Coaches should be highly skilled at building relationships. In our experience, whether a teacher adopts a new teaching practice has as much to do with the IC's communication skills as with whatever intervention the coach has to share. Simply put, if teachers like a coach, they usually will try out what the coach suggests. If they don't like the coach, they'll resist even good teaching practices.

Jim Collins's study of great organizations offers additional insight into the desirable attributes of effective coaches. Great leaders, Collins (2005) writes, "are ambitious first and foremost for the cause, the movement, the mission, the work—not themselves—and they have the will to do whatever it takes to . . . make good on that ambition" (p. 11).

The attributes Collins identifies in great leaders are also found in the best ICs. They need to be ambitious for change in their schools and willing to do, as Collins emphasizes, "whatever it takes" to improve teaching practices. If a coach is too passive about change, chances are that little will happen in the school. At the same time, if a coach is too self-centered or aggressive, there is a good chance the coach will push teachers away.

Effective coaches embody what Collins (2001) describes as a "compelling combination of personal humility and professional will" (p. 13). They are affirmative, humble, and deeply respectful of teachers, but they are unwilling to rest unless they achieve significant improvements in teaching and learning in their schools.

Evaluating Coaches

Evaluation is a major mechanism for continuous improvement of any coaching program. Evaluating ICs can offer unique challenges because no one in a district, including the principal, may ever have been a coach before, and there may be no guidelines for evaluating coaches.

One way to address this challenge is to involve coaches in the process of creating guidelines, standards, and tools to be used for their evaluation.

Involving coaches in the process of writing their evaluation guidelines accomplishes at least three goals. First, it enables school districts to develop a rubric for evaluating coaches that is especially designed for coaches. Second, it increases coaches' buy-in to the guidelines and the process of being evaluated since they created them. Third, the dialogue coaches have while creating the guidelines is an excellent form of professional learning.

CONCLUSION

ICs make a very important contribution to school improvement by partnering with teachers to help them find better ways to reach more students. ICs who work from the partnership perspective can employ the components of coaching as a methodology for sharing proven practices with teachers. In some cases, they might focus on The Big Four practices of (1) classroom management, (2) content enhancement, (3) instruction, and (4) assessment for learning. When coaches understand effective tools to address The Big Four, when they know how to work with teachers, and when they work in schools that embody the success factors listed earlier, there is every reason to assume that they will have an unmistakable positive impact on how teachers teach and how students learn in schools.

REFERENCES

Allen, D. (2001). *Getting things done: The art of stress-free productivity.* New York: Penguin.

Bernstein, R . J. (1983). *Beyond objectivism and relativism: Science, hermeneutics, and praxis.* Philadelphia: University of Pennsylvania.

Billmeyer, R., & Barton, M. (1998). *Teaching reading in the content areas: If not me, then who?* (2nd ed.). Denver, CO: Mid-continent Research for Education and Research.

Block, P. (1993). *Stewardship: Choosing service over self-interest.* San Francisco: Berrett-Koehler.

Block, P. (2001). *The answer to how is yes: Acting on what matters.* San Francisco: Berrett-Koehler.

Collins, J. (2001). *Good to great: Why some companies make the leap . . . and others don't.* New York: HarperCollins.

Collins, J. (2005). *Good to great and the social sectors: A monograph to accompany* Good to Great. Boulder, CO: Collins.

Danielson, C. (1996). *Enhancing professional practice: A framework for teaching.* Alexandria, VA: Association for Supervision and Curriculum Development.

Eisler, R. (1998). *Chalice and the blade: Our history, our future.* New York: HarperCollins.

Eisler, R. (2000). *Tomorrow's children: A blueprint for partnership education for the 21st century.* Boulder, CO: Westview.

Feyerabend, P. (1988). *Against method* (Rev. ed.). London: Verso.

Friere, P. (1970). *Pedagogy of the oppressed.* New York: Continuum.

Gottman, J. M. (2001). *The relationship cure: A five-step guide for building better connections with family, friends, and lovers.* New York: Crown.

Greenleaf, R. K. (2001). *Servant leadership: A journey into the legitimate nature of power and greatness* (L. C. Spears, Ed.). Mahwah, NJ: Paulist.

Jensen, B. (2000). *Simplicity: The new competitive advantage in a world of more, better, faster.* New York: HarperCollins.

Kegan, R., & Lahey, L. (2001). *How the way we talk can change the way we work: Seven languages for transformation.* San Francisco: Jossey-Bass.

Knight, J. (1992). Strategies go to college. *Preventing School Failure, 38*(1), 36–42.

Knight, J. (1999). *Partnership learning: A dialogical method for planning and delivering staff development sessions.* Paper presented at the meeting of the American Educational Research Association, Montreal, Canada.

Knight, J. (2007.) *Instructional coaching: A partnership approach to improving instruction.* Thousand Oaks, CA: Corwin Press.

Knight, J. (2009a). *The Big Four: A framework for instructional excellence.* Manuscript in preparation.

Knight, J. (2009b). *Partnership learning: Scientifically proven strategies for fostering dialogue during workshops and presentations.* Manuscript in preparation.

Knowles, M. S. (1988). *The modern practice of adult education: From pedagogy to andragogy* (Rev. ed.). Englewood, CO: Prentice Hall Regents.

Kuhn, T. S. (1970). *The structure of scientific revolutions* (2nd ed.). Chicago: University of Chicago.

Marzano, R. J., Pickering, D., & Pollock, J. E. (2001). *Classroom instruction that works: Research based strategies for increasing student achievement.* Alexandria, VA: Association for Supervision and Curriculum Development.

Schein, E. H. (1992). *Organizational culture and leadership* (2nd ed.). San Francisco: Jossey-Bass.

Senge, P. M. (1990). *The fifth discipline: The art and practice of the learning organization.* London: Random House.

Sprick, R., Knight, J., Reinke, W., & McKale, T. (2006). *Coaching classroom management: A toolkit for coaches and administrators.* Eugene, OR: Pacific Northwest Publishing.

U.S. Army. (2004). *The U.S. Army leadership field manual.* New York: McGraw-Hill.

3

Literacy Coaching

Cathy A. Toll

INTRODUCTION

Cathy A. Toll's understanding of literacy coaching grew out of her extensive background doing, as she mentioned to me in conversation, "just about everything in education." Cathy's positions included working as a teacher leader, a school administrator, a literacy coach, and eventually a coach of coaches. "When literacy coaching showed up," Cathy said, "the succinct way to say it is I recognized that I had already been coaching in many of my leadership roles and found that I had something to give to literacy coaches that seemed to be helpful. And it was rewarding to find that I could provide that kind of help."

Cathy's doctoral studies at Penn State allowed her to broaden her knowledge even more. The combination of her practical experience in schools and the theoretical foundation she gained through academic study provided an excellent foundation for Cathy's future work. "I came to coaching," she says, "with this array of experiences and with a strong theoretical background in the issues of change, growth, and power. And they all seemed to come together when I started to work as a coach and with coaches. I think everything I do is based in theory, but it really is a kind of practice too. And there have been times when the theory or research led the practice, and other times when the practice led me right to the theory."

What has resulted from Cathy's work is a rich collection of resources, theoretical and practical, for people interested in literacy coaching. Cathy has written extensively about literacy coaching in several books, including *The Literacy Coach's Survival Guide: Essential Questions and Practical Answers* (2005), *The Literacy Coach's*

Desk Reference: Processes and Perspectives for Effective Coaching (2006), and *Lenses on Literacy: Conceptualizations, Functions, and Outcomes* (2007).

Writing this chapter about literacy coaching, Cathy found herself, she says, "Writing about what was on my mind and the minds of my colleagues at the time I wrote the chapter, and I tried to frame it around those matters." Her chapter addresses five themes, providing a kind of state-of-the-field overview for us. First, Cathy includes a description of the work that literacy coaches often do and a description of what a "fresh alternative" to literacy coaching might entail. Then, she provides an overview of the extent of literacy coaching in schools across America.

Cathy also summarizes the research on literacy coaching and expresses her view that more research needs to be conducted so that we better understand such issues as how teachers experience coaching. Following this, Cathy extends our understanding of coaching by discussing various outcomes we might expect from literacy coaching, including some outcomes that may not be explicitly sought by coaches and other educational leaders. Cathy further deepens our understanding of coaching by discussing the many inaccuracies in the way literacy coaching is represented in the literature. At the conclusion of her chapter, Cathy offers several practical steps for examining any coaching program.

All in all, this chapter provides readers with insight into several complex but important aspects of literacy coaching. Further, the chapter clarifies to some extent what literacy coaching is and is not; a discussion is likely relevant for any approach to coaching. In my conversation, Cathy shared her metaphor for coaching: "I grew up in Wisconsin, and so when I hear *coach*, the first person that comes to mind is Vince Lombardi. But I don't think of a literacy coach as being like an athletic coach. I like to think instead of the coach that took Cinderella to the ball because it took her from her where she was to where she wanted to be." That, of course, could well be an apt metaphor for any of the approaches to coaching included in this publication.

Most educators are aware of the phenomenon known as literacy coaching. They have worked with a literacy coach themselves, spoken to colleagues about literacy coaching, seen the topic of literacy coaching on a conference agenda, or encountered the term in professional literature. However, despite their common awareness, educators mostly have uneven and varied understandings of literacy coaching. This chapter discusses literacy coaching in the United States to provide a common perspective on the phenomenon. It does not offer literacy coaching as a model of coaching, because it is not that. Rather, literacy coaching is a category of instructional coaching that focuses on literacy and related aspects of teaching and learning; various programs of literacy coaching implement a variety of coaching models.

The ubiquitous nature of literacy coaching reflects the speed by which coaching came onto the educational scene. Yes, Joyce and Showers (1982) were studying educational coaching 25 years ago, and Bean (2003) finds references to coachlike duties in descriptions of the work of reading specialists as far back as the 1920s. Two programs, the Literacy Collaborative and America's Choice, included literacy coaches before coaching became a well-known national trend. However, large-scale attention to the phenomenon of literacy coaching arose with the presence of literacy coaching in the federal guidelines for Reading First (U.S. Department of Education, 2002). Those guidelines specified that professional development for teachers should consist of "ongoing, continuous activity, and not consist of 'one-shot' workshops or lectures" and specifically mentioned "coaches and other teachers of reading" (U.S. Department of Education, 2002, p. 26).

Thus, literacy coaches were hired for Reading First programs throughout the United States, and the trend toward coaching was noted as well by schools without Reading First funding and by educators beyond the K–3 scope of Reading First. The speed by which this occurred could be described using Michael Fullan's (1982) observation that many educational innovations are approached in a "ready, fire, aim" manner, which leads to serious consideration of the innovation *after* its implementation is well under way.

The current status of literacy coaching can be considered according to these themes:

- The work of literacy coaches
- The extent of literacy coaching
- The research base for literacy coaching
- The outcomes of literacy coaching
- Inaccuracy in representing literacy coaching

I discuss each theme in the bulk of this chapter and conclude with directions for further investigation and practical suggestions for those exploring models of literacy coaching.

THE WORK OF LITERACY COACHES

Educators and policymakers have mostly expected literacy coaches to perform duties already performed by other existing school leaders. Professional developers, supervisors, and technical experts have worked in schools for decades, and in many settings, literacy coaches have been asked to fulfill these already-familiar roles. Some examples follow:

- A principal asks the literacy coach to inform her about which teachers are not teaching reading for the 90-minute block required by Reading First. (In the past, supervisors, usually principals or assistant principals, monitored teachers' implementation of grant requirements.)

- Teachers of middle school science ask the literacy coach for a workshop on best practices for teaching new vocabulary. (In the past, reading specialists, curriculum coordinators, or external professional development providers led workshops for teachers.)
- A literacy coach demonstrates for a group of fifth-grade teachers how to use supplemental materials provided by the publisher of the basal reading series to help students use "fix-up strategies" when their reading is no longer making sense. (In the past, publishers' representatives or reading specialists provided technical assistance in using purchased materials.)

The problem with this approach to literacy coaching is that schools have had supervisors, professional developers, and technicians for many years but have not yet produced success for all children as literate learners. Replicating these roles in the duties of literacy coaches does nothing new to advance children's learning. Granted, in some cases the new individuals in the role of literacy coach approach their work with greater energy, experience, or knowledge; however, if the limitations of previous supervisors, professional developers, and technicians was their lack of energy, experience, or knowledge, then the problem was one of personnel and should not be addressed by an entirely new category of educator.

In addition to the replication of familiar roles by literacy coaches, there has been a lack of clarity about which of these roles should be performed. Some literacy coaches act like technicians, some like supervisors, some like professional developers. Others act like cheerleaders, enthusiastically recognizing signs of success and standing ready to lend a hand when asked. I have argued elsewhere, however, that what is needed is a *fresh alternative* approach to literacy coaching. A literacy coach who is a fresh alternative is one who performs duties different from the duties of existing school personnel, a role that may enable educators to do more than we have already done to facilitate students' success (Toll, 2007).

Fresh alternative literacy coaches are partners with teachers, working alongside them as coequals who first listen and learn from teachers, then assist them in goal setting and planning for action. These literacy coaches are truly providing job-embedded professional development, because they begin with teachers' needs, interests, and questions, and support teachers in reflecting, gathering information (i.e., data), and making informed instructional decisions. Where literacy coaches are taking the fresh alternative approach, they are finding that their work makes more sense to them and to the teachers they work with, they are honoring teachers' knowledge and experience, and they are providing services that have not often been formally provided in school settings.

An example of fresh alternative literacy coaching could be found in the work of LaDonna, a middle school teacher and coach. The school leadership team at her school has identified science and social studies courses as those in which students struggle the most to read assigned materials and has set a schoolwide goal related to comprehension and vocabulary learning in those areas. LaDonna therefore has identified the teachers of science and social studies as those in the pool of teachers with whom she will work as a priority during the current school year.

LaDonna begins by meeting individually with the 16 teachers in the pool. She begins each coaching conversation with this question: When you think about the learning that you want your students to do in science [or social studies] and when you think about the reading that you want them to do in order to learn, what gets in the way? LaDonna listens carefully, frequently paraphrasing what she has heard to ensure that she understood accurately. She takes careful notes about what the teachers say and inquires to learn more about the nature of the obstacles that prevent students from learning successfully in the teachers' classrooms.

LaDonna's questions are always open and honest (Palmer, 2004) in that they are genuine inquiries, about which LaDonna does not know the answer, rather than the rhetorical questions generally asked by some literacy coaches. She wants to understand the concerns of her teacher partners as well as what they have tried and what they envision as success if these concerns are addressed. Three of the social studies teachers express the same concern, that the textbook is too difficult, and LaDonna suggests that these teachers might collaborate with her as a team to investigate possible solutions. She learns that one of the science teachers has attended a conference where he learned about scientific inquiry as a way to foster science learning as well as meaningful scientific reading, and they agree to cofacilitate a book study of *The New Science Literacy* (Their & Daviss, 2002) for interested teachers in their school or the other two middle schools in the district. Meanwhile, LaDonna learns that two of the newer science teachers would like to incorporate more digital texts into their classrooms, to replace the science textbook whenever possible, and that two of the history teachers are struggling to help several English-language learners to read and write about their content. So it goes, as teachers share their struggles and interests and LaDonna listens and learns.

In follow-up meetings with these teachers, some scheduled weekly, others every two weeks, and one scheduled only monthly for the time being, LaDonna helps her teaching partners to establish goals, envision success, and plan to create that success by trying new teaching strategies, rearranging their course structures, drawing on additional resources, and learning more about students' own scientific literacies. She offers a great deal of assistance in these endeavors but also remembers that the teachers she is working with are ultimately responsible for their learning and their classrooms, and the more she supports teachers' own thinking and learning, the more she builds their capacity to make informed instructional decisions. This is LaDonna's ultimate goal as a coach.

The example of LaDonna highlights several features of a fresh alternative approach to literacy coaching. Such coaching is

- Rooted in the needs, interests, and concerns of the teachers being coached.
- Based on ongoing coaching conversations.
- Adapted to the style and pace of the coach's teaching partners.
- Focused on increasing student success by supporting teachers to build capacity.

EXTENT OF LITERACY COACHING

The number of literacy coaches in the United States and the number of schools and districts employing literacy coaches are not known. We do know that virtually every Reading First school has a literacy coach, and there are Reading First schools in all 50 states, the District of Columbia, U. S. territories, and Native American Indian reservations. In addition, the federally funded Striving Readers program has supported literacy coaches in secondary schools around the United States, and literacy coaches are being funded by states, local districts, and foundations to work in elementary, middle, and high schools, as well as programs of special education, early childhood education, and education for English-language learners.

In a 2005 survey (Roller, 2006), the International Reading Association (IRA) gathered information about literacy coaches among its members. However, the study appears limited in its helpfulness. It is conventional wisdom that literacy coaches in middle schools and high schools are less likely to be members of IRA than elementary coaches and that some literacy educators choose to affiliate with the National Council of Teachers of English rather than with IRA. In addition, the generalizability of the information from the IRA survey is questionable, given that it had a response rate of 13.2%.

What can be noted anecdotally about the extent of literacy coaching is that workshops and presentations on literacy coaching are well attended at national conferences, books on literacy coaching are best-sellers for major publishers, and every educational publisher has included one or more selections on literacy coaching in recent catalogues. literacy coaching is now included in the standards for reading specialists developed by IRA and used as Specialized Program Area standards by the National Council for the Accreditation of Teacher Education.

RESEARCH BASE FOR LITERACY COACHING

A cry has been issued among literacy researchers and practitioners: we must conduct research that demonstrates a positive effect of literacy coaching on student achievement (Northwest Regional Educational Laboratory, 2006). The urge for such research makes sense: we are in an era when student learning outcomes are focused on extensively, and literacy coach positions have been created explicitly to improve those outcomes. Existing studies of large-scale coaching programs have not made such a link (see, e.g., Bacevich & Salinger, 2006; Brown, Reumann-Moore, Hugh, du Plessis, & Christman, 2006; Neufeld & Roper, 2002, 2003; Supovitz, 2001), although smaller studies do demonstrate a connection between student achievement and coaching (see, e.g., Norton 2001; Onchwari, 2005). Studies do exist that find stronger achievement in students whose teachers worked with literacy coaches rather than a similar group of teachers who didn't work with literacy coaches, but those studies do not explicitly establish that it is the literacy coaching that made the difference (Fisher, Frey, Lapp, & Flood, 2004; Foundation for California Early Literacy Learning, 2001). There could be other factors influencing the change in student achievement; for instance, a school in which literacy coaches function successfully is likely to have strong leadership and teachers explicitly interested in professional growth, two characteristics identified by school reform literature as themselves leading to greater student achievement.

Researchers, including those at the RAND Corporation and at Research for Action, are currently engaged in work that they hope will establish a connection between coaching and student achievement. No doubt legions of literacy coaches, as well as those who have funded them, including the U.S. government, are eager for these studies to show that literacy coaching does indeed make a difference for children.

Meanwhile, the value of literacy coaching is indeed supported by research on educational coaching more generally (Joyce, Murphy, Showers, & Murphy, 1989; Knight, 2004), adult learning (Cave, LaMaster, & White, 1998; Yorks, 2005), teacher professional development (National Staff Development Council, 2001), teacher reflection and inquiry (Gamston, Linder, & Whitaker, 1993; Hatch, White, & Faigenbaum, 2005; Supovitz, 2001), specific teaching practices (Brown et al., 2006), increased teacher collaboration (Symonds, 2003), and school reform (Fullan, 2003). Such research positions literacy coaching one step away from student achievement; for instance, literacy coaching has qualities of teacher professional development that have been shown to be effective in supporting student achievement.

I have pondered whether it is too narrow a definition of research or merely a failure of imagination that prevents educators, researchers, and policymakers from seeing that a phenomenon (literacy coaching) that leads to conditions demonstrated as supporting greater student achievement (such as teacher reflection and job-embedded professional development) is indeed supported by research. If one believes that the client of the literacy coach is the teacher, and I do, then one may be hard-pressed to engage in sound research that establishes a more direct connection to students.

In other words, research on the effectiveness of literacy coaching may depend on an examination of coaching's effect on teachers, not on students.

OUTCOMES OF LITERACY COACHING

Although literacy coaching's effect on student success has yet to be established in a strong way, the effect of literacy coaching on teachers is clear. It is producing outcomes related to desired changes in teacher behavior, feelings, thinking, and collaboration (Toll, 2005), as well as changes in teachers' identities (Toll, 2007). In addition, literacy coaching in its various incarnations leads to support for particular political positions. I have discussed these outcomes extensively in *Lenses on literacy coaching* (Toll, 2007). Here, I summarize.

Depending on the model implemented, literacy coaching might target the following: changes in teachers' behavior, such as a more acceptable use of teaching materials or the implementation of particular teaching strategies; changes in teachers' feelings, such as a greater acceptance of grant regulations or a more positive attitude toward a required program of literacy instruction; changes in teachers' thinking, such as a greater use of particular data in instructional decision making or deeper reflection on students' home literacies; or changes in teachers' collaboration, such as greater instructional decision making between classroom teachers and special educators or the establishment of teacher study groups. Clearly, this range of potential changes demonstrates the range of outcomes that literacy coaching might affect. Teachers who are happier with the required instructional program are likely to be very different from teachers who are thinking more deeply about students' home literacies.

The outcomes suggested in the previous paragraph reflect the overt outcomes sought by those who develop, lead, and implement programs of literacy coaching. In addition, as with any phenomenon, there appear to be outcomes that are not explicitly sought. Some of those outcomes also relate to teachers themselves, in the form of teacher identities. literacy coaching might inadvertently support constructions of teacher identities, such as the following: The Obedient Teacher, who always does as she or he is told; The Good Teacher, who has a positive attitude and demonstrates caring and consideration in all things; The Problem-Solving Teacher, who identifies needs and concerns and then finds solutions or answers; and The Teacher With Agency, whose actions and interactions are recognized as changing the conditions of schooling for students and teachers alike.

Anthropologists find that one's identity is constantly shaped by and shaping one's environment and is also shaped by the *figured worlds* of one's environment. Holland, Skinner, Lachichotte, and Cain (1998) define a figured world as "a socially and culturally constructed realm of interpretation in which particular characters and actors are recognized, significance is assigned to certain acts, and particular outcomes are valued over others" (p. 52). Thus, when literacy coaching leads to the construction of new teacher identities, those identities influence the construction of coaching as well. For instance, if a literacy coach's engagement with a teacher leads the teacher to identify himself as an Obedient Teacher, the coach will likely construct her identity in a way that supports the teacher in technical or supervisory roles.

Clearly, the changes desired in teachers as well as the shaping of identities are political, in that the enactment of power varies according to the changes sought or the figured worlds in which one participates. In addition, literacy coaching frequently supports particular political positions, which are explicitly recognized by policymakers and theorists who study the educational landscape. I find four political aims that are served by various conceptualizations of literacy coaching: (1) increasing the perception that schools as we know them are seriously broken, demonstrated by the need for coaches to "fix" ineffective teachers; (2) supporting an epistemological stance about truth and knowledge, particularly that knowledge is passed on as a quantifiable entity that can be measured and that truth is revealed by experimental research; (3) changing the manner in which schools are organized and managed, by enacting leadership roles beyond those of the principal and supporting collaboration among educators; and (4) privileging teacher knowledge, experience, and decision making in schools, demonstrated by efforts to begin with teachers' own needs and concerns and to honor practitioner knowledge and craft. These political aims have been written about elsewhere (see, e.g., Apple, 2004; Shannon, 1998; Spring, 2005), and I have elaborated on coaching's ability to support such politics (Toll, 2007).

INACCURACY IN REPRESENTING LITERACY COACHING

The study of literacy coaching and the implementation of programs of coaching are hampered by unclear representations of coaching in the literature. This lack of clarity is found in three areas: inaccurate use of the term *literacy coach*, multiple titles for those in coaching roles, and confusion between programs and models of coaching. I discuss each briefly.

Use of the Term *Literacy Coach*

A literacy coach works primarily with teachers; one could say that the client of the literacy coach is the teacher. However, the term *literacy coach* is sometimes used to describe a person who works primarily with students, typically in a tutoring capacity. It is understandable that the concept of *coach* might appeal to those seeking a tutoring program that feels supportive, and therefore they might seek a term that describes a personal commitment to the learner; *coach* may convey these ideas more than *tutor* (see, e.g., Bacon, 2005). The well-intended use of *reading coach* or *literacy coach* in these instances is confusing and makes it more difficult to assess the status of literacy coaches of the kind described in this article and in the bulk of the professional literature.

Beyond the difference between coaches who work with teachers and those who work with students, there is confusion about the actual duties of literacy coaches (Deussen, Coskie, Robinson, & Autio, 2007). Recent studies of coaching in two large programs found that literacy coaches spent less than 50% of their time working with individual teachers or small groups of teachers and spent as much as 30% of their time doing administrative tasks (Bean, Turner, Draper, Heisey, & Zigmond, 2008; Marsh, McCombs, & Naftel, 2008). Clearly, we are not studying coaching when we are studying work that includes coaching less than half the time.

What *are* the duties that make up the task of literacy coaching? I suggest to literacy coaches that they focus on three: one-on-one conferences with teachers, facilitation of small-group discussions among teachers, and demonstration lessons in teachers' classrooms, which build on the conversations that coaches have with teachers. Many coaching programs assume a fourth duty, which is observing teachers in their classrooms. In fact, many literacy coaches and their supervisors believe that coaching must begin with teacher observations. I suggest that observation is successful only when teachers request it; otherwise, it too often echoes supervisory observations and often leaves teachers feeling like literacy coaches are not their equals but "experts" if not "judges" (Toll, 2005, 2006).

Multiple Titles

The duties of a literacy coach are performed by educators in a variety of roles, in a variety of programs, and with a variety of funding sources. Because these duties were conceptualized at different points in time or by different agencies, groups, or individuals, a myriad of titles has been used for those performing the role of *literacy coach*. Among the titles I have found are reading coach, instructional coach, content coach, dual-role coach, reading specialist, lead teacher, intervention specialist, instructional teacher leader, implementation coach, learning specialist, teaching and instruction specialist, Title I reading teacher, and curriculum specialist. My hunch is that readers of this chapter could contribute dozens more. Such lack of consistency and the confusion caused by unclear titles add to the confusion around the status of literacy coaching.

Confusion Between Programs and Models

In informal conversation, formal conference presentations, and even occasionally professional writing, educators confuse programs and models.

One could speculate whether this confusion is due to ignorance, sloppiness, or perhaps desperation to increase the generalizability of what we know about literacy coaching by treating programs as models. Whatever the case, I find too often that specific programs—say, the program of literacy coaching in the Boston public schools or the coaching being implemented in the Alabama Reading Initiative—are referred to as models.

A model is a representation of theories and concepts (Ruddell, Ruddell, & Singer, 1994), not the enactment of a plan. Some programs of literacy coaching have been developed based on theories and concepts, and therefore one might be able to deduce a model from them. On the other hand, many programs of coaching have been developed because individuals or groups had funding available and needed to "do something." This brings us full circle to a point I made at the beginning of this article: Programs of literacy coaching cropped up suddenly all over the country. In their best efforts to put those programs into practice, many literacy coaches and their leaders acted quickly and in light of their existing understanding of coaching. Well-intentioned as these programs may be, and successful as some of them are, they are not models. When programs are mistaken for models, we assume theoretical and conceptual bases that may not exist.

CONCLUSION

literacy coaching has been put into place in schools throughout the United States (and, of course, beyond). Due to the demand for speedy implementation, literacy coaching is being implemented in multiple ways and with multiple outcomes. The research in support of literacy coaching is developing, but it has not yet met the demand for large-scale demonstration of literacy coaching's effect on student achievement. Additional limitations in assessing the status of literacy coaching come from inaccurate use of language related to literacy coaching and the absence of a thorough survey of literacy coaches.

Further investigation is needed in the two areas discussed herein. As stated earlier, the extent of literacy coaching in the United States has not been accurately assessed. Such information could help educators and policymakers to understand the scope of literacy coaching and the number of teachers and students influenced by it. Second, efforts to research the effectiveness of literacy coaching would benefit from a broader conceptualization of research models and a more precise definition of the appropriate scope of literacy coaching's effectiveness. Right now, most research is either descriptive or evaluative of particular literacy coaching programs. The cry for research demonstrating the effect of literacy coaching will surely produce more efforts to statistically correlate coaching with student achievement scores. While both program descriptions and evaluations and large-scale statistical analyses have their place, a wider scope of research will produce richer information. As well, a discussion of what it is that literacy coaching can and should influence may moderate the drive for a connection between coaching and student test scores.

I see some other areas for further investigation. literacy coaching has yet to be studied closely from the perspective of the teachers who work with literacy coaches. Given that such teachers are the "targets" of coaching, the field will benefit from systematic investigation of teachers' perspectives and experiences. As well, connections between programs of literacy instruction and literacy coaching have not been explored; it is possible that the implementation of certain programs of instruction is better done with coaching than other programs, or that the beliefs behind certain programs of instruction are more compatible with the philosophy of job-embedded professional development. A third area for study is literacy coaching from the perspective of systems thinking. Finally, although I have written somewhat about literacy coaching in relation to politics and power, I believe that more needs to be said about how literacy coaching as a phenomenon may reflect the spirit of the times.

For those who are reading this chapter as an introduction to literacy coaching and who are trying to understand and discriminate among various approaches to literacy coaching, I would suggest these practical steps for examining any particular program of coaching:

- Check whether there is confluence between the recommended coaching practices and research on adult learners.
- Look for clarity in the coach's role, which will support actual coaching and will not lead to a variety of duties that are outside the scope of job-embedded teacher professional development.
- Evaluate the chance for teacher capacity-building, particularly by looking for signs that teachers will be supported in thinking more deeply about their instructional decisions.
- Ensure that there are opportunities for gauging the success of the coaching program using multiple sources of evidence, such as number of teachers engaged in coaching and the extent of their engagement, breakdown of coaches' duties and percentage of time spent in actual coaching, signs of increased reflection and informed decision making in teachers' discussions of their work, increased collaboration among teachers, and signs that student success has increased.

The extensive scope of literacy coaching and the concomitant rate of funding of coaching programs yield interest, criticism, and speculation regarding coaching's effectiveness and potential duration. This overview of literacy coaching is offered as a way to better understand literacy coaching while also thinking beyond existing knowledge to the formation of new questions about the phenomenon of literacy coaching.

REFERENCES

Apple, M. W. (2004). *Ideology and curriculum* (3rd ed.). New York: Routledge.

Bacevich, A., & Salinger, T. (2006). *Lessons and recommendations from the Alabama Reading Initiative: Sustaining focus on secondary reading.* Washington, DC: American Institutes for Research.

Bacon, S. (2005). Reading coaches: Adapting an intervention model for upper elementary and middle school readers. *Journal of Adolescent & Adult Literacy, 48,* 416–427.

Bean, R. M. (2003). *The reading specialist: Leadership for the classroom, school, and community.* New York: Guilford.

Bean, R. M., Turner, G., Draper, J., Heisey, N., & Zigmond, N. (2008, March). *Coaching and its contributions to reading achievement in Reading First Schools.* Paper presented at the annual meeting of the American Educational Research Association, New York.

Brown, D., Reumann-Moore, R., Hugh, R., du Plessis, P., & Christman, J. (2006). *Promising inroads: Year one report of the Pennsylvania High School coaching initiative.* Philadelphia: Research for Action.

Cave J., LaMaster, C., & White, S. (1998). *Staff development: Adult characteristics.* Retrieved September 13, 2004, from http://www-ed.fnal.gov/lincon/staff_adult

Deussen, T., Coskie, T., Robinson, L., & Autio, E. (2007). *"Coach" can mean many things: Five categories of literacy coaches in Reading First* (Issues & Answers Report, REL 2007, No. 005). Washington, DC: U.S. Department of Education, Institute of Education Sciences, National Center for Education Evaluation and Regional Assistance, Regional Educational Laboratory Northwest.

Fisher, D., Frey, N., Lapp, D., & Flood, J. (2004). Improving literacy achievement and professional development through a K–12 urban partnership. In D. Lapp, C. C. Block, E. J. Cooper, J. Flood, N. Roser, & J. V. Tinajero (Eds.), *Teaching all the children: Strategies for developing literacy in an urban setting* (pp. 137–152). New York: Guilford.

Foundation for California Early Literacy Learning. (2001). *California Early Literacy Learning, Extended Literacy Learning, Second Chance at Literacy Learning.* Redlands, CA: Author.

Fullan, M. (1982). *The meaning of educational change.* New York: Teachers College Press.

Fullan, M. (2003). *Change forces with a vengeance.* London: Routledge-Falmer.

Gamston, R., Linder, C., & Whitaker, J. (1993). Reflections on cognitive coaching. *Educational Leadership, 51*(2), 57–61.

Hatch, T., White, M. E., & Faigenbaum, D. (2005). Expertise, credibility, and influence: How teachers can influence policy, advance research, and improve performance. *Teachers College Record, 107,* 1004–1035.

Holland, D., Skinner, D., Lachichotte, W., & Cain, C. (1998). *Identity and agency in cultural worlds.* Cambridge, MA: Harvard.

Joyce, B., Murphy, C., Showers, B., & Murphy, J. (1989). School renewal as cultural change. *Educational Leadership, 46*(3), 70–77.

Joyce, B., & Showers, B. (1982). The coaching of teaching. *Educational Leadership, 40*(1), 4–8.

Knight, J. (2004). Instructional coaching. *Stratenotes, 13*(3), 1–5.

Marsh, J. A., McCombs, J. S., & Naftel, S. (2008, March). *Building teacher capacity through literacy coaching: Findings from the Florida middle school study.* Paper presented at the annual meeting of the American Educational Research Association, New York.

National Staff Development Council. (2001). *NSDC's standards for staff development.* Retrieved June 18, 2005, from http://www.nsdc.org/standards/index.cfm

Neufeld, B., & Roper, D. (2002). *Off to a good start: Year I of collaborative coaching and learning in the Effective Practice Schools.* Cambridge, MA: Education Matters.

Neufeld, B., & Roper, D. (2003). *Expanding the work: Year II of collaborative coaching and learning in the Effective Practice Schools.* Cambridge, MA: Education Matters.

Northwest Regional Educational Laboratory. (2006). *What we know—and don't know—about coaching. A conversation with professor Michael Kamil.* Retrieved June 18, 2008, from http://www.nwrel.org/nwedu/12-01/qanda/

Norton, J. (2001). A storybook breakthrough. *Journal of Staff Development, 22*(5), 22–25.

Onchwari, G. (2005). *An evaluation of the effectiveness of the national Head Start Bureau early literacy mentor-coach initiative on teacher literacy practices and children's literacy learning outcomes.* Unpublished doctoral dissertation, Indiana University, Bloomington.

Palmer, P. (2004). *A hidden wholeness: The journey toward an undivided life.* San Francisco: Jossey-Bass.

Roller, C. (2006). *Reading and literacy coaches report on hiring requirements and duties survey.* Retrieved June 18, 2008, from http://www.reading.org/downloads/resources/reading_coach_survey_report.pdf

Ruddell, R. B., Ruddell, M. R., & Singer, H. (Eds.). (1994). *Theoretical models and processes of reading.* Newark, DE: International Reading Association.

Shannon, P. (1998). *Reading poverty.* Portsmouth, NH: Heinemann.

Spring, J. (2005). *Political agendas for education: From the Religious Right to the Green Party* (3rd ed.). Mahwah, NJ: Erlbaum.

Supovitz, J. A. (2001). Translating teaching practice into improved student achievement. In S. H. Fuhrman (Ed.), *From the capitol to the classroom: Standards-based reform in the states* (pp. 81–98). Chicago: University of Chicago Press.

Symonds, K. W. (2003). *Literacy coaching: How school districts can support a long-term strategy in a short-term world.* San Francisco: Bay Area School Reform Collaborative.

Their, M., & Daviss, B. (2002). *The new science literacy: Using language skills to help students learn science.* Portsmouth, NH: Heinemann.

Toll, C. A. (2005). *The literacy coach's survival guide: Essential questions and practical answers.* Newark, DE: International Reading Association.

Toll, C. A. (2006). *The literacy coach's desk reference: Processes and perspectives for effective coaching.* Urbana, IL: National Council of Teachers of English.

Toll, C. A. (2007). *Lenses on literacy coaching: Conceptualizations, functions, and outcomes.* Norwood, MA: Christopher Gordon.

U.S. Department of Education. (2002). *Guidance for the Reading First program.* Retrieved November 20, 2006, from http://www.ed.gov/programs/readingfirst/guidance.doc

Yorks, L. (2005). Adult learning and the generation of new knowledge and meaning: Creating liberating spaces for fostering adult learning through practitioner-based collaborative action inquiry. *Teachers College Record, 107,* 1217–1244.

4

Cognitive Coaching

Jane Ellison and Carolee Hayes

INTRODUCTION

The first time that Carolee Hayes heard Art Costa coaching someone, she realized, as she told me in conversation, "that Cognitive Coaching[SM] was a totally different way of working." For Carolee, "it was more aligned to my values and beliefs about respecting the professionalism of teachers." At that time, Carolee was working as a staff developer in a district where the coauthor of this chapter, Jane Ellison, was a principal. Carolee suggested that Jane learn more about Cognitive Coaching, and Jane had the same reaction as Carolee, seeing Cognitive Coaching as honoring and respecting teachers, truly the way that professional educators should work with other professional educators.

After their introduction to Cognitive Coaching, Jane and Carolee became frequent collaborators with Art Costa and Bob Garmston, who first developed this approach to coaching in 1984. Fifteen years after the model was created, in 1999, Jane and Carolee were asked to establish the Center for Cognitive Coaching, to continue the study and dissemination of knowledge about Cognitive Coaching. Carolee describes how she and Jane came to be asked to establish the center:

> In 1999, they [Art Costa and Bob Garmston] approached us about putting together an international organization that would sustain the work. I will

AUTHORS' NOTE: The following chapter contains content from the book *Effective School Leadership: Developing Principals Through Cognitive Coaching* (Ellison & Hayes, 2006b). Reprinted with permission of Christopher Gordon Publishers, Inc.

Cognitive Coaching[SM] is a service-marked term, but for literary purposes, the service mark will not appear throughout the reminder of this chapter.

never forget them telling us that we would sustain the work 50 years past their death, continuing to have an impact on the educational setting. That was probably about the most honoring moment of my professional career.

Cognitive Coaching and the Center for Cognitive Coaching have been embraced widely across the world. Started almost 25 years ago, Cognitive Coaching is now present in all continents except Antarctica. There are Cognitive Coaching trainers and consultants in all 50 states, and major initiatives are under way currently in Australia, Singapore, Bangkok, Mexico, and Italy.

In this chapter, Jane and Carolee provide an overview of Cognitive Coaching, an approach to coaching in which the coach sees her or his purpose as developing self-directed people. In a time when so many teachers feel like they are being told what, how, and when to teach, Cognitive Coaching is intended to help people help themselves, prompting them and their coaches to ask what it means to be self-managing, self-monitoring, and self-modifying. Cognitive Coaching aims at giving teachers choice and control.

The authors also introduce the five States of Mind central to the work of a Cognitive Coach: efficacy, flexibility, consciousness, craftsmanship, and interdependence, and the underlying assumptions of Cognitive Coaching, that people are self-sufficient and resourceful, naturally driven to seek out learning opportunities and growth. Additionally, the authors distinguish Cognitive Coaching from other forms of support for professional learning.

Jane and Carolee also provide an introductory overview of the Cognitive Coaching process, which they introduce through the metaphor of a map, specifically, three coaching conversation maps for planning, reflecting, and problem resolving. They also introduce several coaching tools that likely could be integrated into many other approaches to coaching, including rapport-building skills, response behaviors designed to mediate thinking, and inquiry.

At the heart of Jane and Carolee's chapter is their elaboration on the central goal of Cognitive Coaching. As its name would suggest, Cognitive Coaching is a process coaches use to improve the thinking practices of teachers and others who are coached. If teachers improve their higher-level cognitive functioning, they will improve the way they teach, and students, in turn, will have significantly better learning experiences.

WHAT IS COGNITIVE COACHING?

Cognitive Coaching supports individuals and workplace cultures that value reflection, complex thinking, and transformational learning. Arthur Costa and Robert Garmston developed the process in 1984 as a way for principals to support teachers' thinking and self-directedness. Their intention was to move beyond a behaviorist philosophy that often focused on installing behaviors into a teacher's daily practice. At the time, monitoring and evaluation was based on compliance with desired behaviors.

Checklists were common as principals, with clipboard in hand, checked off teacher behaviors. The teacher's words and actions were commonly scripted followed by a conversation where the principal praised the correct behaviors and talked to the teacher about the missing behaviors. Cognitive Coaching was a breath of fresh air to professional practice. It is grounded in the belief that the thought processes of the teacher are what drive practice. Instead of seeking compliance, Cognitive Coaching develops thoughtful professionals who are self-directed. The Cognitive Coaching process is not rote or directive, but instead uses structures for supporting the teacher's own planning, reflecting, and problem resolving. It is a set of tools designed specifically to enhance performance by supporting the teacher's internal thought processes.

As Cognitive Coaching became more widely used in educational institutions, it was clear that the skills and methods had application beyond teacher supervision. Teachers realized that the process works well with students and enhances their thought processes. Principals found that Cognitive Coaching can be used in meetings to assist groups in working at higher levels and being reflective in their practice. The skills of Cognitive Coaching also are useful with parents in conferring about their child's progress. Cognitive Coaching is a process that assists any group or individual in becoming more self-managing, self-monitoring, and self-modifying. These applications are described in the book *Cognitive Coaching: Weaving the Threads of Learning and Change Into the Culture of an Organization* (Ellison & Hayes, 2006a).

The term *Cognitive Coaching* is service-marked, which means whenever the term is used, it should refer to Costa and Garmston's work. The term *coaching* is generic and can refer to many different models; Cognitive Coaching is specific to one model. Cognitive Coaching becomes not only an interactive strategy intended to enhance the self-directedness of others; it becomes internalized into a way of being and an important part of an individual's identity. It is this unique attribute of Cognitive Coaching that makes the work so powerful and, as many people have reported, so life changing.

RESEARCH ON COGNITIVE COACHING

Over 20 years of research on coaching teachers using this methodology has shown significant results (Edwards, 2005):

- Cognitive Coaching was linked with increased student test scores and other benefits for students.
- Teachers grew in teaching efficacy.
- Cognitive Coaching impacted teacher thinking, causing teachers to be more reflective and to think in more complex ways.

- Teachers were more satisfied with their positions and with their choice of teaching as a profession.
- School cultures became more professional.
- Teachers collaborated more.
- Cognitive Coaching assisted teachers professionally.
- Cognitive Coaching benefited teachers personally.
- Cognitive Coaching benefited people in fields other than teaching.

This chapter provides a framework for the basic constructs of Cognitive Coaching. Those who choose to embrace this way of working will benefit from taking more extensive training that will guide them in becoming knowledgeable and skillful with the principles and practices of Cognitive Coaching (www.cognitivecoaching.com).

THE MISSION OF COGNITIVE COACHING

Cognitive Coaching is a model that guides a person's actions and provides a process for working from the following mission:

> The mission of Cognitive Coaching is to produce self-directed persons with the cognitive capacity for high performance both independently and as members of a community. (Costa & Garmston, 2002, p. 16)

Missions define our purpose and reason for existing. Each word in the mission statement clarifies a way of working with intentionality.

The verb *produce* suggests that educators must be results-oriented with a focus on outcomes for the individuals with whom they work. Cognitive Coaching focuses on impact by assisting in identifying the results one is striving for and clarifying the success indicators and strategies for doing so. Additionally, the Cognitive Coach assists the coachee in examining data, reflecting on their meaning, and committing to action for the future.

Self-directed persons are one of the outcomes of a person who holds the mission of Cognitive Coaching in the forefront of his or her mind. Costa and Garmston (2002) define self-directedness through three distinct yet intertwined qualities—*self-managing, self-monitoring,* and *self-modifying.* Self-managing people are able to articulate their goals and intentions. They hold a clear vision for their own achievements and are strategic in planning for goal achievements. *Self-management* includes specificity about indicators of success. People with skill in self-management are deliberate about considering prior knowledge and experiences. They are careful to control the tendency to leap to action and instead gather information and consider options and relevant data. *Self-monitoring* requires constant vigilance of oneself and one's environment. Self-monitoring people gather data as an ongoing process. They draw on self-knowledge as a checkpoint for attending to what is working and not working. Self-monitoring is a process requiring attention to one's metacognition as well as external cues. In self-monitoring, an individual is constantly comparing the current conditions to the intended plan. To be truly self-monitoring requires attention to alternatives and choice making in the moment. It demands focus through attentive listening and observing. To be *self-modifying,* an individual must evaluate his or her actions and decisions against intentions and goals. Self-modification requires reflection and introspection. A disposition toward continuous growth serves the self-modifying person. That disposition includes constructing meaning from experience and commitment to make changes based on the new learning. Self-modification draws from the self-monitoring process to focus forward and deliberate on future actions.

The phrase in the mission statement, *cognitive capacity,* differentiates Cognitive Coaching from other models of coaching or supervision. The unique focus of this work is to develop an individual's ability to engage in higher levels of cognitive functioning (e.g., evaluating, analyzing, inferring). The concept of capacity assumes that the cognitive abilities can be developed. Cognitive functions are not mutually exclusive of emotions. Each is part of a system of biochemically interdependent responses incorporated into one singular system (Damasio, 1994). Cognitive Coaching addresses the intertwined nature of the cognitive and affective systems. Leaders who are coached have increased capacity for complex thinking and for addressing their own emotions and those of others. Cognitive Coaching draws on the research on teacher cognition and supports increased capacity for planning, reflecting, and problem resolving. Additionally, Cognitive Coaching supports the development of emotional and social intelligence as defined by Daniel Goleman.

In his most recent book, Goleman (2006) states that as human beings, we are wired to connect with each other. "Neuroscience has discovered that our brain's very design makes it *sociable,* inexorably drawn into a brain-to-brain linkup whenever we engage with another person" (Goleman, 2006, p. 4).

Cognitive Coaching expands the traditional work of an educator to include developing internal cognitive, social, and emotional capacities within others. When individuals are coached, they have a richer understanding of how to develop those capacities in others, and they simultaneously have their cognitive and affective capacities expanded. The mission of Cognitive Coaching describes cognitive capacity as a means for high performance in two domains—*independently* and *in community.* Cognitive Coaching draws on the concept of holonomy, the study of wholeness (Costa & Garmston, 2002). Central to the mission is a focus on the duality of human existence. Each of us lives an autonomous life with our own thoughts and emotions, unique talents and skills, and a personality unlike anyone else's. Simultaneously, we live as members of systems, be those family systems or organizational systems. We are influenced by the systems in which we live and concurrently, as individuals, influence the systems. The self and system are interconnected, interdependent, and inseparable. However, the dual nature of this reality creates tensions between our internal self and the systems self. Those tensions have been defined as tensions of holonomy (Costa & Lipton, 1996).

Resolving the tensions allows us to rise to the challenges of human growth and development and to live more productive lives, serving others and ourselves. Through Cognitive Coaching, individuals become more skillful in resolving the inherent tensions within themselves and their jobs. The Cognitive Coach is intentional in providing assistance in finding resources to balance and manage the tensions. Those resources are called *States of Mind*.

Tensions of Holonomy

Ambiguity and Certainty

Knowledge and Action

Egocentricity and Allocentricity

Self-Assertion and Integration

Inner Feelings and Outer Behaviors

Solitude and Interconnectedness

SOURCE: Costa, A., & Lipton, L. (1996). *Holonomy: Paradox and promise.* Unpublished manuscript. Reprinted with permission of Art Costa.

FIVE STATES OF MIND

Cognitive Coaching draws on an impressive list of many well-respected researchers, including the following: Lev Vygotsky, Richard Bandler and John Grinder, Carl Jung, Richard Shavelson, David Berliner, Carl Glickman, Arthur Koestler, Reuven Feuerstein, Albert Bandura, Gregory Bateson, Noam Chomsky, John Dewey, Robert Goldhammer and Morris Cogan, Antonio Damasio, Carl Rogers, and Abraham Maslow. At the core of the work, and unique to this model, is the concept of States of Mind. This is the original work of Costa and Garmston. The States of Mind describe and illuminate the resources necessary to become intentionally holonomous and self-directed. They are abstractions that provide a conceptual framework for understanding the internal drives within each of us. The five States of Mind that are central to the work of a Cognitive Coach are efficacy, consciousness, craftsmanship, flexibility, and interdependence.

1. Efficacy

Teacher and school *efficacy* are among the most highly researched aspects of educational literature. Albert Bandura (1997) describes self-efficacy as belief in one's capabilities to organize and execute the courses of action required to produce given attainments. In an educational setting, efficacy is an internally held sense that one has the knowledge and skills to impact the learning processes in the school to attain desired results. Efficacy exists within individuals and for schools. For example, with high efficacy, a teacher knows her actions make a difference across the school community. Each interaction contributes to the overall learning of the community. High teacher efficacy means teachers hold a belief that their actions will result in student learning. Ongoing efforts will pay off with results. When a person has low efficacy, there is a strong external locus of control, often manifesting itself as blame and victimization; for example, "These kids come from such deprived homes," or "I had such better results when I had a different population of students."

Efficacy is a foundational State of Mind, being a resource that gives us a sense of motivation, hope, and a belief in our own ability to influence and change our world. Research on efficacy has shown to have consistent findings (Tschannen-Moran, Woolfolk Hoy, & Hoy, 1998):

- Efficacy is self-fulfilling. With increased efficacy, teachers make greater effort resulting in improved results. With lower efficacy, less effort is expended leading to fewer results and decreased efficacy.
- Efficacy leads to openness to new ideas and experimentation to support learning.
- Efficacy increases resilience and the willingness to persist in efforts in light of challenges.
- Efficacy decreases criticism of students when they are not successful and draws up their planning and organization.
- Efficacy decreases the likelihood a teacher will make a special education referral.
- Efficacy increases a teacher's enthusiasm for teaching.
- Efficacy at the school level relates to a healthy organizational climate.
- School efficacy relates to an orderly and positive environment and more classroom-based decision making.

The process of Cognitive Coaching in and of itself builds efficacy.

2. Consciousness

Consciousness leads to self-awareness and allows for examination of other States of Mind. It requires attention to one's own metacognition. Highly conscious people listen to their own listening. In working with others, they notice biases interfering with their ways of understanding, they think about how their preferences affect their perceptions, and they track the processes of their thinking. The following are examples of the kinds of internal questions a conscious person might ask. Such consciousness provides capacity for reflection before, during, and after an experience:

- Am I being logical or emotional?
- How is my prior knowledge of this situation affecting my thought processes?

- What judgments am I making?
- How can I gain another perspective on this?
- What might I do to become more data-based?

In addition to internal attention, the conscious person is monitoring external cues and data in an ongoing manner. In working with a teacher, the coach pays attention to the subtle, nonverbal cues in addition to the words being spoken. The principal observing a classroom is aware of the need to attend to both the teachers and the learners. Focus is given to both types of data. Every experience is lived at two levels, one with attention to self and one with attention to others. The executive capacity to manage both simultaneously is a sign of highly developed consciousness. In addition, the conscious person makes connections between past and present experiences, seeking patterns and connections. The ability to do that kind of thinking is what distinguishes us from other species and mammals (Damasio, 1994).

3. Craftsmanship

Craftsmanship is an internal drive toward personal and group excellence. It manifests itself behaviorally in a drive for continuous improvement. It is not about becoming a perfectionist, but instead focusing on clear criteria for quality. It is about measuring one's performance against a standard and seeking ongoing means for moving toward a higher standard. Craftsmanship is data-driven. The teacher with high craftsmanship invites the use of data in determining areas of growth for her students. She pushes the envelope, always holding higher and higher expectations for students. She models her value on growth in her actions and expectations. She commends successes by giving specific feedback on the sources and examples of striving for higher performance. Simultaneously, she analyzes cause and effect before setting future goals. Craftsmanship is not judgmental, but seeks ongoing self-assessment using criteria for excellence. From the self-assessment stage, craftsmanship leads us to examine our actions and their outcomes with an intention to refine them for development and growth toward even more successful performance and outcomes.

4. Flexibility

Flexibility is the State of Mind that allows us to move beyond our natural tendencies toward egocentricity. Egocentricity is necessary for survival; it allows us to monitor our internal states, knowing when to withdraw from a situation and even telling us when we need to take shelter and food. However, egocentricity simultaneously limits our ability to see and understand our world beyond our internal frameworks and lenses. Low flexibility is the source of low creativity and high rigidity. We are trapped by our egocentricity, becoming blind to new and different ways of seeing. Margaret Wheatley (2005) describes listening for flexibility:

> There are many ways to sit and listen for the differences. Lately, I've been listening for what surprises me. What did I just hear that startled me? This isn't easy—I'm accustomed to sit there nodding my head as someone voices what I agree with. But when I notice what surprises me, I'm able to see my own views more clearly, including my beliefs and assumptions. (p. 212)

The flexible teacher is open to understanding the multiple perspectives of his or her students and embracing the diversity. As Wheatley (2005) states, "It's not the differences that divide us. It's our judgments that do. Curiosity and good listening bring us back together" (p. 212). Taking those multiple perspectives enhances a leader's ability to unite diverse factions. Flexibility is a doorway to interdependence.

Flexibility is also a touchstone for creativity and problem solving. A flexible person explores multiple alternatives, viewpoints, and possibilities. We spoke with a participant in Tennessee whose school was struggling with tardiness. Many efforts had been tried, including student consequences and appeals to parents. Thinking flexibly, the principal purchased alarm clocks for students that were distributed with talks about self-management and self-monitoring. Behaviors began to change. The flexible position moved from blaming and punishing to inviting alternative behaviors.

5. Interdependence

Interdependence is a resource that allows us to move beyond a self-centered view of the world to a view that assists us in seeing ourselves as part of something larger. Interdependence assists us in moving between egocentricity (self-centered), allocentricity (other-centered), and macrocentricity (system-centered). Interdependence draws on our ability to see the nature of our relationships instead of thinking in isolation:

> Those of us educated in Western culture learned to think and manage a world that was anything but systemic or interconnected. It's a world of separations and clear boundaries: jobs in boxes, lines delineating relationships, roles, and policies describing what each individual does and who we expect them to be. (Wheatley, 2005, p. 100)

The recognition that individuals need each other lies at the heart of every system. From that realization, individuals reach out, and seemingly divergent self-interests develop into a system of interdependency. Thus, all systems form through collaboration, from the recognition that we need another in order to survive. (Wheatley, 2005, pp. 102–103)

Mutuality and reciprocity are critical attributes of the State of Mind of interdependence. Interdependent people see themselves inside a system and appreciate the flow of resources. They understand the need to contribute to the system and appreciate the value they receive from the system.

Given the growing body of research on the importance of building collaborative cultures to impact student achievement, effective educators will move beyond a hierarchal and authoritarian structure of leadership. To do so, they will need to have their own internal resource of high interdependence with their staff and the school district. Equally important, they will have a skill set for creating increasing interdependencies within their school.

So how do coaches utilize their knowledge of States of Mind to support self-directed learning? Cognitive Coaches listen closely to the thoughts of the coachee. As they listen, they are not only hearing the content of the words being delivered, but at a deeper level, they are listening for what the words say about the person's States of Mind. As the coaches explore the States of Mind, the thinking of the coachee deepens, expands, and takes on new dimensions. The direction is unknown to the coaches because the new thinking is created inside the coachee. The coaches deftly use States of Mind as a means to create new possibilities, new thinking, and new resources for the people being coached.

ASSUMPTIONS OF COGNITIVE COACHING

Cognitive Coaching is grounded in the assumption that humans seek learning and growth as inherent parts of their being. It presumes resourcefulness and sufficiency in others. Cognitive Coaching is a process that provides conditions for maximizing the individual's drive for self-directedness.

A toddler illustrated this to his grandmother. The grandmother was observing her young grandson struggle with a puzzle. Wanting to see him succeed, she offered her assistance. In his innocent way, with his limited language, he responded to her offer with these words: "Grandma, I do it I-self." What a powerful spoken message early in life about the natural drive to be self-directed. The grandmother wisely listened to her grandson's words and backed away, observing him work tirelessly to make the puzzle pieces fit. After much ado, he had some successes and some frustration with the more complex aspects of the puzzle. As he reached the point of maximum effort with low success, he shifted his posture with his grandmother by saying, "Grandma, I need some help." This story illustrates the faith in human capacity within Cognitive Coaching. We are naturally self-directed, striving for a sense of freedom as a learner. We are equally dependent on our environment to support our need to go beyond our current capacity. Cognitive Coaching allows for the human nature within us to find its place in a nurturing environment. It provides support for managing the tensions of autonomy and community.

Cognitive Coaching is a mental model for cognitive development. It assumes that when thinking is mediated, cognitive growth will occur. The word *mediation* is derived from middle, like the word *median.* The mediator, using a set of coaching skills, intervenes between a person and a task or between a person and an experience. When a person faces a task or problem to be solved, the mediator or coach uses Cognitive Coaching maps and tools to assist the person in thinking clearly about his or her goals and resources. In mediating between a person and experience, the coach assists the person in reflecting on available data about the experience, analyzing the meaning of the information, and constructing new learning that will lead the person forward to future applications. The same process occurs in reflection. The coach intervenes between the person and the experience and invites analysis and new insight. From the reflection, the individual is able to project the learnings into future applications. The intention of the coach is to assist the learner in clarifying, developing, and modifying his or her internal schema (Costa & Garmston, 2002). That is the process for creation of new learning. Without mediation of thinking, there is little likelihood that internal thought structures will be modified.

Robert Kegan's (Kegan, 1995; Drago-Severson, 2004) constructive-developmental theory illustrates how the processes of Cognitive Coaching influence adult development. The theory operates on a fundamental assumption that growth and development are processes that are ongoing and never-ending throughout life. If those growth processes are to be sustained, interventions to reshape and expand internal meaning-making structures are necessary. Kegan differentiates informational learning and transformational learning. Informational learning adds value to what a person knows and the skills he or she can demonstrate. Transformational learning changes the way a person knows. As ways of knowing shift, leaders develop in their ability to deal with greater complexities and challenges in their environment. Kegan names three stages of adult development, sometimes given different names: the Socializing, the Self-Authoring, and the Self-Transformational.

Adults at the Socializing level can be characterized as dependent on others as sources of their values. Experiences are tests of whether others value them. The environment is the source of well-being. Criticism and conflict are perceived as negative and become threatening to the self. Transition to the Self-Authoring level is evidenced by a stronger sense of values being internally developed, and an internal set of standards becomes a measuring tool for success. Self-Authoring people are constantly questioning whether they are living in a way that is congruent with their own values. At the Self-Transformational level, the adult is most capable of dealing with a world that is nonlinear, ever-changing, and highly demanding. Conflict is an inherent part of life and is seen as a source of deeper understanding and improvement. Most adults never reach the stage of becoming Self-Transforming. They remain trapped in earlier stages because they are not in an environment that mediates their development; instead it only adds skills and information to their repertoire.

Kegan assists us in having mental models for promoting transformational development (Kegan, 1995; Drago-Severson, 2004). Like children, adults need an environment that provides developmentally appropriate supports while simultaneously offering challenges. It is the critical combination of support and challenge that allows the adult to construct new ways of being and knowing. Without that environment, the conditions for development are nonexistent. Cognitive Coaching is a perfect match to developmental-constructivism. It supports teachers and principals with a listening, nonjudgmental ear. Additionally, it invites inquiry, a reshaping and reconstructing of one's thinking, and challenges the deep structures of a person's mental models, beliefs, values, and identity. Without this kind of intervention, educators become trapped in a professional development and support system that is informational only. True growth is limited rather than expanded. Cognitive Coaching can create conditions for transformational learning.

Cognitive Coaching is a constructivist model of learning. It rejects behaviorist notions that ignore the capacity of the human mind to create knowledge, examine the meaning of knowledge, and make decisions about how to act on knowledge. The coach intentionally structures human interactions to maximize productive analysis of one's work and environment to act more effectively as a professional.

As professionals, we have a responsibility to those we serve to be continuously learning. There is ample evidence (Joyce & Showers, 1995) to indicate that without coaching, educators have little likelihood of moving knowledge learned in training into important arenas of application. Cognitive Coaching is grounded in an assumption that explicit processes are required to facilitate learning. Learning is not linear, but it is also not haphazard. Attention to structures and processes for learning enhances the likelihood for results and capacity for forward momentum.

Cognitive Coaching is a nonjudgmental process. The person being coached makes his or her own judgments. The coach builds trust by being nonjudgmental. The coaching environment frees the person to take risks and examine long-held assumptions without fear. Cognitive Coaching is congruent with the body of research describing the importance of environmental conditions for thoughtful practice. Under stress, the brain reverts to old pathways that move the actor toward fight or flight. Those patterns are counterproductive for the conditions and needs of today's educators. By contrast, Cognitive Coaching enhances the environmental conditions necessary to sustain the neural capacity to work at the neocortical or higher-level thinking part of the brain. If we want to be thoughtful, reflective practitioners, we have a responsibility to provide systems of support to make that happen. The skills of the Cognitive Coach enhance and support the most basic neural needs to develop our most exquisite capacities.

FOUR SUPPORT FUNCTIONS

Costa and Garmston (2002) have developed a model of four functions for professional support: Cognitive Coaching, collaborating, consulting, and evaluation. These functions allow those who are supporting others to be clear about the purpose of their interactions and to apply functions to their work based on need rather than some prescribed process. Costa and Garmston refer to this as a capability: "Know one's intentions and choose congruent behaviors" (p. 64). All four support functions are intended to support growth and development, but they do so in very different ways. Although all four have a place in systems of support, Cognitive Coaching has the greatest potential for transformational learning. It is an ongoing process whereby the coach invites regular reflection based on the needs of the coachee, thus increasing capacity with the coachee's internal resources. It is a constructivist-developmental process, one of the most compatible of the four support functions with transformational learning.

Evaluation is probably the most familiar in educational settings. It refers to making judgments about one's performance based on a well-understood set of external standards. While evaluation is an important accountability measure for districts, it has little potential for transformational growth as it is externally imposed and rarely constructivist in nature. The implementation most often relates to personnel systems rather than growth.

Consulting is also a familiar form of support in the world of schools. Consultants work to support others by providing expertise and knowledge to them with the intention to expand their informational learning. This is often seen in the form of mentor programs where others are assigned to teachers and principals to share their knowledge and experiences. The mentors help their mentees "learn the job" and problem solve with them. While very helpful, without an added Cognitive Coaching component, these are not effective in transformational learning, the most effective source of adult development.

Another support function, collaboration, allows a team or pair of educators to work together to plan, problem solve, or inquire together. The notion of collaboration is about a community of learners, sharing their ideas and creating learning together.

A key feature that differentiates the four support functions is the source of judgment in each. In Cognitive Coaching, the judgments are made by the coachee; for example, "I was not happy with the meeting today because . . ." In collaboration, the judgments are shared by the collaborators; for example, "We seem to agree that by disaggregating our data, we are becoming more effective in addressing learner deficits." The consultant provides judgments about the criteria for performance using his or her expertise to define them; for example, "When you can document that you are spending 30% of your time on learning walks, you can expect to see some gains from the process." In evaluation, the criteria are set through defined standards and the evaluator makes judgments about the person's performance in relation to the data; for example, "Your work is a level 3 on our performance criteria for instructional leadership. Here are the data I am using to make that rating."

COGNITIVE COACHING CONVERSATION MAPS

Cognitive Coaches are guided in their interactions by three coaching maps. When we think of a road map, we think of a symbolic representation of some territory we might like to explore. It serves as a guide for assisting us through some terrain, focusing us on staying on course and getting where we want to go. We know the map is only a depiction and that we have to make midcourse corrections as we traverse the territory. Cognitive Coaching maps serve a similar function. They give us templates for conversations for planning, reflecting, and problem resolving. They are not scripts, but guides through the territory of the teacher's thinking. They serve to focus the conversation, keeping it on course and supporting productive use of time. The maps reflect research on effective planning, reflecting, and problem resolving. As coaches internalize the maps, it frees them to focus fully on truly listening to the internal maps of the teacher's mind, revealed in their conversations. Further, it gives the coach guidance in patterns of questioning that build capacity for self-directed learning. The Cognitive Coaching model is based on three maps, each with different purposes.

The Planning Conversation Map serves to assist a teacher in preparing for an upcoming event. It is generic and can be used for multiple purposes (e.g., planning a staff meeting or lesson, preparing for a parent conference, long-range planning related to school improvement). This map has two focuses—one on the event and one on the person doing the planning. It ends with a reflection on the coaching. The first three regions of the map focus on the event. In doing so, the planner has the opportunity to mentally rehearse the event, gaining greater clarity and craftsmanship about the event's desired outcomes and the ways of assessing those outcomes. The teacher anticipates effective strategies and considers ways to monitor and adjust as the event progresses. The fourth region, the personal learning focus, shifts the teacher's thinking from the event to an internal focus. The teacher is asked to identify areas of learning and growth. This region may be the most critical region of the map as it is the source of an internal focus and goal setting for learning. Without this element, the map is shallow, providing only thinking for the event, but no deeper commitment to professional growth and meaning making from the experience. The final region of the map invites reflection on the conversation, providing thinking to synthesize for the teacher and feedback to the coach.

The Reflecting Conversation Map serves the teacher in analyzing and learning from experiences. It invites a person to move from a significant experience to making meaning of the experience in a manner that leads to transferring learning into the future. Without reflection, teachers are doomed to repeat patterns of behavior. Contrasted with the common educational practice of planning, few educators are given the opportunity to reflect and few have internalized the processes of reflection. This map provides a structure that moves teachers from focusing on events (episodic thinking) to gleaning key learnings and generalizations from experiences. In doing so, the map is compatible with how human brains remember. We do not remember specifics, but instead store generalizations and guiding principles: For example, inclusion is a key factor in decision making; budgeting is something that is often misunderstood by staff. Those larger frames inform us in the future. Smaller frames (e.g., that was a challenging staff meeting because three teachers were upset about how the final decision was made) do not inform us for the future. They only cause us to recycle an event over and over.

In the reflecting conversation, the coach is careful to not invite storytelling, a simple reiteration of the experience. Instead the coach supports the reflector in linking impressions with data that support those impressions. The critical focus of this map is on analyzing causal factors. The coach supports high consciousness by assisting the thinking about each decision and each part of the experience. As those are analyzed, the teacher begins to construct new learning about factors that contributed to the outcomes, successes, and failures in the experience. From that analysis, the reflector is able to gain new insights that lead to generalizations for future application. The final region of the map, reflect on the process, is the same as in the Planning Conversation.

The Problem-Resolving Map draws on brain research about the human mind under stress. It is a map a coach might use with teachers who are seemingly low in resources and unable to find forward direction. Examples might be as follows:

- A teacher is uncertain about how to implement a new program.
- A teacher is having a difficult relationship with his assistant.
- A difficult parent issue seems without resolution.
- A teacher is discouraged by the pressure to deliver improved test scores.

The Problem-Resolving Map differs from the other maps in that it is more conceptual and less focused on specific steps to explore. The States of Mind are the source of questions in all of the three maps, but especially critical in this map. The coach is attuned to the emotional and cognitive needs of the coachee, balancing the two.

The map first attends to an acknowledgement of the existing state, that is, what is the current reality for the coachee. This is important because under threat, the brain experiences neurochemical changes causing loss of cognitive capacity. The structure and processes of the map support enhanced cognition. The map begins with a process called pacing, which paraphrases the existing state of the person. Attention is given to both emotion and content of the existing state; for example, "You're hurt because your boss is not seeing your contributions."

The map's structure leads the coach to refocus the coachee's energy toward the desired state. The coachee begins to envision a better future, for example, feeling valued. The increase in the brain's neurotransmitters occurs when language is given to creating an image of something more positive. The coach uses language to assist the problem resolver in expressing a more desirable way of being. Finally, using the States of Mind as sources of energy, the coach questions the problem resolver to develop internal resources related to the desired state.

Skilled coaches develop flexibility in using the maps. They sometimes use only some of the regions of the map in their mediation of the teacher's thinking. Other times they modify the sequencing of the maps to align with the needs of the teacher. Coaches use the maps both formally and informally. A short conversation in the hall might cover just a few elements of the map and the coach could leave the teacher with a question to ponder. Such conversations do not bring closure to a coachee's thinking. The brief hallway conversation is still coaching and leaves the person more resourceful. The coach knows that work can continue with the coachee in future conversations. The focus of coaching is on serving the needs of the person in the moment, not on completing the maps.

COACHING TOOLS

Cognitive Coaches work from a toolkit of effective communication skills that support creating an environment of trust. If the coach is to grow transformationally, there must be challenge *and* support. The coach's toolkit is congruent with those intentions. One teacher called her coaching sessions her "brain massage." When you think of the qualities of a skillful massage, there is an opportunity to tune out other stimuli and focus on self. The atmosphere is relaxed and slowed in pace. However, with deep massage, like deep thinking, there is often some pain and challenge.

Rapport skills allow the Cognitive Coach to create comfort in the moment and let the coachee know that the coach is truly present and listening intently. The kind of listening that is seen when the coach attends fully, using verbal and nonverbal skills, is rarely seen in an educator's day. The rapport is intended to create optimal conditions for thinking.

Cognitive Coaches are knowledgeable in response behaviors designed to mediate thinking. Those behaviors include pausing, paraphrasing, and probing for specificity. Our culture has come to equate speed with intelligence. Similarly we equate productivity with speed (Wheatley, 2005). The pause provides time to think for both the coach and the teacher. It allows for space to engage in the behaviors of complex thinking and reflection. Pausing has been shown to create an increased level of cognitive functioning in students. It is our experience that the same is true for adult learners.

Paraphrasing, well executed, is a fundamental tool for mediating thinking. When people hear their own words reflected back in a rephrased manner, it is often the first time they attend to the meaning of their own thinking. It is the social construction of placing one's thinking in the middle between the coach and teacher and examining it with one's own words and then examining it a second time through the coach's paraphrases that causes a reshaping and deeper examination of the internal thought processes that may have been previously unexpressed. Without language being put to the inner thoughts, they remain inaccessible and cannot be modified. Cognitive Coaches use a variety of paraphrasing types to cause teachers to hear their own feelings, key concepts, and generalizations. The most complex paraphrases give teachers access to their inner beliefs, values, assumptions, goals, and mental models.

Probing for specificity is one way a coach increases the teacher's precision and craftsmanship. Words are simply an externalization of thinking. When words lack specificity, it is often a reflection of lack of clarity in thinking. Take, for instance, a teacher who says, "It's important to me that my students collaborate." If the teacher is to genuinely target student collaboration, he or she will need to have a clear picture about the meaning of collaboration. Does it mean that teachers share texts, coplan, examine student work, or use common assessments? The Cognitive Coach would assist the teacher in moving toward clarity by following, "It's important to me that my students collaborate," with a probe such as, "If your students were genuinely collaborating, what might be some of the behaviors you would expect to see?" Another probe might be, "What does collaboration mean to you?" Probes bring focus and clarity to words that allow us to move them to action.

Inquiry is another tool a coach uses. Inquiry differs from probing in that it has the intention to broaden thinking to more divergence. The coach, speaking to a teacher about his or her value around collaboration, might inquire by asking, "What might you anticipate happening for student thought processes if they were to collaborate?" or "As you envision a more collaborative classroom, what possible downsides might there be?" Effective inquiry is open-ended and has no agenda. It is an invitation to explore. Inquiry has intellectual risk embedded in it as it may cause one to think about things that one had not considered before, or it may make visible things that are uncomfortable, challenging, or even threatening. This is the heart of using Cognitive Coaching for transformational learning. Inquiry moves the person into the territory of challenge. In pairing inquiry with the other coaching tools, it also creates a sense of support. When people are invited to think through inquiry, they begin to internalize the process of inquiry and become more self-directed in developing a professional identity as an inquirer.

IDENTITY AS A MEDIATOR OF THINKING

The thinking of Cognitive Coaches distinguishes them from other types of coaches. The focus on self-directed learning requires that Cognitive Coaches think about their role as neutral and nonjudgmental about the topic of conversation. Although Cognitive Coaches are unbiased about *what* the person is thinking, they are biased that the person *is* thinking.

The metacognition of Cognitive Coaches is based on their identity as mediators of thinking. Our identity is who we believe we are and is usually held unconsciously. Although it may be unconscious, it is reflected in all our words and actions and is apparent to all those with whom we live and work. Our identity influences our perceptions, interactions, choices, and ultimately the way we fulfill our roles and responsibilities in life.

The term *mediator* comes from the work of Reuven Feuerstein (2000) and refers to mediated learning experiences. Feuerstein describes a mediated learning experience as one in which a person processes the experience at deeper levels because a mediator is interposed between the event and the learner. Such mediated learning experiences lead to deeper, more pervasive change.

Costa and Garmston (2002) explain mediator in the following way:

> The word *mediate* is derived from the word *middle*. Therefore, mediators interpose themselves between a person and some event, problem, conflict, challenge or other perplexing situation. The mediator intervenes in such a way as to enhance another person's self-directed learning. (p. 56)

When one's identity is that of a mediator of thinking, one believes that he or she is someone who can be neutral and nonjudgmental in supporting another person's thinking toward being self-directed. A mediator of thinking does not solve other people's problems for them because that would be robbing them of an opportunity to grow. Metaphorically, a mediator shines a spotlight of awareness on the other person's thinking. Ultimately, mediators of thinking believe in the human capacity for continual growth, in themselves and in others, and also in their capacity to empower others.

It is as a mediator of thinking that each of us holds the greatest potential for supporting growth and development of another person. When a coach mediates a teacher's thinking, the teacher's learning is enhanced, and there is an increased likelihood of change. From these mediated learning experiences, teachers are able to more fully develop their potential for success as leaders.

METAPHORICAL ORIENTATIONS

Costa and Garmston (2002) contrast four metaphorical orientations that people sometimes take when they are not being a mediator of thinking. The metaphorical orientations are parent, expert, friend, and boss. As metaphors, they serve to help us understand the presuppositions and goals we have when we are not engaging neutrally without judgments. For many coaches, it is the orientation of expert that is problematic to developing one's identity and capacity as a mediator of thinking. Past experience and positive reinforcement for offering advice and suggestions often interfere with becoming a mediator of thinking. In fact, the job title "consultant" communicates to others that you are an expert, someone to be consulted on designated topics.

People who have an expert orientation place high value on their ability to help others by sharing their expertise. Their sense of self-worth is based on how much they know and how much they can share that knowledge and skill with others. Oftentimes they have been promoted and sought out in an organization as a person to call on to have things "fixed." Letting go of an expert orientation as a default position must happen before a coach can develop the identity of a mediator of thinking. It doesn't mean that the coach will never share his or her expertise. When the decision is made to share expertise, it will be based on the coachee's need to receive it and not the coach's need to share it.

The expert orientation is the basis for the support function of consulting. If a coach begins a conversation in the consulting support function, he lowers the efficacy of the person and builds dependency on the coach. Given the percentage of time that teachers will spend with coaches, versus the amount of time they will spend on their own, the coaches who enter conversations as consultants are not doing all that they can to build the self-directedness of the coachees.

Entering a conversation from a neutral, nonjudgmental perspective enables coaches to determine whether Cognitive Coaching is the most appropriate support function to support self-directedness. Additionally, it enables coaches to determine what information they might need to offer while collaborating, consulting, or evaluating. When one's identify is that of a mediator of thinking, he or she defaults to the support function of Cognitive Coaching. Just as a computer defaults to a certain font when you turn it on, mediators of thinking default to the support function of Cognitive Coaching when they enter into an interaction with another person. It is from this neutral perspective that one can make decisions about other ways to support the teacher.

THE COGNITIVE COACHING PROCESS

Every human interaction is an opportunity to mediate another person's thinking. We do not choose to mediate in every interaction, but the choice is always available. In viewing coaching as ongoing, we begin to view our work as a process of continuous improvement and development. Although most educators come to their work with skills, the job is organic, changing, and evolving. Effective educators seek opportunities to reflect on practice and broaden and deepen their thinking and internal thought structures. Without a coaching process, opportunities for reflection and focused thinking become infrequent. Cognitive Coaching provides a structure for and expectation of reflective practice. Cognitive Coaching is not a process of evaluation. Evaluation exists to make judgments about performance. It is a key feature of effective human resource management, but it is generally ineffective in developing professionals with increased capacity for rich cognition and self-directedness. The process of Cognitive Coaching institutionalizes the expectation that educators will be supported as growing professionals.

REFERENCES

Bandura, A. (1997). *Self-efficacy: The exercise of control.* New York: W.H. Freeman.

Costa, A., & Garmston, R. (2002). *Cognitive Coaching^{SM}: A foundation for renaissance schools.* Norwood, MA: Christopher-Gordon.

Costa, A., & Lipton, L. (1996). *Holonomy: paradox and promise.* Unpublished manuscript.

Damasio, A. (1994). *Descartes error: Emotion, reason and the human brain.* New York: HarperCollins.

Drago-Severson, E. (2004). *Helping teachers learn.* Thousand Oaks, CA: Corwin Press.

Edwards, J. (2005). *Cognitive Coaching research.* Highlands Ranch, CO: Center for Cognitive Coaching.

Ellison, J., & Hayes, C. (2006a). *Cognitive Coaching: Weaving threads of learning and change into the culture of an organization.* Norwood, MA: Christopher-Gordon.

Ellison, J., & Hayes, C. (2006b). *Effective school leadership: Developing principals through Cognitive Coaching.* Norwood, MA: Christopher-Gordon.

Feuerstein, R. (2000). Mediated learning experience. In A. Costa (Ed.), *Teaching for intelligence II: A collection of articles* (p. 275). Arlington Heights, IL: Skylights.

Goleman, D. (2006). *Social intelligence.* New York: Bantam Dell.

Joyce, B., & Showers, B. (1995). *Student achievement through staff development* (3rd ed.). Alexandria, VA: Association for Supervision and Curriculum Development.

Kegan, R. (1995). *In over our heads: The mental demands of modern life.* Cambridge, MA: Harvard University Press.

Tschannen-Moran, M., Woolfolk Hoy, A., & Hoy, W. K. (1998). Teacher efficacy: Its meaning and measure. *Review of Educational Research, 68*(2), 202–248.

Wheatley, M. J. (2005). *Finding our way: Leadership for an uncertain time.* San Francisco: Berrett-Koehler.

5

Coaching Classroom Management

Wendy M. Reinke,
Randy Sprick, and Jim Knight

INTRODUCTION

Randy Sprick's interest in classroom management started with his experiences coaching teachers in their use of Engelmann's direct instruction approach. Randy would spend a week or a month onsite coaching teachers in the use of Engelmann's materials. Although he was supposed to provide coaching on the reading program, he found himself spending 50% of his time coaching teachers on classroom management. From those experiences, Randy published his first book on classroom management, *Solution Book: A Guide to Classroom Discipline* (1981), and followed that with several others, including *Discipline in the Secondary Classroom: A Positive Approach to Behavior Management* (Sprick, 2006), *CHAMPs: A Proactive and Positive Approach to Classroom Management* (Sprick, Garrison, & Howard, 1998), *Foundations: Establishing Positive Discipline* (Sprick, Garrison, & Howard, 2002), and a host of other practical publications aimed at creating safe and civil public schools.

I was introduced to Randy's excellent work by my friend Jodi King, from Cecil County, Maryland. While I was visiting Cecil County schools, I mentioned to Jodi that our coaches in Topeka, Kansas, needed a way to assist with classroom management in some teachers' classrooms. Jodi quickly told me that I "really should read

(Continued)

(Continued)

Randy Sprick's work," and with the fervent passion of a believer, she gave me a copy of Randy's book, *CHAMPs: A Proactive and Positive Approach to Classroom Management* (Sprick et al., 1998), on the spot. As fate would have it, the next day I found myself stuck on an airplane on a runway for several hours. By the time my flight finally delivered me home to Kansas, I had read the book, and I understood why Jodi was so enthusiastic about Randy's work.

Two weeks later, I found myself in Portland attending Randy's workshop titled "*Foundations: Establishing Positive Discipline Policies*." Over lunch, Randy and I discussed my work on coaching in Kansas, and he generously offered to visit and consult on our project and work with our coaches. This visit sparked Randy's interest in our instructional coaching model, and he soon found himself at one of my workshops on instructional coaching in Baltimore, Maryland, where, as it turns out, he introduced me to Wendy M. Reinke.

Wendy learned about Randy's work at the University of Oregon, where she had gone to pursue her interest in helping students with serious behavior problems. In her first year at school, Wendy took a class that Randy taught on behavioral consultation. That class, and Randy's advice, convinced her to do her doctoral research on behavioral consultation, and Wendy, naturally, asked him to sit in on her dissertation committee because of his expertise in working with teachers.

The method for gathering data that Wendy developed for her dissertation, "The Classroom Check-Up" (CCU; Reinke, 2006), and her depth of knowledge about data gathering in general were very helpful for coaches, and soon Wendy was also working with our coaches in Topeka. The three of us, Wendy, Randy, and I, and a dynamite coach from the Topeka project, Tricia McKale Skyles, began exploring how the classroom management ideas could be employed through the use of the instructional coaching model (which I described in more detail in Chapter 2). The final outcome of these collaborations, aside from the very rewarding professional friendship we all share with each other, is the book *Coaching Classroom Management* (Sprick, Knight, Reinke, & McKale, 2007).

This chapter describes high-leverage tools that coaches can use to help teachers create positive learning communities in their classrooms and that are described in greater length in *Coaching Classroom Management* (Sprick et al., 2007). Additionally, the chapter describes several variables that coaches can observe to help teachers monitor their progress in managing behavior. Through effective data gathering, coaches can make the invisible visible, by helping teachers monitor such student variables as engagement and disruptions, and teacher behaviors such as offering praise and providing opportunities to respond. The coaching methods described in this chapter will not be used in every classroom simply because many teachers manage classroom behavior masterfully. However, we have found that if a teacher is struggling to keep students on task or to reduce disruptions, that teacher's coach will need to know how to help him or her to regain control of the class before much else can be done. We hope this chapter offers a quick summary of many of the starting points for teachers and coaches who are working on classroom management.

The connection between academic achievement and student behavior is difficult to deny, particularly when you are faced with a classroom of students with challenging behavior. Managing students' disruptive classroom behavior can be a consuming task that reduces the amount of time teachers spend on instruction. Effective classroom behavior management is directly tied to high levels of student involvement and academic achievement, making it an important component of teaching. However, the link between effective instruction and behavior is often neglected. It is not uncommon for teachers to enter the workforce with little or no coursework on effectively managing student behavior. Hence, it's not surprising that teachers state that classroom management is one of their primary concerns (Maag, 2001). In fact, a recent nationwide survey conducted with teachers across all grade levels indicated a strong need for additional training and support in classroom management (Coalition for Psychology in Schools and Education, 2006).

The increasing numbers of students with challenging behaviors entering school and the movement for inclusion of special education students present new complexities for teachers working to manage classroom behaviors. Neglecting the connection between academic achievement and student behavior is costly to students and teachers. Poor classroom management has been linked to long-term, negative, academic, behavioral, and social outcomes for students (Kellam, Ling, Merisca, Brown, & Ialongo, 1998; National Research Council, 2002; Reinke & Herman, 2002), whereas teachers who struggle with classroom management may feel ineffective, demoralized, and are likely to leave the profession altogether. Nearly half of new teachers leave the profession within five years, many citing student misbehavior as a primary reason for leaving (Ingersoll, 2002).

There is a clear need for training in classroom management, but one-shot training is not enough (Sprick et al., 2007). While traditional professional development can educate teachers on innovative and effective practices to bring back to the classroom, classroom management strategies can be tricky and less easily transferred from workshop to reality. There are a few reasons for this. First, effective teaching requires a teacher to do many different things at once (e.g., monitor independent work, answer questions, and keep students on task). When a teacher is faced with disruptive behavior, he or she is required to make a decision at that moment. There is not often time to review notes from a workshop or look up a potential strategy in a book. Additionally, misbehavior, particularly refusal to follow a direction, poses a threat to the teacher's authority. When under stress, we are all more likely to revert to familiar behaviors, such as reacting with anger or getting into a power struggle with the student, and less likely to implement a behavior we have recently learned. Thus, when a teacher is forced to make a quick decision about what to do when confronted with student misbehavior, he or she may revert to less effective management strategies that were in place prior to the freshly discovered strategies picked up from a training workshop. It takes practice and support to effectively implement new classroom management strategies. Second, any change in how the teacher manages behavior in the classroom will inevitably result in unanticipated reactions from students. Without additional supports, the teacher may be discouraged from persisting in the new management strategy.

One method for supporting teacher implementation of effective classroom behavior management practices is through the use of coaching. Teachers, especially during the initial stages of implementing new strategies in the classroom, need additional support. A coach provides these supports by preparing the teacher for potential reactions and by offering guidance and feedback until the new behavior has been successfully incorporated into everyday practice (see Fixen, Naoom, Blasé, Friedman, & Wallace, 2005).

The purpose of this chapter is to familiarize you with a model for coaching classroom management. We provide an overview of this coaching model, outline the critical components of effective classroom management, and introduce you to the CCU, a structured model for collaboratively designing interventions to improve classroom management.

OVERVIEW OF THE COACHING MODEL

An effective coaching model begins with a structure that explicitly communicates the roles of administrative staff, coaches, and teachers. In a nutshell, administrators have responsibility for creating a vision for how the school will approach behavior management, providing training opportunities, and creating accountability for implementation of the vision. The coaches have responsibility for knowing the vision, spending time in classrooms with teachers, and assisting teachers in successfully meeting the accountability standards set by the administrators. The coaches should be supportive and nonthreatening, with the communication skills and interpersonal rapport to be able to build and maintain effective relationships with teachers. Teachers have the responsibility of working in collaboration with coaches to improve behavior management in their classroom. Everyone is working toward the ultimate goal of creating positive outcomes for the students.

To clarify the difference between the role of the administrator and that of coach, it is important to distinguish between two classifications of coaching: evaluative and nonevaluative coaches. Evaluative coaches are those individuals in the school who play an important role in coaching, which by the nature of their position and job description is one of authority relative to most teachers. For instance, the administrator as coach tends to be evaluative, since he or she is involved in teacher evaluations. Whereas the nonevaluative coach's role is to solely help support teachers with behavior management. Ideally, for the purposes of coaching classroom management, anyone in an administrative or supervisory role should consider his or her role in coaching to be evaluative, and anyone coaching nonevaluatively should be allowed to work with teachers confidentially, without directly reporting to an administrator or linking with teacher evaluations. Providing teachers with access to nonevaluative coaches, particularly with regard to gaining supports in classroom management, will produce the best results in that the coaching process poses no risk to one's job security. However, this idealistic scenario is not always the case, but one that both administrators and coaches should make every effort toward. At the very least, the teacher, the coach, and the building administrator must each know all expectations regarding who reports to whom and what the coach will be required to report to the school administrator about what takes place during the coaching relationship.

ROLE OF THE ADMINISTRATOR

Effective classroom management begins with effective leadership from the building administrator. The principal or administrator involved in the coaching process has the role of creating a vision with regard to behavioral expectations within the school. Defining this vision is the first step toward creating a positive climate and common purpose among staff and students. Envision a school where most misbehavior is prevented and that which does occur is managed effectively. Next, choose a model for classroom management. Some schools or districts already have a model in place. If this is not the case, carefully consider choosing a model that is consistent with the best findings in research and provides plenty of "how-to" information. What is most important when identifying or developing the structure for coaching is that teachers, administrators, and coaches all have a shared understanding of what constitutes effective classroom management, why it's important, what it looks and sounds like, and how it should be implemented.

A good classroom management model addresses prevention, teaching expectations, encouragement, and correction. A schoolwide approach to discipline and behavior support is optimal. If your school is not currently implementing schoolwide behavior supports, consider doing so. For instance, your school might utilize schoolwide positive behavior support initiatives such as *Foundations* (Sprick, Garrison, & Howard, 2002), *Positive Behavior Intervention & Supports* (PBIS; see Horner & Sugai, 2000), or *Building Effective Schools Together* (BEST; see Sprague & Golly, 2004). In addition to schoolwide programs for behavior support, there are models specific to establishing classroom management procedures that can be implemented within a schoolwide system or simply within the classrooms in your school. One such model for helping to organize how teachers, administrators, and coaches structure classroom management that is based on effective research is the CHAMPs approach set forth in *CHAMPs: A Proactive and Positive Approach to Classroom Management* (see Sprick et al., 1998), and *Discipline in the Secondary Classroom: A Positive Approach to Behavior Management* (see Sprick, 2006).

CHAMPs operates from a conceptual framework that addresses five categories in which expectations should be precisely taught:

CHAMPs Approach

Conversation	Can students talk to each other during this activity?
Help	How do students get teachers' attention and their questions answered?
Activity	What is the task or objective? What is the end product?
Movement	Can students move about during this activity?
Participation	How do students show they are fully participating? What does work behavior look or sound like?

Teachers using the CHAMPs approach are encouraged to use principles of effective classroom management to create their own plan, identify decisions they need to make about their plan, and then follow logical steps to implementation. Coaches working within schools implementing the CHAMPs approach to classroom management can work with teachers on developing and incorporating effective management practices while giving ongoing support.

Other models of classroom management include The Classroom Organization and Management Program (COMP) developed by Dr. Carolyn Evertson and Marzano's Classroom Management That Works: Research-Based Strategies for Every Teacher, to name a few. Regardless of what model for classroom management your school chooses as the foundation of coaching classroom management, it is important that the model utilizes research-based principles of effective classroom management. Be wary of models or approaches to classroom management that are non–research based or punitive in nature. Committing to implementing classroom management practices that are proactive, positive, and research based will provide optimal outcomes for teachers and students.

The best behavior management strategies address five areas of behavioral intervention: prevention, expectations, monitoring, encouragement, and correction. We have developed the acronym STOIC to bring these variables easily to mind (Sprick et al., 2007):

STOIC Intervention Planning

Structure for success

Teach expectations

Observe and monitor

Interact positively

Correct fluently

For instance, teachers *structure for success* by organizing classrooms and class activities to discourage misbehavior and encourage student engagement. Teachers *teach expectations* for how to successfully function within that structure. Teachers *observe and monitor* by circulating through the classroom unpredictably, scanning frequently. Teachers *interact positively* by proving both contingent praise (e.g., praising a student for correctly raising his hand to answer a question) and noncontingent positive attention (e.g., greeting students each morning). Teachers *correct fluently* by responding to undesired behavior calmly, consistently, briefly, and immediately. A fluent correction does not disrupt the flow of instruction. The following scenario provides an example of correcting fluently: During a lesson the teacher asks Johnny to provide the answer to a question. Immediately, Kennedy (another student in the classroom) blurts out the answer. The teacher states, "Kennedy, that was talking out of turn. Please wait until you are called on," and returns to instruction by asking Johnny another question. The flow of instruction was not disrupted and Kennedy was provided a clear correction. A correction that was not fluent may look like this: Kennedy blurts out the answer. The teacher stops instruction, walks over to Kennedy's desk, and in an angry tone states, "Kennedy, we have talked about this before; you need to wait until you are called upon before you give an answer. Now, let Johnny answer the question himself. We all know that *you* know the answer. I want to know if Johnny knows the answer."

The approaches outlined by CHAMPs and STOIC intervention planning are all based on empirically supported practices, meaning that these strategies have been researched and shown to be effective in improving student behavior in the classroom. Therefore, the CHAMPs approach and STOIC intervention planning can be used to guide the use of effective, research-based classroom management plans.

The STOIC model for intervention planning can also be utilized as an overarching guide to establishing an effective coaching model. For instance, administrators and coaches can collaborate to *structure for success* by creating a vision, selecting a research-based classroom management model, and training all staff in the selected model to ensure that everyone has the necessary skills to implement the model. The administrator and coaches can *teach expectations* by communicating the roles of coaches, administrators, and teachers within the coaching model to ensure that all members understand the expectations and can be successful in their role. The administrator and coaches *observe and monitor* how the classroom management model is being implemented within classrooms by conducting walk-throughs and giving feedback to teachers. The administrator and coaches both *interact positively* with school staff and model the use of contingent and noncontingent positive attention. The administrator and coaches both *correct fluently* by providing feedback to teachers as needed in implementation of the classroom management model (with coaches always remembering that their corrective feedback is nonevaluative and designed to help teachers successfully meet expectations).

Staff Training

Once an effective model for classroom management has been identified, a training plan will need to be formalized. Without staff training in the model, whether it be the CHAMPs approach or another model, there will be no implementation. Ongoing training yields better results than a one-shot workshop. An effective training plan is one in which training is distributed over time, allowing participants to try out new techniques and later discuss what worked and what did not.

While plans for training staff will vary in what they look like, effective training plans will include the following: (1) ongoing training and support to ensure that faculty understand and practice implementing the strategies laid out in the chosen classroom management model, (2) a plan for orienting new teachers to the model, (3) a plan for monitoring implementation of the classroom management model in classrooms (e.g., administrator walk-throughs), (4) a plan for identifying and training coaches, (5) allocation of the amount of time that coaches will be available to support teachers, (6) ongoing support for coaches (e.g., networking opportunities for coaches, study groups for coaches), and (7) a visible show of administrative commitment regarding the importance of good classroom management and a commitment to coaching as a vehicle for achieving that end.

There are a number of options for how to structure effective training for classroom management. For instance, training sessions could be staggered with a one- or two-day training session in the summer before school begins, with quarterly half-day follow-up trainings. Other options include having monthly faculty study meetings on particular modules of the classroom management model selected. The book *Coaching Classroom Management* (Sprick et al., 2007) suggests that administrators arrange for brief discussion and practice opportunities, or mini-inservices, during staff meetings. The book provides a series of mini-inservice activities, including modules on finalizing your classroom management plan, brainstorming interventions for a class that is not responding to the attention signal, handling an emotional outburst from a student, and maintaining student motivation through the last month of school (see Sprick et al., 2007, for a complete list and actual activities).

Once the training program is up and running, administrators will need to devise a plan for orienting newly hired faculty or staff who missed the initial training session on the selected classroom management model. Mentoring first-year and relocated teachers as part of the plan can really help with long-term success of the model within the school. Additionally, new staff can be encouraged to meet regularly with a coach or mentor to discuss implementation.

Administrator Walk-Throughs

Once initial training has been conducted, and the faculty and coaches have the knowledge necessary to implement the classroom management model, ongoing monitoring of how well teachers are implementing the model is needed to ensure success. Research shows that student behavior is more responsible and motivated when adults actively observe. This same principle applies to adults. Therefore, administrator visits to the classroom can improve staff implementation of effective classroom management. Even the most motivated teachers with the best intentions can become busy, fall into past patterns, and fail to implement as well as they would like. Administrator walk-throughs simply bring the importance of implementation to the forefront.

Administrators should have a game plan before entering a teacher's classroom. With a good game plan, a 3- to 5-minute walk-through will allow for observation of both instructional and behavior management issues in each classroom (see Sprick et al., 2007, for a full description of how to conduct administrator walk-throughs). First, plan to observe student behavior. Are the students engaged, respectful toward one another and the teacher, and are they complying with posted expectations? Next, observe for student engagement. Does the teacher provide instructional opportunities to respond to and do the students respond correctly? Are the students on task? Last, observe teacher behaviors. Is the teacher actively observing, using praise effectively, and correcting misbehavior fluently? Forms that guide the observation during administrator walk-throughs will help ensure that the observations are more objective.

Walk-throughs provide the administrator with the opportunity to provide feedback to teachers. Prior to any visit, the administrator should prepare the teachers by describing exactly what they will be looking for and how feedback will be provided. Then, on completion of the visit, the administrator can summarize the data collected during the visit, providing positive feedback as well as corrective feedback. If there are a number of variables that need to be improved, the administrator can encourage the teacher to ask for assistance from one or more of the instructional coaches in the building who have been trained in the building's classroom management model.

Selecting and Supporting Coaches

The selection, training, and ongoing support of the coaches need careful consideration to ensure success. Coaches supply the link in the feedback circuit as a neutral third-party observer. Teachers will feel empowered, rather than abandoned, when they have access to coaching options that include colleagues they respect. Therefore, the more coaching options the better (e.g., instructional coaches, content-area coaches, psychologists, and others whose professional duties intersect teachers in a nonevaluative manner). However, one caveat is that teachers should limit involvement with coaching to one or, at the most, two coaches. This avoids the issue of teachers becoming overwhelmed with competing suggestions or too much information.

It is helpful for administrators to provide a structure to ensure success for coaches. This structure includes the quantity of time in which coaches are allocated to be available for teachers, for being present in the classroom, and the proportion of time they devote to coaching relative to other duties. Communication of these expectations with teachers and staff will help clarify expectations as well as share information about the support available.

It is important to note that successful coaching of classroom management starts with effective leadership. The school administrator is a key player in the success of any coaching model. In particular, the school administrator can set the tone by showing strong support for the coaches within the building. Therefore, one key component to any coaching model is ongoing administrative support. This support can include allocating resources to coaches for ongoing training and networking opportunities. Additionally, administrators can show the importance of coaching and classroom management by encouraging teachers to seek out coaches to support them in implementation.

The administrator wears many hats toward shaping classroom management: to develop a vision for the school, choose a classroom management model, arrange training in that model, inform staff of what is expected, monitor implementation, provide feedback to staff, and encourage teachers to seek out coaches. The role is a continuous cycle of improvement that is never fully complete. Staff members should recognize that they are never in it alone, that their colleagues are available for help, and that a system of coaching is in place that empowers, recognizes, and values the contributions of each individual.

Role of the Coach

The coach has the responsibility of understanding the classroom management model set forth in the school. As such, the coach is expected to know enough about effective classroom management to help teachers overcome challenges and break through barriers to managing their classrooms effectively. Coaches will need to be familiar with research-based interventions and strategies of classroom management and understand the dynamics involved in classroom behavior and misbehavior, recognizing the variables that can be manipulated to bring about positive outcomes for students. In addition to being knowledgeable about effective classroom management, coaches should be helpful, supportive, and nonthreatening. An effective coach uses good communication skills and interpersonal rapport to build and maintain effective relationships with teachers.

Every coaching relationship is unique, but there are several stages that characterize the typical coaching cycle. These stages, or components to coaching, include the following: (1) enroll the teacher, (2) identify interventions, (3) explain the process, (4) model techniques, (5) observe the teacher, (6) explore data, and (7) review results. These stages are fairly chronological but don't necessarily need to occur in this order. Chapter 2 provides a detailed review of these components of coaching. What follows provides a brief overview.

Enroll the Teacher

Before the coach and teacher can work toward improving classroom management, the coach will need to enroll the teacher. We do not recommend that the administrator "assign" a teacher to a coach or require teachers to meet with a coach if they are not interested in doing so. Instead the coach can employ various tactics to attract teachers' interest. These tactics are not limited to, but may include, large-group presentations (i.e., stand up in front of a school's faculty and explain what they have to offer), small-group meetings, one-on-one interviews, informal conversations, or principal referrals that offer coaching as a possible strategy to struggling teachers. The goal of enrollment is that the coach is viewed as a preferred option, not an obstacle, a prop, or a punishment.

Identify Interventions

Prior to the development of any intervention, plan to collect data from several sources. The three primary sources of data include the teacher, classroom observation, and the students. The classroom teacher can provide information through self-reflection, self-evaluation, and self-monitoring. For instance, a teacher might conduct a self-evaluation by completing a checklist or track the occurrences of a certain behavior in the classroom. Information collected in this manner can be very useful in determining the starting point of any intervention. Additionally, classroom observations can provide a great deal of information. Classroom observations can be formal, such as described later as part of the CCU, or informal, such as taking notes on teacher and student behavior. Finally, students themselves can be a very fruitful source of information. For instance, asking students what they know about classroom rules and expectations can be the ultimate test to whether the strategies are working effectively.

Explain the Process

At some point in the coaching partnership, the coach will need to explain research-based teaching practices, data collection and feedback, and interventions. Certainly there is some trial and error in the process toward finding the best ways to effectively communicate. However, a few pointers can help in getting the coach started. First, fully understanding what is being described is important. If a coach does not fully understand an intervention, he or she runs the risk of teaching something wrong and creating misrules that are often difficult to change once put into action. Second, conversations that are free of clichés, buzzwords, and jargon, and include language that implies what needs to be done (e.g., "The number of disruptions in your classroom will decrease if you increase the number of praise statements you make."), are more readily understood and more likely to be put into action by the listener. Last, weaving stories or analogies into descriptions can really make things come alive. Some of the most important conversations that occur between the coach and teacher are those of the role of the coach and the intended outcomes. Making these conversations clear will improve the process.

Model Techniques

Modeling is one of the most powerful tools a coach has in his or her toolkit. Modeling allows the teacher to see firsthand how an effective practice can reach students with whom he or she is struggling. A coach can get the most out of modeling by preparing the teacher ahead of time. For instance, a coach can instruct the teacher on collecting the types of data the coach collects when he or she observes in the classroom. Then, the coach can use this data as part of the collaborative conversation with the teacher following the modeling session. Having teachers collect data during the modeled lessons allows them to focus on the most important parts of the lesson, ensures that the teachers do not become distracted by other tasks, and informs them of the observation practice that the coach will be involved in later.

Observe the Teacher

Observation is a process that informs and guides the initial intervention as well as revisions to the intervention over time. The process is circular, continuing until the teacher and coach determine that the interventions have been successfully incorporated into the everyday flow of the classroom (see Figure 5.1). Following a modeling session, coaches can conduct an observation in which they collect the same data that the teacher gathered during the modeling session. Classroom observations are a joint process with both the teacher and coach having an important role before, during, and after the observation. Collaboration across each step helps both the coach and teacher feel comfortable with the process, making the relationship feel less evaluative.

Explore Data

Once an observation is complete and data have been gathered, the next step is discussing the results with the teacher. This discussion can be challenging, but it can be less tricky if structured in a way in which the coach and teacher investigate the data collaboratively. The goal of the collaborative exploration of the data is to structure the conversation so that the teacher and coach work together as partners toward increasing positive outcomes for the students. Including positive direct, specific, and nonattributive feedback and avoiding comments that imply negative judgments about teaching practices during the discussion can be helpful in building a trusting relationship. Exploring the data in this collaborative manner will not only make it more likely that the teachers see themselves as equal partners, but will often lead to better plans to improve instruction than those generated solely by the coach.

Review Results

Coaches can conduct an after-action review (AAR) at any point in the coaching process. The collaborating teacher can be involved, but the focus of the review is on what the coach has done, rather than on the teacher's performance. The AAR provides an efficient way for coaches to reflect on, summarize, and internalize what was learned during the course of a partnership with a teacher. The review is built around four questions: (1) What was supposed to happen? (2) What really happened? (3) What accounts for the difference? (4) What will I do differently next time? Coaching provides ongoing opportunities for learning through experience. Coaches learn

Figure 5.1   The Monitor, Review, Revise Cycle

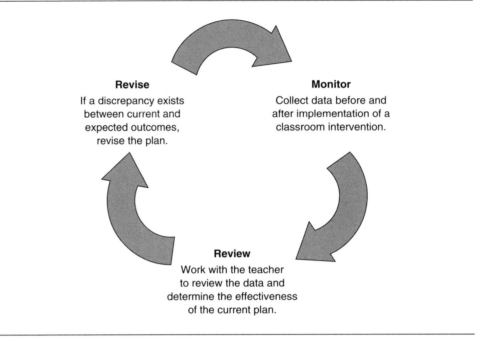

Revise
If a discrepancy exists
between current and
expected outcomes,
revise the plan.

Monitor
Collect data before and
after implementation of a
classroom intervention.

Review
Work with the teacher
to review the data and
determine the effectiveness
of the current plan.

SOURCE: Sprick, Knight, Reinke, & McKale (2007).

something new every time they work with a teacher. Taking the time to review and capitalize on the experiences by pausing to reflect, adjusting coaching practices, and setting new goals will help coaches become leaders for positive change in their school.

THE CLASSROOM CHECK-UP

Linking assessment to intervention has become a mantra in education. Several critical classroom management variables have been identified that provide coaches with a feasible, efficient, and effective way of making this link. The CCU is a model for coaching developed to provide a consistent systematic process for assessing these critical classroom variables, determining areas for improvement, developing interventions collaboratively with teachers, and providing ongoing feedback and support to teachers (Reinke, Lewis-Palmer, & Merrell, in press). Coaches can utilize the CCU to structure the support provided to teachers around implementing effective classroom management strategies.

The CCU links assessment to intervention by including an appraisal of the teachers' current use of critical classroom management variables followed by feedback to the teacher and the collaborative design of a classroom intervention. Interventions are based on objective data and collaborative discussions between the coach and the classroom teacher. Areas of need are identified from data gathered from observation and discussions between the teacher and coach. Then, the coach and teacher brainstorm potential interventions. The result is the creation of individualized classroom interventions that the teacher feels are important and is invested in implementing in his or her classroom.

In this section, we provide an overview of important classroom management variables, including opportunities to respond, praise, and reprimands. These variables can be easily observed in the classroom setting and linked to research-based interventions. Then we provide a description of the CCU and evidence for its use as an effective coaching tool.

Critical Classroom Management Variables

Opportunities to Respond

In teacher-led activities, high task involvement occurs when long periods of student talk are avoided and teachers retain control of the pacing of instruction (Kounin & Doyle, 1975). Increasing the rate of opportunities for students to respond during instruction generates more learning, provides important feedback to the teacher, and increases on-task behavior. This has been shown in several studies. Increasing the rate of opportunities to respond resulted in improved performance in reading and math (Skinner, Belfiore, Mace, Williams-Wilson, & Johns, 1997). Additionally, positive effects have been noted for academic engagement (Carnine, 1976) and decreased disruptive behavior (West & Sloane, 1986).

Academic opportunities to respond can be easily observed by counting the number of instructional questions, statements, or gestures made by the teacher that seek an oral response, and recording each opportunity directed at either an individual student or to the entire class. Opportunities to respond have an academic response component to them and do not include directives that are related to behavior only (i.e., "Pick up your pencil"). Research indicates that 4 to 6 responses should be elicited from students per minute of instruction on new material with 80% accuracy, and 9 to 12 opportunities to respond should be provided during drill-and-practice work with 90% accuracy (Council for Exceptional Children, 1987).

Correct Academic Response

In conjunction with directly observing opportunities to respond, the accuracy of student responses can be determined by collecting the number of correct academic responses. A correct academic response occurs when an opportunity to respond is directed toward one student or a group of students and the correct response is provided. To calculate the percentage of correct academic responses, divide the number of correct responses by the number of opportunities provided. This allows the teacher to determine if the instruction material correctly matches the current ability of the students. If student accuracy is below 80% for new material or below 90% for drill-and-practice work, then a review of the material may be in order (Council for Exceptional Children, 1987).

Praise

Praise is another important classroom management strategy that can be readily observed. Increasing positive interactions between teachers and students in classrooms has profound effects on student outcomes. Teachers who deliver high amounts of praise experience lower off-task and disruptive behaviors from their students (Shores, Cegelka, & Nelson, 1973), allowing more time for instruction. Additionally, praise increases intrinsic motivation of students and helps them feel more competent (Cameron & Pierce, 1994).

The number of praise statements provided can be observed by counting statements or gestures that indicate teacher approval of desired academic or social behaviors. Additionally, praise can be separated into specific and general praise, allowing the coach to provide more detailed feedback to the teacher.

Specific Praise Versus General Praise

Teacher praise is most effective when it is behavior specific (Brophy, 1983). Specific praise specifies to students the behavior for which they are being praised, making teacher expectations clear. Teacher praise can be counted as being specific when explicit feedback for the desired student behavior is provided (e.g., "China, I like the way you are *listening*."). Teacher praise is counted as being general if no specific feedback for the desired student behavior is provided (e.g., "Class, you are doing a great job!" or "China, nice work."). Nonverbal praise such as thumbs up, stickers, and high fives is considered general praise.

Reprimands

Another important classroom management strategy utilized by teachers is the use of reprimands. The number of reprimands can be observed by counting comments or gestures made by the teacher indicating disapproval of student behavior. Reprimands are recorded when directed to the whole class, group of students, or individuals. Then, a positive-to-negative ratio can be calculated by totaling the number of praise statements and the number of reprimands. The suggested ratio of praise to reprimand is 3:1. If the ratio of praise to reprimands is not optimal, a

Table 5.1   Components of the Classroom Check-Up

Step 1: Assess Classroom	☑ Teacher interview ☑ Classroom ecology checklist ☑ Classroom observations
Step 2: Feedback	☑ Coach provides feedback on assessment findings ☑ Feedback includes strengths and weaknesses
Step 3: Menu of Options	☑ Teacher and coach collaboratively develop a menu of options for intervening to create positive classroom outcomes
Step 4: Choose Intervention(s)	☑ Teacher chooses intervention(s) to implement ☑ Coach provides ongoing support in the implementation of the intervention(s)
Step 5: Monitor, Review, and Revise	☑ Teacher self-monitors implementation of intervention ☑ Ongoing classroom observations with exploration of the data and joint decisions on the maintenance or revision of the intervention plan

teacher can choose to increase his or her use of praise in the classroom in an effort to change the ratio. Increasing praise in the classroom has a direct link to decreasing disruptive classroom behavior.

Student Disruptive Behavior

The only way to tell if classroom management strategies are working is by collecting the number of disruptive behaviors occurring in the classroom. Disruptive behaviors are recorded when the statements or actions of an individual student or group of students interfere with ongoing classroom activities. It is easiest if disruptions are coded as discrete events (e.g., two students fighting is one disruption, one student talk-out is one disruption).

The CCU involves a series of steps: (1) assessing the classroom, (2) providing the teacher with feedback, (3) developing a menu of possible interventions collaboratively with the teacher, (4) choosing and implementing the intervention, and (5) monitoring the implementation and effectiveness of the intervention (see Table 5.1). The CCU provides a guide to coaches and teachers working together to create positive outcomes for students. The components of coaching outlined earlier and STOIC intervention planning are utilized within the CCU framework.

To understand the classroom dynamics and the interactions between the teacher and students, you have to see it for yourself. Therefore, the first step in the CCU is the collection of data from the teacher and through classroom observations. Looking for specific behaviors in the classroom during a brief 10-minute observation is done to inform intervention (see Sprick et al., 2007, for relevant data collection forms and guidelines). The behaviors of interest include the teacher behaviors and student behaviors listed earlier as critical classroom management variables. These variables are connected with improved outcomes for students.

More than one observation of the classroom should be conducted before using the information to inform intervention. Ideally, three to five classroom observations should be conducted during teacher-led instruction. This helps avoid the problem of designing an intervention based on one particularly bad day in the classroom. It is most useful for the teacher to identify a time for observation during teacher-led instruction when students exhibit the most challenging behaviors.

Once observations are conducted, the second step of the CCU involves exploring the data. Feedback is provided to the teacher in an objective manner using the CCU feedback form. The form guides the discussion of data between the coach and teacher. On the form, each variable collected is presented to the teacher, indicating whether it is in the green zone (i.e., keep doing what you are doing), the yellow zone (i.e., you may want to consider doing something different), or the red zone (i.e., do something different). Using the optimal range for the variables outlined in Table 5.2, the coach can provide objective feedback on areas of strength (green zone) and weakness (yellow and red zones) in current classroom management procedures.

Next (Step 3), the teacher identifies areas that he or she is interested in improving, and in collaboration with the coach, they brainstorm ideas for intervention. It is important to note that the brainstorming of interventions is guided by the coach's knowledge of effective classroom management strategies, the STOIC model for intervention planning, and the overarching classroom management model for the school. Once the brainstorming is complete, the teacher selects one or several strategies for improving classroom management (Step 4). In the final step, the monitor, review, and revise component of the CCU (recall Figure 5.1), the teacher monitors his or her implementation of these intervention strategies in the classroom, and the coach continues to conduct observations in the classroom. Several classroom observations should follow implementation of the intervention for two reasons:

1. Continued observations will allow teachers to see if they have actually changed their rate of targeted variables (e.g., praise is increasing). This is known as performance feedback. Performance feedback is a powerful tool in changing behavior. Studies have documented the effectiveness of performance feedback on behavior change with teachers (Noell et al., 2000).

Table 5.2   Guidelines for Feedback to Teacher

Behavior	Red	Yellow	Green
Percentage Correct Academic Responding (Number of opportunities to respond or number of correct academic responses)	Less than 75% new material Less than 80% drill and practice	75% new material 80% drill and practice	80% new material 90% drill and practice
Opportunities to Respond	Less than 10/10 per minute	10–39/10 per minute	40 and greater/ 10 per minute
Ratio of Interactions (Praise: Reprimand)	Less than 1:1 or < 1 praise statement per minute	At least 1:1 Consistently	At least 3:1 Consistently
Specific Versus General Praise	No red zone All praise is good	Less specific praise than general praise	More specific praise than general praise
Disruptions	10/10 per minute	5–9/10 per minute	0–4/10 per minute

2. Continued observations also allow the teacher to see if classroom disruptive behavior is decreasing as a result of the intervention. In other words, is the intervention working? If there is no change in student behavior, then the intervention will need to be rethought or changed slightly. This should continue until desired change is seen in student behavior.

The CCU has been tested using a multiple-baseline design across four classrooms (see Reinke et al., in press). The results provide evidence that the CCU increased teacher implementation of effective classroom management strategies, especially total use of praise, use of behavior-specific praise, and decreased use of reprimands. These findings were particularly true when ongoing performance feedback was provided to the teachers. Furthermore, the changes in teacher behavior contributed to positive changes in student behavior through decreased classroom disruptions. Additionally, in this study, changes in teacher and student behavior at one-month follow-up were promising. At the time of the follow-up, teachers were no longer receiving daily visual performance feedback and they were not self-monitoring their own behavior. Despite this, the gains observed during the intervention phases, to some extent, remained. Perhaps the maintenance of teacher behavior came as a result of improved skills, confidence and fluency with use of the skills, and reinforcement from positive changes in student behavior. As such, the CCU can be used by coaches to guide intervention development with teachers.

The purpose of coaching is to bring about change. Change can be difficult. For a coaching program to have any hope of leaving a lasting positive impact on the lives of students, leaders must know what changes they hope to bring to the school and successfully address personal and organizational-level barriers to change. Thus, the effectiveness of a coaching program is modulated by the clarity of the shared vision, the way individuals in the program experience change, and the quality of communication within coaching relationships. If the coaches and the administrator within the school do not have a shared vision of what they are trying to accomplish with classroom management, change is unlikely to be substantive, productive, or long lasting. Additionally, administrators and coaches alike can find ways to make change less threatening. This includes administrators being ready with clear and consistent expectations, prepared materials, and data to back up assertions. Coaches should be ready to model in the classroom, observe teachers, and provide targeted, data-based feedback. Last, there is no substitute for effective communication. Communication breakdowns are major impediments to building strong relationships among school colleagues. Administrators are effective leaders when they can communicate clearly, empathetically, and without judgment or prejudice. Coaches need to build strong, safe relationships with each teacher-collaborator to conduct observations and provide feedback without psychic barriers and defense mechanisms getting in the way. Effective communication makes this more likely.

Administrators and coaches can utilize the information outlined in this chapter to construct a coaching program that produces clear and lasting improvement. Understanding that effective classroom management is a key component to effective instruction is imperative. Adopting a school-wide or districtwide model of classroom management creates a common language among teachers, coaches, and administrative staff. Administrators can show strong support for the classroom management and the coaching model by setting aside time for professional development for all staff in the classroom management model, conducting walk-throughs to assess teacher implementation of effective management, and encouraging teachers to seek out assistance from nonevaluative coaches. Coaches should work within a systematized framework, such as the CCU, to ensure that reliable data are collected to inform the monitor, review, revise cycle of collaborative coach-teacher partnerships. Together, administrators, coaches, and teachers can create changes within the school to meet the goals and vision of a school where most misbehavior is prevented, producing positive outcomes for students both academically and behaviorally.

REFERENCES

Brophy, J. (1983). Classroom organization and management. *Elementary School Journal, 83,* 265–286.

Cameron, J., & Pierce, W. (1994). Reinforcement, reward, and intrinsic motivation: A meta-analysis. *Review of Educational Research, 64,* 363–423.

Carnine, D. W. (1976). Effects of two teacher-presentation rates on off-task behavior, answering correctly, and participation. *Journal of Applied Behavior Analysis, 9,* 199–206.

Coalition for Psychology in Schools and Education. (2006). *Report on the Teacher Needs Survey.* Washington, DC: American Psychological Association, Center for Psychology in the Schools and Education.

Council for Exceptional Children. (1987). *Academy for effective instruction: Working with mildly handicapped students.* Reston, VA: Author.

Fixen, D., Naoom, S., Blasé, K., Friedman, R., & Wallace, F. (2005). *Implementation research: A synthesis of the literature.* Tampa: University of South Florida.

Horner, R., & Sugai, G. (2000). School-wide behavior support: An emerging initiative. *Journal of Positive Behavior Interventions, 2,* 231–232.

Ingersoll, R. M. (2002, August 15). High turnover plagues schools. *USA Today,* p. 13A.

Kellam, S. G., Ling, X., Merisca, R., Brown, C. H., & Ialongo, N. (1998). The effect of the level of aggression in the first grade classroom on the course and malleability of aggressive behavior into middle school. *Development and Psychopathology, 10,* 165–185.

Kounin J., & Doyle, P. (1975). Degree of continuity of a lesson's signal system and the task involvement of children. *Journal of Educational Psychology, 67,* 159–164.

Maag, J. (2001). Rewarded by punishment: Reflections on the disuse of positive reinforcement in education. *Exceptional Children, 67,* 173–186.

National Research Council. (2002). *Minority students in special and gifted education.* Washington, DC: National Academies Press.

Noell, G. H., Witt, J. C., LaFleur, L. H., Mortenson, B. P., Ranier, D. D., & LaVelle, J. (2000). Increasing intervention implementation in general education following consultation: A comparison of two follow-up strategies. *Journal of Applied Behavior Analysis, 33,* 271–284.

Reinke, W. M. (2006). *The classroom check-up: A brief intervention to reduce current and future student problem behaviors through classroom teaching practices.* Unpublished doctoral dissertation, University of Oregon, Eugene.

Reinke, W. M., & Herman, K. C. (2002). Creating school environments that deter antisocial behaviors in youth. *Psychology in the Schools, 39,* 549–559.

Reinke, W. M., Lewis-Palmer, T., & Merrell, K. (in press). The Classroom Check-Up: A classwide teacher consultation model for increasing teacher praise and decreasing disruptive behavior. *School Psychology Review.*

Shores, R. E., Cegelka, P., & Nelson, C. (1973). Competency-based special education teacher training. *Exceptional Children, 40,* 192–197.

Skinner, C. H., Belfiore, P. J., Mace, H. W., Williams-Wilson, S., & Johns, G. A. (1997). Altering response topography to increase response efficiency and learning rates. *School Psychology Quarterly, 12,* 54–64.

Sprague, J., & Golly, A. (2004). *Best behavior: Building positive behavior supports in schools.* Longmont, CO: Sopris West.

Sprick, R. (1981). *Solution book: A guide to classroom discipline.* Chicago: Science Research Associates, Inc.

Sprick, R. (2006). *Discipline in the secondary classroom: A positive approach to behavior management.* San Francisco: John Wiley & Sons.

Sprick, R., Garrison, M., & Howard, L. (1998). *CHAMPs: A proactive and positive approach to classroom management.* Longmont, CO: Sopris West.

Sprick, R., Garrison, M., & Howard, L. (2002). *Foundations: Establishing positive discipline* (2nd ed.). [CD-ROM]. Eugene, OR: Pacific Northwest Publishing.

Sprick, R., Knight, J., Reinke, W. M., & McKale, T. (2007). *Coaching classroom management.* Eugene, OR: Pacific Northwest Publishing.

West, R., & Sloane, H. (1986). Teacher presentation rate and point delivery rate: Effect on classroom disruption, performance accuracy, and response rate. *Behavior Modification, 10,* 267–286.

6

Content Coaching

Transforming the Teaching Profession

Lucy West

INTRODUCTION

Lucy West first developed many ideas for this chapter—which are elaborated in more detail in the book she coauthored with Fritz Staub, *Content-Focused Coaching: Transforming Mathematics Lessons* (West & Staub, 2003)—when she was employed as a director of mathematics for Community School District 2 in New York City. Lucy was fortunate at that time, because her superintendent asked her to focus entirely on improving instruction in the school level, and this allowed her to spend 80% of her time working in schools with teachers and principals as a district administrator. Addressing such a challenging mandate, Lucy found herself developing an innovative (some might say revolutionary) method for accelerating professional learning.

District 2 in New York City was bringing to life new approaches to professional learning. At that time the district was led by Superintendent Anthony Alvarado, and many educators in the district were reading widely, exploring and inventing new ways of communicating, organizing, and developing professionally. "We were reading many, many different authors at the time," Lucy recalls, "and many of them were from fields outside of education. Yet, we kept our eyes firmly on the goal of improving learning by improving instruction—there was no 'flavor of the month' mentality in District 2."

(Continued)

(Continued)

As Lucy's work with teachers helped her shape the philosophy and practices she has come to refer to as content coaching, she moved into more senior positions in the city, eventually serving as deputy superintendent, supervising a regionwide adoption of content coaching with K–12 math and literacy coaches. The success of her coaching model and the overall success of District 2 naturally attracted the attention of researchers such as Richard Elmore, Lauren Resnick, and Fritz Staub. Fritz Staub, a visiting scholar from Switzerland, collaborated with Lucy, documenting what Lucy here refers to as content coaching. In her chapter, Lucy explains that content coaching is grounded in the effort-based principles of learning articulated by Lauren Resnick—the fundamental belief being, Lucy quotes Resnick, that "effort creates intelligence." Resnick's effort-based principles of learning and systems theory shape the way Lucy understands instruction, as well as the way she understands professional learning and where coaching is situated in the landscape of a professional development initiative. In her chapter, Lucy talks about the importance of "mindful engagement" with materials rather than fidelity that is understood to be "a dictum to follow a script." Lucy believes teachers should move away from a mechanistic or programmatic approach to learning that fosters relatively unreflective teaching and sees learning as the regurgitation of information. She passionately emphasizes the importance of teachers and content coaches collaborating to skillfully design lessons that engage students at all levels and prompt robust learning.

In addition to offering a vision for professional teaching practice and robust learning, Lucy also offers a sophisticated overview of what she refers to as "the work" of content coaching. The chapter provides a brief description of (a) the planning preconference, (b) a framework and guide for lesson design, (c) ways in which teachers and coaches might work together during a lesson, and (d) the postconference. Thus, the chapter is very helpful in providing a practical description of what content coaching is and what content coaches do. However, Lucy is adamant that content coaching is not a programmatic approach, with coaches following a script. Rather, content coaches ask questions that engender dialogue, provoke changes in thinking, and place teacher professionalism and evidence of student learning at the heart of all interactions. The content coach, as Lucy has told me in conversation, does not try to manipulate the teacher to think a certain way. Rather, the coach meets the teacher where he or she is and works with the teacher to cocreate effective ways to plan, implement, and reflect on lessons.

Content coaching is a practical and powerful method for improving instruction and student learning. The *essence* of content coaching is simple: to improve learning, teachers must focus on relevant, important, rich content. Robust lessons center around big ideas in a given domain and give students opportunities to grapple with significant problems or issues using reasoning and discourse particular to that domain. For example, mathematicians may seek to prove a conjecture logically, whereas literary critics might attempt to make inferences about characters based on excerpts from a text. The premise of content coaching rests on the hypothesis that improved instruction significantly improves learning.

The *practice* of content coaching is sophisticated and nuanced. Content coaching is an iterative process centering on thoughtful lesson design, skilled enactment of lessons, reflective analysis of student learning, and use of that analysis to construct ensuing lessons. Content coaches possess knowledge and understanding of the content of their discipline, awareness of which concepts within that discipline are appropriate for students at various stages, knowledge of current learning theories, a varied repertoire of instructional strategies aligned with those theories, and an understanding of organizations as living, dynamic systems. The goal of content coaching is to cultivate teachers' academic habits of reasoning and discourse associated with their particular discipline and to help them develop a specific skill set that will enable them to cultivate those same habits in their students, habits that will promote student appreciation and understanding of the subject at hand. Unlike some models of coaching, which focus almost exclusively on building collaborative professional learning cultures, content coaching views attending to content as a critical aspect of the coaching process.

THE BIG PICTURE

Content coaching is *evolving* in tandem with the standards movement, the trend toward the professionalization of teaching (Saphier, 2005), growing research findings on the nature of learning (Dweck, 2002; National Research Council, 2005; Resnick, 1995), and complexity or systems theories of change (Elmore, 2004; Fullan, 2004; Senge, 1990; Wheatley, 2001). Content coaching is grounded in a set of principles of learning articulated by Lauren Resnick and initially practiced in Community School District 2, New York City (1995–2003), during the time the model was under development (see Figure 6.1). The principles of learning underpinning the model are gleaned from the research and based on an emerging theory of intelligence called the incremental theory of intelligence. The theory of incremental intelligence, in turn, is emerging from the fields of biology, brain research, and cognitive psychology. The theory posits that we can indeed become smarter by becoming cognizant of who we are as learners and by applying the right kinds of effort and metacognitive strategies to whatever it is we want to learn or accomplish. In practice, this theory of intelligence implies that educational models should be more effort based and less ability based. Resnick and Hall (2000) speak to the shift in emphasis from ability to effort when they say the following:

> There is a third logical possibility about the relationship between ability and effort, one that holds the potential to resolve the tension between aptitude- and effort-oriented belief systems. The third possibility, the newest vision, is that an effort-based system actually can *create* intelligence. Ability is created through certain kinds of effort on the part of learners and reciprocally on the part of educators who

are working with those learners. Jeff Howard expresses this notion in a way that particularly captures young people's imagination: Smart isn't something you are, it's something you get. (p. 3)

The policies of most American schools (e.g., tracking systems, gifted programs, excessive use of special education) stem from an ability-based view of intelligence, which contributes in part to the kind of achievement gaps we see across the nation. Such a view sees children through a lens that may prove debilitating to many, a view that leads educators—thinking they are protecting the self-image of students and preventing their failure—to deny them access to rigorous curriculum and to challenging experiences. The denial of such a curriculum is a reflection of a lack of belief in students' capabilities. These ingrained, insidious, ubiquitous, and unexamined beliefs proliferate in our schools, in spite of avowals that "every child can learn." The result is a large number of students drowning in a sea of low expectations, denied an optimal opportunity to learn. Unfortunately, supervisors and coaches too frequently hold similar views about teachers, such as "some people are born to teach; others just haven't got the knack," which leads to a failure to invest in the coaching that could help teachers develop their knowledge and skills.

Figure 6.1   Effort-Based Principles of Learning

• Socializing intelligence	• Self-management of learning
• Academic rigor in a thinking curriculum	• Learning as apprenticeship
• Accountable talk	• Fair and credible evaluations
• Clear expectations	• Recognition of accomplishment

SOURCE: Resnick & Hall (2000).

It turns out that Asian societies are more prone to effort-based beliefs (Stiegler & Hiebert, 1999) that result in effort-based professional learning opportunities like Lesson Study. Lesson Study is a Japanese model of improving teaching practice in part through collaborative attention to the details of a lesson, by a group of teachers ranging from novice to veteran, generally in primary school with assistance from university faculty. It is an example of implementing an incremental theory of intelligence in professional practice. Teaching is a complex and learnable craft (Saphier, 2005). People can learn to become very competent teachers. One is not necessarily "born" a great teacher. In other words, we can take the effort-based theory of intelligence and apply it to adult learning as well as to student learning. Content coaching aims to do just that.

PRINCIPLES OF LEARNING AND COACHING

These principles of learning are foundational in the work between coach and teacher just as they are in the classroom. The principles incorporate a learning stance that posits that all substantive learning requires effort. Intelligent effort results in the development of capacities we may not "naturally" possess. To put it simply, "effort creates intelligence" (Resnick, 1995). Content coaching is an effort-based process through which professionals learn to be more effective teachers.

Accountable Talk

Content coaching employs the same set of principles with adults that most of us want to see employed in classrooms, for example, dialog. It is well documented that people learn through conversation (Allington, 2000; Resnick, 1995). In content coaching we engage in substantive discourse around core instructional issues. The discourse (accountable talk) is accountable to the professional community, the academic domain, and to rigorous reasoning based on evidence (Resnick, 1995).

In our coaching sessions, we wonder aloud about the important dilemmas and complexities of meeting standards, getting high test scores, and, most important of all, ensuring that all our students are really learning important content. As we discuss such issues, we reflect on our talk to become aware of our professional habits of discourse. If we are committed to respectful, honest, focused dialog, we will more likely be able to facilitate robust, rigorous dialog in our classes.

In many coaching sessions, we reflect on the discourse of students and how the teacher might facilitate student talk and learn from that talk. In class, we invent techniques or try on research-based strategies designed to get our students talking about their thinking, and we then contemplate what student comments reveal about their understanding.

Self-Management of Learning

Each of the principles of learning can be used to influence how a lesson will be enacted and to shape the work among adults. *Self-management of learning* (Dweck, 2002; Resnick, 1995), also referred to as *habits of mind* (Costa & Kallick, 2000), is another principle that could be considered on both the adult and student levels. What habits of mind or learning strategies do each of us employ as we work to refine our craft? Can we articulate what we do as we try to learn a new instructional strategy or deepen our content knowledge? Do we know when to ask for assistance, where to go for information, when to persevere, and when to let go and give ourselves time and space for things to percolate? Such habits of self-reflection and self-awareness are crucial life skills and are all namable, learnable strategies that successful people employ. When we become conscious of such strategies personally and professionally, we can name them. Once we can name them, we can incorporate the cultivation of these life skills in our lesson designs so that our students can adopt them and learn to take charge of their own learning. This holistic approach to teaching and learning is foreign to many teachers, especially to secondary teachers who often view their job as teaching "math" or "science" rather than as also teaching *students* how to learn math or science.

Socializing Intelligence

The idea of working together to shape the learning among us might be called "socializing intelligence" (Resnick & Nelson-Le Gall, 1997). It is a principle that builds on Vygotsky's finding that we learn through social interactions. In fact, as professionals, we "enculture" one another just as we enculture our students. One of the prevailing cultural aspects of too many schools is the culture of isolation—teachers working independently from one another as if what they do or don't do in their classrooms has no impact on the school as a whole. Each teacher works in a vacuum, designing lessons and struggling to meet student needs, with neither input from others nor the opportunity to provide input to others, as if they were isolated heroes with the weight of the world on their shoulders. In many schools, teachers are aware that a colleague's class is not one they would want their own child to be assigned to, and yet no one takes any productive steps toward upgrading the instruction in that room. Teachers who need help don't receive it, and teachers who have great success are often loath to share their secrets because the school culture is a competitive or "star" environment rather than a collaborative learning environment. Many veteran teachers become exhausted and cynical in such cultures.

Sometimes, as a survival strategy and to keep passion alive, teachers may tap informal networks for advice or companionship in the work. These informal networks, however, often lack focus, structure, or administrative support and ebb and flow under the dictates of time pressures and conflicting demands. In some schools today, there is a movement toward common meeting periods. While this is a step toward collaboration, unless the purpose of "common periods" is clearly centered on improving instruction and learning, we often perpetuate the very culture we are trying to change. Teachers may use the time to discuss administrative issues or to complain about administrators, other teachers, parents, and students, and myriad other things. As to what's working in the school or classroom, they may take a stand of "I know" rather than "I wonder" or "what if," and on issues of disagreement, they may just end up agreeing to disagree. Agreeing to disagree essentially leaves everyone comfortably right where they started.

Content coaching is one means of beginning to "reculture" schools into collaborative *learning* environments in which adults work together to help each other and to assist *all* the students in their community to succeed.

Educators see the school as "the village" in which each student is everyone's student. Adults "publicly and explicitly" engage in learning as "learners," thereby giving their students a living model of what "lifelong learning" looks like. In a content coaching environment, common periods are used to design and analyze lessons, study student work, and collaboratively invent ways to assist students who aren't succeeding when we employ the prevailing instructional practices. Teachers often coteach and talk with each other in front of their students about the choices they're making or the questions they have. They walk the talk of taking risks and learning together publicly.

Learning as Apprenticeship

Another principle of learning is that of making the learning as experiential as possible. The coteaching example provided earlier is an "experiential" approach to improving practice. The people who are coteaching might be coach and teacher or two teachers who are peer coaching one another. Coaching can be thought of as an "apprenticeship model" of teaching. The important distinction about the content coaching apprenticeship model is that it is not idiosyncratic in nature. It employs the accumulated knowledge we have as a profession about teaching and learning and provides tools to develop coherence across practitioners. Content coaching is a principled practice that assumes that "best practice" is always evolving as new research informs the field. Content coaching takes a "scholarly" approach to the study of teaching and learning and focuses specifically on the pedagogical content knowledge needed for a particular domain.

THE WORK

Content coaching defines "the work" as lesson design, enactment, diagnosis, and enhancement of student learning—the instructional core. Content-focused coaching does not advocate for a specific program, set of materials, or one particular instructional strategy. Content coaches keep an eye on the bigger picture—effective instruction as *evidenced by student learning.* We engage in respectful, meaningful, ongoing dialog centering on the core issues of teaching and learning. We consider all resources, including curriculum materials, as *tools.* The job of the educator is to select and utilize the appropriate tools in the service of learning. No tool can do all things. Using a carpenter's toolkit as an analogy, you don't want to use a screwdriver when you need to hammer a nail. A worksheet would not be the appropriate tool for grappling with complex ideas. Group work is a good choice when the problem is rich enough to engage more than one person. Individual interviews or writing samples would be useful tools for discovering what individual students are thinking.

Too often coaches are hired to be "salespeople." The district wants the coach to convince the teacher to "buy into" the use of particular materials or strategies instead of engaging with teachers to solve authentic dilemmas related to teaching and learning identified by the district and teachers. (I am not meaning to imply that teachers have carte blanche to ignore an adopted curriculum. I discuss this further later.) Whatever strategies or materials that are being used must make sense to the practitioner using them. It is possible to build coherence and also provide for individual freedom when everyone keeps an eye on student learning as the bottom line. This stance is critical to developing powerful and satisfying solutions to complex problems.

TOOLS OF THE PROFESSION

Curriculum materials, programs, pacing guides, standards, and assessments are tools. The use of a specific tool implies agreement with the beliefs informing the tool. Think of a compass. If you use a compass to find your way through the woods, you believe that the earth has a magnetic force, that the needle on the compass always points north, that there are four cardinal directions, and so forth, and that use of this tool can take you in the direction you want to go. If you lack belief in the tool or feel it's faulty, you won't choose to use it. If we learn by examining our beliefs and by trying out and reflecting on new ones, then a *well-designed* and *well-understood* tool can, in fact, assist the process of change and improvement (hence the investment by the National Science Foundation into "standards-based" curriculum materials). I emphasize *well-understood* because too many times new programs, curriculum materials, or other *tools* are foisted on educators without the provision of enough time and support for people to grapple with and understand the underlying theory or beliefs embedded in the tool. People who question the implementation of a new text are often seen as "resistant" rather than as voices representing the need for more deliberate and in-depth inquiry into the use of the new tools. Inadequate, up-front inquiry often results in people attempting to use the new tools through the filter of their old beliefs or to resist using the tools at all. When this happens, superficial implementation is the result. The conflict and frustration this causes leads to endless debates—the math wars, for example, or whole language verses phonics. Content coaching takes a radical stance away from this policy-driven approach to implementation of curriculum materials and proposes a *mindful engagement* with programs and materials. Fidelity then becomes something to explore and investigate rather than a dictum to follow a script.

Teaching is a very complex activity (Bromme, 1992; Stiegler & Hiebert, 1999; Leinhardt, 1993). It can be looked at from many perspectives and discussed at different levels of abstraction, depending on one's knowledge, theories, and beliefs. The conceptual frame presented here reflects a profound change in the definition of teaching—from teaching as *mechanically implementing curriculum* to *mindfully making use of curriculum.* Teaching requires sophisticated reasoning in choosing and prioritizing lesson goals and designing lessons that enable a given group of students to reach given standards. (West & Staub, 2003, p. 5)

What this means in practice is that although a lesson under discussion may be "the next lesson in the book," it is incumbent on the coach and the teacher to consider the lesson as described in the book to be the starting point for discussion, not the recipe for the lesson. This is an important distinction to understand. In many forms of coaching, coaches are expected to assist teachers in implementing a particular set of curriculum materials as written. Often the mantra is as follows: "teach the materials as they are written at the pace recommended in the pacing calendar" (a pace sometimes provided by the publisher or authors and sometimes by the district). This is what we refer to as "mechanistic teaching." It implies that every student, in every class, needs the same thing on any given day. In addition, the lessons described in many programs and curriculum materials are designed in bite-sized pieces, meaning they focus on one small idea or skill at a time in the belief that over time the student will put all the pieces together and thereby understand the whole picture. These notions fly in the face of everything we know about how people learn. Yet policies requiring this type of practice abound.

At the same time that teachers are being told to "follow the curriculum as written" to ensure "fidelity" to its enactment at a prescribed pace, they are also being told to differentiate the lesson to meet the range of needs of every one of their students. The first directive is a push to "cover the curriculum," and the second comes from an acknowledgement of student differences. To follow the first is often to run roughshod over the needs of many students. These opposing directives cause a dissonance and are a source of great frustration for teachers.

The standards movement is one effort to try to move the field away from naïve and mechanistic approaches to teaching, but unfortunately, with the advent of "No Child Left Behind" legislation, it has had an unintended impact of emphasizing the importance of high-stakes test scores over substantive learning.

THE STANDARDS MOVEMENT

In fact, the standards movement has two premises: all students can learn to high standards *and* individual students will need differing amounts of time and types of interventions to meet the standards. Curiously, the standards movement has spawned a great deal of debate about what is to be learned as well as an array of sanctions for those who do not meet standards within a specified time frame based on one or two test scores. Less emphasis has been placed on flexible time and individualized interventions than on the idea of meeting the standards. Our schools are designed like factories of the early 20th century (Resnick, 1995; Senge, 1990), whose aim was the efficient mass production of a product. Materials came to the factory, were run along an assembly line, and ended up integrated into something of value in the marketplace. Working with this model, we devised schools where all six-year-olds were expected to enter a classroom in the fall, study the same things for the same amount of time (whether or not some of them already knew some of these things), and leave the classroom in June as finished first graders, ready to advance en masse to the next grade with its set of skills. Not originally designed to address the needs of individual learners, our schools have not made the transition to flexible, vibrant learning organizations capable of dealing effectively with individual differences. Furthermore, we are not as sophisticated as we need to be about exactly what interventions will result in helping a range of students meet high standards. Thus educators who become mindful of a need for change have to learn to move in a new way in an old system while we all work to transform the system to one that supports the very goals it purports to support—high standards and respect for individual learning differences.

Content coaching takes a different, more complex view of teaching and learning than the mechanistic view of the factory. Based on what we already know and emerging information about learning and teaching, it is not only possible to think deeply about lessons, about the mindful use of materials, and about evidence of student understanding or lack thereof, but it is essential that we do so. We can think about lessons in relation to a unit of study, a set of standards, essential questions, learning styles, prior knowledge, and a host of other things. By thinking in this way, we can better meet the standards and the demands of testing than we can by mechanically implementing lessons. We are not saying that every teacher should "do his own thing" or ignore the materials that may be "mandated for use" by the district. We are saying that there is a *mindful* way of using materials and a mechanistic way of using materials and that how one uses materials is as important as which materials are selected. There is a continuum of teacher stances when it comes to curriculum. At one end of the spectrum is the stance of following the book page by page, and at the opposite end is the stance of creating everything from scratch. Neither extreme is useful in today's world.

Mindful use of materials of course implies that teachers and coaches are deeply familiar with the design of the materials and the underlying theory (if any) in their design. It requires that they have a solid grasp of the content they want to teach and a large and flexible repertoire of effective teaching strategies to engage the specific learners who are sitting in front of them. This mindful use of materials is the focus of the content coach, to assist teachers in becoming skillful practitioners through thoughtful dialog around the what, how, why, and who questions described later.

THE USE OF TOOLS IN COACHING SESSIONS

In a content coaching session, for example, it would not be enough for the coach to say, "The pacing calendar dictates we do this lesson today, therefore, we are doing it." In addition to the pacing calendar, the coach would take into account what the students already know and can do based on their prior work and knowledge and would consider whether the lesson proposed actually meets their needs. The coach would also keep in mind that the "what" to be taught can be addressed in myriad ways, and that sometimes by connecting the focus of the proposed lesson to ideas with which the students are already familiar, the coach can create a lesson that will both honor the intended content of the pacing calendar and the needs of his or her students. In other words, we engage with the tools in our toolkit in a thoughtful manner that encourages teachers to be both accountable to the community and to be creative and resourceful enough to meet the true needs of their students. This is a *both/and* approach. We can both teach for understanding and be accountable to the assessment and standards demands of our context.

In addition to the tools described earlier, content coaches are guided by a set of tools that are drawn from both theory and practice. These tools situate the work into the big picture (see Figure 6.2) and provide a scaffold (see Figure 6.5) for diving into the details of crafting a powerful lesson. We discuss these tools in greater detail later in the chapter.

THE COACHING DIALOG

Content coaching is a dialogical practice that is designed to cultivate high-quality instruction. The premise behind engaging in dialog to improve instruction is that improved instruction comes from an internal change in thinking, not just from an external mandate. Dialog changes thinking. In dialog, we each "stimulate the other to think." It is both "creative and re-creative" (Shor & Freire, 1987, p. 2). In true dialog, we reexamine our ideas and invent new, more informed perspectives. "We can rigorously approach the ideas, the facts, the problems, but always in a light style, almost with a dance-like quality, an unarmed style" (Shor & Freire, 1987, p. 2).

The process of content coaching includes a preconference planning session and a postconference debriefing session. Dialog between coach and teacher may also occur during the enactment of the lesson. The nature

Figure 6.2   A Framework for Lesson Design

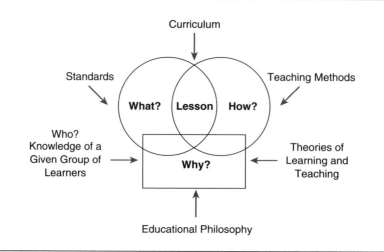

SOURCE: Adapted from Staub (1999, 2001).

of the dialog is one of curiosity, possibility, and support. The coach is genuinely interested in the teacher as a human being and as an educator with ideas, passions, beliefs, anxieties, and skills to be discovered and interwoven into the work. Skillful content coaches are authentically engaged in finding "mutual purpose" in relation to the work. They are *not* attempting to manipulate the teacher into using specific materials or a new practice or even a particular lesson, although all of these options may be discussed in the course of a coaching relationship. In other words, coaches are not invested in "convincing" teachers of anything. They are partners in exploring with teachers authentic concerns, issues, and hypotheses about teaching and learning. Conversations focus on the instructional core: the planning and implementation of lessons, reflecting on these lessons through the diagnosis of student talk and work, and designing interventions to improve student learning.

CONTENT COACHES CONTRIBUTE THEIR EXPERTISE

The nature of the content coaching dialog is one of partnership and shared decision making. The coach's content knowledge and pedagogical expertise are acknowledged and used. Thus in this model of coaching, *the coach can have substantive input into the lesson.* This practice is different from some other models of coaching in which the coach mainly asks thought-provoking questions for the teacher to consider while the teacher essentially plans the lesson. When teachers' content knowledge is lacking or their instructional repertoire is limited or when they are inexperienced, they may not be ready to design sophisticated lessons without input from a more knowledgeable partner. In fact, the coaching process can be frustrating for the teacher if the coach only uses inquiry and never provides suggestions.

This approach is one that is used in athletic coaching. An athlete who hires a coach is doing so because the coach has insight that the athlete lacks. When the coach shares his or her insight about what is off in the athlete's golf swing, for example, and offers suggestions about how to correct it, then the athlete can "try on" the new practice and ask for additional feedback. The same is true for lesson design. When teachers are unsure about why their students are not learning or what the underlying "big idea" of a lesson is, for example, a coach can provide insight into the content of that lesson as well as the range of student understanding for teachers to attend to in their lessons. On the elementary level, it is often the case that teachers are not steeped in mathematics content and may have a fairly fragile understanding of the concepts they are being asked to teach. Content coaching seeks to scaffold a teacher's content knowledge during the planning process of a lesson by actively engaging the teacher in the mathematics from a "big idea" and "habits of mind" perspective. Then the coach and teacher step back to reflect on how mathematics is embedded in the selected activity. (Coaching is a valuable aid to the teacher but alone will not sufficiently develop robust content knowledge. Institutes, workshops, and coursework are also necessary and should be part of a menu of professional learning opportunities for teachers who need to deepen their understanding of the content they teach.)

The content coach can also assist the teacher in identifying central concepts and their underlying ideas. For example, in elementary school mathematics, it is important that students develop a robust and flexible understanding of the base-10 number system. Place value is a big idea in a network of related smaller ideas about our number system that when understood in relation to one another, lead to the capacity to work within the number system with confidence and skill. It is not easy for young students to begin to understand place value in any depth without many varied and contextualized experiences specifically designed to help them make sense of this system. The content coach will assist a teacher in identifying the network of big and small ideas at play and in selecting from available resources activities that give students access to these concepts. For example, one idea in the network of ideas related to place value is that a digit immediately to the left of the decimal point is 10 times greater than the one to the right. This multiplicative relationship is much more difficult to comprehend than is the activity to "circle the number in the tens place." Because a student can correctly circle a digit in a specific "place" does not necessarily mean the student understands the multiplicative relationship in place value.

A content coach will help a teacher see the levels of understanding students may have when grappling with the "big ideas," such as place value. In doing so, the coach is building the teacher's capacity to analyze student understanding, predict student responses, and plan lessons that address the range of student needs in any given class. (I use mathematics examples because my main focus in the field is mathematics, but content coaching is applicable to any academic domain; see Resources A and B.)

AN INQUIRY STANCE IN ACTION

The content coach also takes an inquiry stance, eliciting the teacher's goals, concerns, observations, questions, and beliefs—an inquiry that should be done with great humility and respect. Sometimes, especially in elementary schools where teachers are responsible for several subjects, the teacher may lack content knowledge in a given domain. Skillful questioning by a coach can uncover weaknesses in understanding and alert a coach to the kinds of support the teacher needs. The coach knows, however, that the teacher has knowledge of his or her own classroom that the coach may lack and that the teacher's own ideas are a good starting point for discussion. Often the first question a coach asks the teacher is, "What is your plan?" or "What ideas do you have?"

Questioning is an art. In our culture, questions are often seen as disguised judgments, interrogations, or manipulations to trip us up. People know by a person's attitude when a question, although asked in identical words, is sincere and when it is judgmental. "What were you thinking?" could mean, "I'm really curious about your thinking," or it could mean, "What kind of stupid move was that?" It is essential that a content coach set the stage for robust questioning that exhibits genuine curiosity and caring. Questioning is a two-way street with both coach and teacher free to ask what they will without fear of being judged. It is our genuine questions, not our preconceived answers, that lead to new insights.

Content coaches understand in the very core of their being that all human beings are natural learners who have wonderful ideas, dreams, and goals of their own. They see their job as taking a journey with the teacher in which both people will become smarter about teaching and learning as they both explore authentic questions about the impact of their lessons on student learning. They use the specifics of lesson planning to consider the philosophy and epistemology of teaching and learning in practice.

THE PRECONFERENCE IS KEY

We emphasize the preconference planning session because the planning session is designed to help ensure a successful lesson. It also helps to ensure that the conversation will be focused and specific rather than general. It is specificity in lesson design that makes all the difference. This emphasis is different from that of some models of coaching that emphasize the debriefing dialog. While we advocate for *both* opportunities for conversation in a coaching cycle, we have found that the planning session is key for transference to practice (see Figure 6.3).

Planning dialogs are considered the most important part of the process as they immerse the practitioner into robust habits of planning that eventually become internalized and over time result in "habits of planning," which, in turn, result in richer lessons. It is often the case that when teachers have been working with a coach for a few months, they will report that when working alone, they can hear the coach's voice "over their shoulder" asking them the kinds of questions asked during a coaching session. This internalization process is necessary for transference to independent practice to take place.

In the preconference dialog, a genuine belief in the power of collaborative lesson planning is at play, and the coach strives to empower the teacher to take an active role in the planning process. It is also understood that through probing and provocative questioning, we often

Figure 6.3   Conferencing: Benefits of the Preconference

Over the years, due to restraints on teacher time, we have had to choose between the postconference and the preconference. Experience has led us to believe that if we must choose, the planning time is more useful then the debriefing time, especially for less experienced teachers.

- Collaborative planning sessions are more likely to ensure that the lessons presented to students will revolve around important big ideas or essential questions.
- Preconferencing allows for crisp articulation of the lesson goals and careful design of instructional strategies.
- Preconferencing focuses the teacher's attention on student learning and asks for deliberate pedagogical decisions designed to foster student understanding.
- Preconferencing encourages the teacher to take an analytical stance toward the written curriculum and empowers the teacher to actively engage with the curriculum.
- Preconferencing provides the coach a window into the teacher's thinking and needs. The coach can identify the following:
  - Issues important to the teacher
  - The learning theory that underpins the teacher's beliefs
  - The teacher's level of content knowledge and confidence
- Preconferencing allows the coach's postconference feedback about the lesson to be based on the shared lesson plan and its implementation.
- If postconference is not possible, feedback can be in the form of notes or e-mail, as the lesson plan and lesson enactment were shared experiences.

SOURCE: Staub, West, & Bickel (2003).

deepen our understanding and invent new solutions to our dilemmas (knowledge creation). Thus the content coach inquires into the teacher's choices and the reasoning behind those choices. Together they design the lesson, and responsibility for its success is shared. But the *teacher* has the ultimate decision-making voice. It is the teacher who chooses to take or leave a coach's suggestion. Teachers are the clients and they decide what "serves them." The lesson is jointly designed and the *responsibility for its success is shared.* If the teacher doesn't fully own and agree with the lesson design, he or she will not be able to artfully execute it (note: if the coach is teaching the lesson, then the final decisions rest with the coach with input from the teacher). Checking for teacher understanding and commitment to the choices made during the preconference is one way to ensure a successful lesson.

A CONTENT FOCUS

In each session, the coach works to ensure that the academic content of a lesson is worthwhile, important, and relevant. The intent is to create lessons that ensure that every student has access to the lesson and that the lesson is rich enough conceptually to challenge even the most informed in the group. Thus, content coaching tackles head-on the ubiquitous question, "How do I address the range of needs of *all* the learners in my class?"

Content plays a key role in our coaching conversations. In a mathematics coaching conference, for example, the coach always ask questions like, "What is the mathematics we want to teach? What are the concepts, strategies, and skills we want students to understand?" In a mathematics coaching session, for example, it is not sufficient to answer, "I'm teaching multiplication," as that is too general. It is also not sufficient to answer, "I'm teaching the facts," as this is not only too vague but also lacks a conceptual frame. Instead, the coach might suggest that we create a lesson that brings the commutative property of multiplication to the fore for students to understand how this powerful property allows them to learn twice as many facts. The ensuing conversation would concern how this property might be made visible and more concrete for students. What context can give them a way to conceptualize the idea that 4×5 and 5×4 both equal 20? What is the same and what is different in the meaning of the number sentences $4 \times 5 = 20$ and $5 \times 4 = 20$? An area model of multiplication might be considered, along with contexts that make meaning of this model. In addition, this exploration might be seen as a way to help students learn their multiplication facts, as they realize that two numbers multiplied together always result in the same answer, no matter their order.

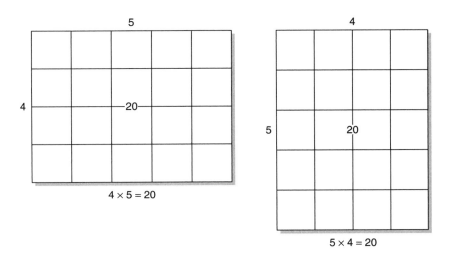

CORE ISSUES OF LESSON DESIGN

The questions a content coach asks center around a set of research-identified core issues of lesson design (see Figure 6.4). When these issues are routinely and adequately addressed in lesson planning, the result is not only lessons that promote greater student understanding, but also development of robust habits of planning among practitioners, habits that naturally lead to the capacity to differentiate a lesson to meet the needs of a range of students, habits that question why something is taught in a particular sequence and at a particular pace, habits that seek out evidence of student understanding or lack thereof and that lead to the development of diagnostic and intervention strategies to assist student learning. When mindful lesson design is practiced systemically, everyone gets smarter.

These overarching issues have been turned into "guiding questions" in our main planning tool, the Guide to Core Issues in Lesson Design (see discussion that follows).

Figure 6.4   Abbreviated List of Core Issues in Lesson Design

- Lesson goals
- Lesson plan and design
- Students' relevant prior knowledge
- Relationship between the nature of the task and the activity on one hand and the lesson goals on the other hand
- Strategies for students to make public their thinking and understanding
- Evidence of students' understanding and learning
- Students' difficulties, confusions, and misconceptions
- Ways to encourage collaboration in an atmosphere of mutual respect
- Strategies to foster relevant student discussion

SOURCE: West & Staub (2003).

THE FRAMEWORK FOR LESSON DESIGN

The Framework for Lesson Design (see Figure 6.2) attempts to situate the core issues into the big picture. It shows the variables that impact lesson design: resources, policies, tools, theories, beliefs, and student prior knowledge. These variables all impact the what, how, why, and who of lesson design (Staub, West, & Bickel, 2003):

- What is the curricular content to be learned by the students?
- How is this content to be taught?
- Why is this specific content to be taught? Why will it be taught in this way?
- Who is the lesson designed to teach?

These basic questions can be discussed and addressed in myriad ways in relation to the curriculum materials, standards, or other tools in a teacher's toolbox and to the particular students in a class. That is to say, they are not dependent on a given program. All the materials and programs available to teachers and schools are understood to be tools, not scripts or panaceas. Learning is contextual and teachers must design lessons that take into consideration the prior knowledge of their students. Resources are only as effective as the skill level and beliefs of the people using them.

When some practitioners focus on the *what* aspect of lesson design, they ask, "What's the next lesson in the scope and sequence, curriculum, or textbook?" The *how* becomes, "What materials need to be gathered and what does the book tell us we should say or do?"

These versions of the "what and how" questions are different from the ones we are thinking about in content coaching. A focus on what comes next in the book or scope and sequence is often symptomatic of a mechanistic approach to teaching, an approach that can never address the following oft-heard lament: "There is such a big range of learners in my class, how can I possibly address all their needs? Many of my students are still struggling with the ideas in the previous lessons in the book. How can they possibly deal with this lesson? Yet, if I don't move on, what am I going to do with those who could understand this lesson in five minutes?" Mechanistic approaches have resulted in narrow lessons aimed at some imagined middle-of-the-spectrum student and do not serve the majority of children. They have also resulted in rhetorical stances that divide rather than inform the field. Rarely do practitioners seriously ponder the *why* questions proposed earlier in any depth beyond statements such as the following: "it's important for the test," "so students can get into college," "for the next grade," or "for the work world." Often these clichés are used to justify practices that are ineffective and lead to trivial pursuits in classrooms. Content coaching encourages practitioners to question deeply the *how, what,* and *why* of their lessons and work to design lessons that go beyond testing requirements toward the development of robust habits of learning and thinking as well as deeper understanding of content.

Content coaches ask practitioners to consider the *who*. Who are the specific students and what do they already know, want to know, and need to understand to not only succeed on "the test" but in life; to not only get a good job but to participate in a healthy democracy and a rapidly changing global reality?

FROM MECHANISTIC TO MINDFUL PLANNING

Content coaching seeks to upgrade the whole nature of lesson planning in this country. Lesson planning is part of the skill set that should distinguish teachers as professionals. When lesson design is done thoughtfully by well-informed teachers, the result is lessons that give all students access to important content and encourage habits of reasoning and discourse germane to a given domain. Presently, the common mindset (and policies that emerge from this mindset) that "anybody can teach as long as they stay a few pages ahead of the students in the textbook" is difficult to combat because the kind of planning many teachers do is exactly that of staying a few pages ahead in the book. In addition, many districts exacerbate this tendency by imposing rigid pacing calendars. Both tendencies imply a mechanistic view of teaching and learning that perpetuates the idea that teaching is a simple act of dispensing information that students might just as easily acquire in a book or online. It seems that we often confound the gathering and regurgitating of information and the capacity to follow directions with real learning. Learning is different from and in addition to simply accumulating information. Among other things, learning requires us to question critically even what may seem obvious (e.g., the status quo, policies or practices or procedures we do not understand or find meaningful or suspect are even detrimental), to analyze and synthesize information, and to process new information in light of what we already think we understand. Furthermore, the process of learning differs from person to person, and these differences must inform us.

There is a history of attempting to create "teacher-proof" materials on the premise that teaching is a mechanistic act and anyone can teach as long as they follow the pacing guide and are familiar with the standards. Anyone who has ever attempted to teach knows the fallacy of this premise. Yet many policymakers and authors of curriculum materials continue to try to mandate or manipulate effective teaching through implementation of scripted programs. Content coaches acknowledge this history and work to transform practice through meticulous lesson design.

Lesson-design takes place at the intersection of *what* and *how*. What is the relationship between curriculum and teachers' work in the classroom? In the United States, curriculum is most often thought of as an "organizational framework"; a "curriculum-as-manual," containing the templates for coverage and methods that are seen as guiding, directing, or controlling a school's, or a school system's, day-by-day classroom work (Westbury, 2000, p. 17). In other words, these manuals set forth *what* to teach and *how* to teach it. For a time, it was even hoped that a "technology of teaching" would lead to fully specified curricula that would guarantee effective teaching no matter who the teacher happened to be. The aim of constructing "teacher-proof" curricula, however, has turned out to be out of reach and based on a naïve conception of what effective teaching involves. Even when curriculum materials specify lessons in some detail, a competent teacher still needs to adapt a given lesson to the context of the particular classroom and to the individual characteristics, needs, and backgrounds of the learners in it. (West & Staub, 2003, p. 6)

The standards movement has attempted to define "what" content should be taught. This movement has been contentious, sprouting "math and phonics wars" and endless arguments about what matters in a subject and how it should be taught. Often the standards are reduced to a laundry list of skills and concepts that must be "covered." Most textbooks are constructed to meet the various and sundry laundry lists of standards, which differ for all 50 states. This results in the cliché, "Curriculum is a mile wide and an inch deep." It also results in needless and endless repetition from year to year because various states require similar concepts at different grade levels, and when teachers follow a textbook, they are often repeating as much as 70% of what was taught in the previous year. The common lament, "We don't have enough time to cover the curriculum," is a catch-22 because the tools that teachers are often using are part of the problem. There have been many attempts since the beginning of the standards movement to create more coherent curriculum materials in both math and literacy, with mixed results.

TEACHER CONTENT KNOWLEDGE AND LESSON DESIGN

Another job of the content coach is to encourage thorough examination of the "big ideas" in an academic domain so that the content (or the *what*) to be taught comes from a perspective of understanding that can lead students to develop the habits of mind associated with that academic domain. The fact that some teachers lack a firm handle on the conceptual underpinnings and organizational structure of content is one reason they have difficulty planning rigorous lessons around "essential questions" or "big ideas" and must, therefore, rely heavily on texts as scripts. This lack of a comprehensive content knowledge breeds in turn an insecurity that prevents them from allowing students to investigate a subject like math or science from an inquiry perspective. The worry is that the teacher might not be able to answer questions posed by students, especially precocious students. Teachers fear they will say the wrong thing or not be able to identify fledgling understanding of important ideas expressed by students who may not be expressing themselves precisely in the language of the domain.

Part of the problem seems to be that our present understanding of planning continues to be largely a mechanistic one. We read our teacher's guide, gather the prescribed materials, ask the questions proposed, and assign students the task suggested. While this basic approach to planning is not entirely without merit, it is insufficient to meet our oft-stated goal of taking all students to high standards. This insufficiency is slowly changing, but it is still prevalent.

Content coaches seek to assist practitioners in building a repertoire of powerful and nuanced instructional strategies to be used purposefully and specifically as appropriate (the how), the effectiveness of which are measured by evidence of student learning, one piece of which could include test scores. Content coaching is advocating something dramatically different and much more powerful than mechanistic, programmatic approaches to teaching and learning.

THE GUIDE TO CORE ISSUES IN LESSON DESIGN

The Guide to Core Issues in Lesson Design is a tool that invites coach and teacher to engage in a dialog that results in skillfully designed lessons that will engage students at all levels.

The guide was created by Fritz Staub, a visiting scholar from Switzerland, myself, and colleagues in Community School District 2, New York City, as well as at the Institute for Learning at the University of Pittsburgh. Fritz brought a European perspective and teaching theory to the work as well as a researcher's eye. During the birthing phases of content coaching, I was the principal investigator of a National Science Foundation Teacher Enhancement Grant that supported a mathematics initiative in Community School District 2 in New York City. District 2 was a lighthouse district studied widely because of its innovative and far-reaching professional learning opportunities. At the time, I was coaching both teachers and coaches and mysteriously getting remarkable results. Fritz and I videotaped dozens of coaching sessions. We were interested in finding out the specific things that coaches did that resulted in identifiable improvement of instruction. Fritz also often accompanied me during my own coaching sessions. He and I pondered questions of lesson design, enactment, coaching moves, and the impact coaching was having on teacher practice. Fritz was then able to hone a theory based on principles of learning and on European ideas about teaching, a theory that informs our book, *Content-Focused Coaching: Transforming Mathematics Lessons* (West & Staub, 2003).

Fritz and I spent many hours studying the coaching sessions and the lessons connected to the sessions. Through this process, Fritz named the coaching moves that positively impacted lessons as evidenced by student learning and transference to instructional practice. Out of our observations and dialog with each other and teachers and coaches in the field, Fritz developed the Guide to Core Issues in Lesson Design as a tool for informing content coaching conversations (see Figure 6.5).

To drill deeply into the specifics of a lesson and develop robust habits of skillful lesson design, content coaches use the Guide to Core Issues in Lesson Design as a kind of map of the terrain of the possible issues that could be considered during a planning session. The guide we developed for a mathematics lesson is shown in Figure 6.4. Resources A and B contain some samples of guides that others have created from the original for literacy or science using the mathematics guide as a template.

This tool is *not* a script. It includes far too many questions to discuss in any one coaching session. (It could be used in its entirety if one is engaged in a full "lesson study" over several sessions on the order of the Japanese model. See Lewis, 2002, and Wang-Iverson & Yoshida, 2005, for more information on Japanese Lesson Study.)

The purpose of this tool is to map the terrain for the core variables affecting teaching and learning and to carefully consider them in lesson design and instructional practices. If you study the guide, you will note that there are several questions that revolve around content and others that focus on finding out what students think and still others that encourage the teacher to be planful about attending to the inevitable range of understanding in any group of students. These questions can also be considered in light of the principles of learning collected by Resnick and colleagues (Resnick, 1995; Resnick & Hall, 1998, 2000; Resnick & Nelson-Le Gall, 1997), and the work of various others (Dweck, 2002). For example, embedded in the following question from the guide is an acknowledgement that it is expected that students will inevitably have to work through confusions or misconceptions: "What can you identify or predict students may find difficult or confusing or have misconceptions about?" There are other questions in the guide that consider how to encourage students to expose their thinking through the development of classroom discourse or "accountable talk," such as the following: "What ideas might students begin to express and what language might they use?" "In what ways will students make their mathematical thinking and understanding public?"

In my experience in working with teachers of Grades K–12 in mathematics, the content questions in the guide are not easy to answer. When we ask teachers, "What is the specific mathematics goal of this lesson?" or "What are the mathematical concepts?" it is fairly common to hear them say things like, "I'm teaching lesson 2.5 today" or "I'm teaching multiplication." When we probe a bit deeper and ask, "What about multiplication are you teaching?" many teachers cannot adequately answer the question.

Figure 6.5   Guide to Core Issues in Lesson Design—Mathematics

What are the goals and the overall plan of the lesson?

- What is your plan?
- Where in your plan would you like some assistance?

(Based on the teacher's response, the coach makes tentative choices about which of the following ideas to focus on.)

What is the mathematics in this lesson? (i.e., make the lesson goals explicit)

- What is the specific mathematics goal of this lesson?
- What are the mathematics concepts?
- Are there specific strategies being developed? Explain.
- What is the skill (applications, practice) being taught in this lesson?
- What tools are needed (e.g., calculators, rulers, protractors, pattern blocks, cubes)?

Where does this lesson fall in this unit and why? (i.e., clarify the relationship between the lesson, the curriculum, and the standards)

- Do any of these concepts or skills get addressed at other points in the unit?
- Which goal is your priority for this lesson?
- What does this lesson have to do with the concept you have identified as your goal?
- Which standards does this particular lesson address?

What are students' prior knowledge and difficulties?

- What relevant concepts have already been explored with this class?
- What strategies does this lesson build on?
- What relevant contexts (money, for example) could you draw on in relation to this concept?
- What can you identify or predict students may find difficult or confusing or have misconceptions about?
- What ideas might students begin to express and what language might they use?

How does the lesson help students reach the goals? (i.e., think through the implementation of the lesson)

- What grouping structure will you use and why?
- What opening question do you have in mind?
- How do you plan to present the tasks or problems?
- What model, manipulative, or visual will you use?
- What activities will move students toward the stated goals?
- How does this lesson engage students in thinking and activities that move them toward the stated goals?
- In what ways will students make their mathematical thinking and understanding public?
- What will the students say or do that will demonstrate their learning?
- How will you ensure that students are talking and listening to each other about important mathematics in an atmosphere of mutual respect?
- How will you ensure that ideas that are being grappled with will be highlighted and clarified?
- How do you plan to assist those students whom you predict will have difficulties?
- What extensions or challenges will you provide for students who are ready for them?
- How much time do you predict will be needed for each part of the lesson?

SOURCE: West & Staub (2003).

Answers tend to be too general (multiplication), too narrow (memorizing facts), or nonexistent (a workbook page from the text). This scenario might play out similarly in a literacy class. The question, "What are you teaching today?" might be answered with, "writing" or "essay writing," rather than, "the distinguishing features of essay writing." Examples like these show a lack of specificity or conceptual focus in the planning habits of many teachers and are reported to be the case by coaches in all content areas when teachers do not have a firm handle on the big ideas of the content they want to teach and a tendency to define a topic by the formats or procedures employed in the domain (e.g., the whole class writing in the form of haiku one day and rhyme the next). Without a clear, articulate, and rich enough content goal, lessons generally flounder or fall flat. The guide is designed to get teachers and coaches to drill down to the very core of the "what, why, how, and who" of the lesson. Just the act of asking the questions begins a journey to more reflective teaching.

MEASURING SUCCESS

Content coaching measures success through the lens of *evidence of student learning* as opposed to the implementation of specific curriculum materials, pedagogical strategies, or use of technology. Evidence of learning is an ongoing inquiry for content coaches. The question, "What constitutes evidence of learning?" is one that is interwoven through the planning sessions, the enactment of the lesson, and the debriefing sessions. Together we wonder how we might know to what degree students understand the content at hand and what we can do about improving or deepening student understanding. Example questions from the guide include the following:

- What can you identify or predict students may find difficult or confusing or have misconceptions about?
- In what ways will students make their mathematical thinking and understanding public?
- What will the students say or do that will demonstrate their learning?
- What ideas might students begin to express and what language might they use?
- How will you ensure that ideas that are being grappled with will be highlighted and clarified?
- How do you plan to assist those students whom you predict will have difficulties?
- What extensions or challenges will you provide for students who are ready for them?

Content coaching is an attempt to deepen the conversation beyond the mere rhetoric of beliefs about teaching practices, or about the nature of learning, and toward the use of evidence of student learning as a focal point for informing teaching decisions. When we focus on evidence of learning, we reveal to ourselves whether our deeply held beliefs are worth holding on to or need to be let go in light of new information. Changing our cherished beliefs is one of the most difficult of human endeavors. Thus, rather than advocating a handful of teaching strategies as "best practice," why not hold all teaching strategies to the test of results? When teachers say, "I've been doing it this way for years," we could invite them to reflect on whether their way of doing things has resulted in 100% of their students demonstrating robust understanding. If not, we could wonder together about the impact of particular instructional strategies on the learning of specific students. Teachers might be willing to note that some students don't seem to learn the material deeply. Their present rationale may be that the students have "special needs" or are "second-language learners" or have "poor home environments." The content coach might nudge teachers into acknowledging that while any and all of that may be true, they have no control over those variables. The one thing teachers can do is be willing to try out additional instructional strategies and diagnose the resulting student work as well as student discourse for insights into how that strategy might be working to make content more accessible. Through dialog and inquiry into "what works," we might discover that there is a place for every teaching strategy ever contrived—at least some of the time with particular learners. On the other hand, we might discover that our ideas about who benefits from our preferred instructional style are mistaken and there are strategies and tools that would serve some students better.

Teaching and learning are complex acts. Finding evidence for what people are actually learning is what underpins the assessment movement, and the search for this evidence has resulted in some misguided and overzealous standardized testing practices. Content coaching is advocating that we pause and reflect collaboratively as explorers with wide-eyed curiosity and a healthy dose of skepticism into the question, "What counts as evidence of student (or teacher) understanding?" Content coaches engage with teachers to find out day to day, moment to moment what our students (teachers) are thinking about and how deeply they understand the content under study, so that we might adjust and adapt our lesson designs to meet the "differentiated" needs of our students (teachers).

WORKING TOGETHER DURING THE LESSON

Content coaching is a practice-based approach to upgrading instruction and learning. Like most coaching models, the coach spends time in the teacher's classroom engaged in teaching or in observing lessons. The role that the coach will play in any particular lesson is negotiated between the coach and the teacher prior to the lesson. The coach may teach the entire lesson with the teacher observing either a specific instructional practice or the talk and actions of students. The teacher and coach may coteach the lesson either as a team or in tandem, or the teacher may teach the entire lesson while the coach observes through an agreed-upon lens.

One of the more controversial practices of content coaching is that the coach might intervene during a lesson when the teacher is teaching. This is done with the teacher's prior consent. It is also done judiciously and never with the intent of "correcting" the teacher. The interventions are not done in a critical manner, but in more of a supportive one. Interventions are done sparingly and for a purpose. In all of my experiences with this practice, there is only one incident that I can recall that was "uncomfortable" for the teacher I was working with. The teacher's discomfort provided an opportunity for coach and teacher to dialog and become clearer about their relationship and the work.

Interventions are made for a number of reasons:

1. *A student expresses an important (mathematical) idea that is relevant to the lesson and the teacher does not notice or realize its relevance.* In this case, the coach might suggest that the student repeat the idea, with the permission of the teacher. The coach might then ask a question of the students related to that idea, which allows the teacher to then pursue the concept and facilitate the discourse.

2. *The teacher's questions may be inhibiting student thinking.* For example, a primary teacher I worked with was asking students to come up with two addend combinations for the number 11. When students made suggestions, she put out counters and asked the class to count with her. She counted each addend and then she counted from 1 to 11. Several of her students were able to compute the sum without counting three times. They knew that 5 and 6 were 11. By having students count three times, this teacher was inadvertently guiding them to use the most primitive strategy for finding sums. In this instance, the coach might intervene and ask students how they might know that 5 plus 6 is 11 without having to count all the pieces. Some students might then share a counting-on strategy while others might share a doubles-plus-one strategy. The teacher, on hearing her students' more sophisticated strategies, might realize that she can ask questions that are designed to make public such thinking.

3. *The coach can "highlight" a moment that the teacher and coach can unpack during the postconference dialog.* Perhaps a student made a comment or asked a question that revealed a misconception or partial knowledge that can be addressed more fully in a future lesson. The coach may want to "highlight" that moment to help the teacher recall it during the postlesson coaching conversation.

In addition to the types of interventions described earlier, content coaches assist teachers as they work with individual students or small groups of students during the work period of a lesson. In this coaching practice, we do not "divide and conquer," we "stick together." What I mean by this is that the coach rarely works with one group of students while the teacher works with another. Instead, they travel from student to student or group to group as a team. One or the other may take the lead when interacting with a particular student or group while the other listens. Then the teacher and coach might step off to one side and have a brief dialog about what occurred. The coach might invite the teacher to try a questioning strategy or suggest that he or she listen for a specific approach that is being demonstrated. This "over the shoulder" coaching is an "apprenticeship" model through which the teacher gradually builds a repertoire of intervention or facilitation skills. This practice addresses the "transfer to practice problem" that plagues so many professional development practices.

The reader may think it seems more practical for the coach to work with a subset of students while the teacher works with others. While there is merit in this thinking in terms of the short-term benefits to a small group of students, content coaches do not usually agree to work directly with students when the teacher is not present. Content coaching is aimed at upgrading the teacher's skills. How will the teacher's skills improve if he or she is not even present to observe when the coach is engaging with the students?

THE POSTCONFERENCE

After a lesson, the coach and the teacher spend time together discussing the lesson through any of several lenses or combination of lenses. They may study student work or reflect on student discourse. To reflect on student discourse, the content coach takes copious and verbatim notes of what was said in the classroom during the lesson. This skill takes practice and is often challenging for coaches to master. It is essential to have verbatim notes to inquire into the various levels of understanding, confusion, misconceptions, and partial knowledge that students reveal when engaged in rich problems and robust discussion. Verbatim notes also allow the coach to be very specific in his or her feedback. Specificity is critical to powerful coaching. Specific feedback coupled with an agreement to try on a new practice or look through a new lens is what promotes growth.

The coach and teacher might discuss the questions that were raised during the lesson. They might wonder about the visuals that were or could have been employed to provide better access for struggling students. In other words, they will revisit the core issues in the guide and this time reflect on what aspects of their design worked and what aspects need to be refined, discarded, or modified.

The most important goal of the postconference is to consider the focus of the next lesson in light of their reflections, particularly their examination of student work and comments. The follow-up lesson may or may not be the next lesson in the book or pacing calendar. The variable that will most strongly influence the next lesson will be the evidence of learning demonstrated by the students. This is often difficult for teachers to fully embrace in today's high-stakes, fast-paced climate. Content coaches attempt to assist teachers as they grapple with the tensions and paradoxes of the art and science of teaching and learning in a high-stakes testing environment. It may be necessary to slow down in order to speed up and dive deep to broaden understanding. The more specific we can be when diagnosing the work of a few students who represent the range of understanding in the class, the more likely we will be able to address the needs of the whole group. The more we design lessons in response to student understanding, the more likely that student understanding will increase. The more student understanding increases, the more test scores rise. The more attention to detail in the lesson design, the more we can let go of the plan and respond to the students as they engage in the messy process called learning.

ONE LAST THING

My work has evolved separately from the work of the Institute for Learning, from District 2, and from the work of Fritz Staub. What is written in this chapter is my perspective and does not necessarily represent the views of anyone else. The way I see it, content coaching is a dynamic and evolving practice. If one is focusing on the conceptual content of a lesson, taking an effort-based stance in relation to teaching and learning, and engaging in robust, frank, and detailed conversations about evidence of learning at both the adult and student levels, then one is probably engaging in content coaching. All of the tools offered in our book, *Content-Focused Coaching: Transforming Mathematics Lessons* (West & Staub, 2003), and herewith, are works in progress. They are tools to be adapted and reworked by practitioners who engage with them. Our goal in creating the tools was to provide a starting place, a framework, an entry level to the practice of robust, responsive lesson design and collaborative planning.

When done well, content coaching is a powerful strategy for upgrading the teaching profession and cocreating vibrant, collaborative learning organizations where all members thrive. Content coaching is one strategy for transitioning to new schools sensitive to the demands of an ever-changing, complex world.

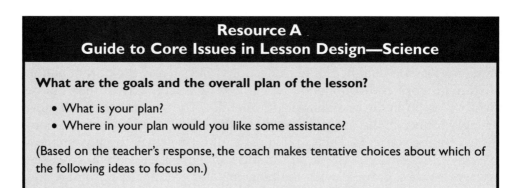

Resource A
Guide to Core Issues in Lesson Design—Science

What are the goals and the overall plan of the lesson?

- What is your plan?
- Where in your plan would you like some assistance?

(Based on the teacher's response, the coach makes tentative choices about which of the following ideas to focus on.)

Making explicit the lesson goals: What is the science content in this lesson?

- What is your goal?
- What are the science concepts?
- Are there specific strategies being developed? Explain.
- What is the skill aspect of this lesson (applications, practice)?
- What tools are needed (e.g., graduated cylinders, thermometers)?

Clarifying the relationship between the lesson and the curriculum: Where does this lesson fall in this unit and why?

- Do any of these concepts and/or skills get addressed at other points in the unit?
- Which goal is your priority for this lesson?
- What does this lesson have to do with the concept you have identified as your goal?
- Which standards does this particular lesson address?

What are students' prior knowledge and difficulties?

- What relevant concepts have already been explored with this class?
- What strategies does this lesson build on?
- What contexts could you draw on in relation to this concept that would be relevant to your students?
- What can you identify or predict students may find difficult or confusing or have misconceptions about?
- What ideas might students begin to express and what language might they use?

Thinking through the implementation of the lesson: How are students assisted during the lesson in reaching the lesson goals?

- What grouping structure will you use and why?
- What opening question do you have in mind?
- How do you plan to present the tasks or problems?
- What model, manipulative, or visual will you use?
- How does this lesson engage students in thinking and activities that move them toward the stated goals?
- In what ways will students make their scientific thinking and understanding public?
- What will the students say or do that will demonstrate their learning?
- How will you ensure that students are talking and listening to each other about important mathematics in an atmosphere of mutual respect?
- How will you ensure that ideas that are being grappled with will be highlighted and clarified?
- How do you plan to assist those students whom you predict will have difficulties?
- What extensions or challenges will you provide for students who are ready for them?
- How much time do you predict will be needed for each part of the lesson?

SOURCE: Adapted by Megan Roberts, Region 9, New York City.

Resource B
Guide to Core Issues in Lesson Design—Writing Workshop

What are the goals and the overall plan of the lesson?

- What is your plan?
- Where in your plan would you like some assistance?

(Based on the teacher's response, the coach focuses on one or more of the following ideas.)

What is the writing in this lesson?

- What is the specific writing goal of this lesson?
- Are there specific strategies being developed?

Where does this lesson fall in this unit of study and why?

- Do any of these elements, strategies, or skills get addressed at other points in the unit?
- Which goal is your priority for this lesson?
- What does this lesson have to do with the elements, strategies, and/or skills you have identified as your primary goal?
- Which standards and/or Principles of Learning does this particular lesson address?

What are students' prior knowledge and difficulties?

- What relevant concepts have already been explored with this class?
- What strategies does this lesson build on?
- What relevant contexts (i.e., other genres, oral language, craft elements) could you draw on in relation to this concept?
- What can you identify or predict students may find difficult or confusing or have misconceptions about?
- In what ways might students begin to express their ideas? What forms (written lists, oral stories, memories, etc.) might the students choose?

How does the lesson help students reach the goals?

- What grouping structure will you use? Why? When?
- What opening statement do you have in mind?
- How do you plan to present the tasks?
- What activities will move students toward the stated goals?
- In what ways will students make their writing, thinking, and understanding public?
- What will we see in the students' writing that demonstrates their learning?
- How will you ensure that students are talking with and listening to one another in an atmosphere of mutual respect?
- How will you be sure that your teaching point is clear to the students (not increase confusion)? Do you have a clear focus with one teaching point?

- How do you plan to assist those students who you predict will have difficulties?
- What extensions or challenges will you provide for students who are ready for them?
- How much time do you predict will be needed for each part of the lesson?

REFERENCES

Allington, R. L. (2000). *What really matters for struggling readers: Designing research-based programs.* Boston: Allyn & Bacon.

Costa, A., & Kallick, B. (2000). Discovering and exploring habits of mind. Alexandria, VA: Association for Supervision & Curriculum Development.

Dweck, C. S. (2002). *Messages that motivate: How praise molds students' beliefs, motivation, and performance (in surprising ways).* New York: Academic Press.

Elmore, R. F. (2004). *School reform from the inside out: Policy, practice, and performance.* Cambridge, MA: Harvard Education Press.

Fullan, M. (2004). *Leadership and sustainability: System thinkers in action.* Thousand Oaks, CA: Corwin Press.

Lewis, C. (2002). *Lesson study: A handbook of teacher-led instructional change.* Philadelphia: Research for Better Schools.

National Research Council. (2005). *Choose effective approaches to staff development.* Retrieved April 29, 2008, from www.nas.edu/rise/backg4b.htm.

Resnick, L. B. (1995). From aptitude to effort: A new foundation for our schools. *Daedalus, 124,* 55–62.

Resnick, L. B., & Hall, M. W. (1998). Learning organizations for sustainable education reform. *Journal of the American Academy of Arts and Sciences, 127,* 89–118.

Resnick, L. B., & Hall, M. W. (2000). *Principles of learning for effort-based education.* Pittsburgh, PA: University of Pittsburgh.

Resnick, L. B., & Nelson-Le Gall, S. (1997). Socializing intelligence. In L. Smith, J. Dockrell, & P. Tomlinson (Eds.), *Piaget, Vygotsky and beyond* (pp. 145–158). London: Routledge.

Saphier, J. (2005). *John Adams' promise: How to have good schools for all our children, not just for some.* Acton, MA: Research for Better Teaching.

Senge, P. M. (1990). *The fifth discipline: The art and practice of the learning organization.* New York: Doubleday.

Shor, I., & Freire, P. (1987). *A pedagogy for liberation: Dialogues on transforming education.* New York: Bergin & Garvey.

Staub, F. C. (1999). *Reflection on content-focused coaching dialogues.* Pittsburgh, PA: University of Pittsburgh, The Institute for Learning.

Staub, F. C. (2001). Fachspezifisch-pädagogisches coaching: Forderung von Unterrichtsexperties durch Unterrichtsentwicklung [Content-Focused coaching in teaching: Fostering teaching expertise through long-term classroom-based assistance in design and enactment of lessons]. *Beitrage zur Lehrerbildung, 19*(2), 175–198.

Staub, F. C., West, L., & Bickel, D. D. (2003, August). *Content coaching.* Paper presented at the meeting of the European Association for Research on Learning and Instruction, Padua, Italy.

Stiegler, J. W., & Hiebert, J. (1999). *The teaching gap: Best ideas from the world's teachers for improving education in the classroom.* New York: Free Press.

Wang-Iverson, P., & Yoshida, M. (Eds.). (2005). *Building our understanding of lesson study.* Philadelphia: Research for Better Schools.

West, L., & Staub, F. C. (2003). *Content-focused coaching: Transforming mathematics lessons.* Portsmouth, NH: Heinemann.

Westbury, I. (2000). Teaching as a reflective practice: What might Didaktik teach curriculum? In I. Westbury, S. Hopmann, & K. Riquarts (Eds.), *Teaching as a reflective practice: The German Didaktik tradition* (pp. 15–39). Mahwah, NJ: Lawrence Erlbaum.

Wheatley, M. J. (2001). *Leadership and the new science: Discovering order in a chaotic world.* New York: Berrett-Koehler.

7

Differentiated Coaching

Jane A. G. Kise

INTRODUCTION

Jane A. G. Kise's interest in coaching and personality types grew out of a few wonderful coincidences, all starting the day she signed up to help with a class at her church. As luck would have it, Jane found herself collaborating with Sandra Hirsh, a world-renowned expert on personality type theory. As Jane says, "working with her, personality type just became something I was passionate about." Together, they wrote several books on using type in organizations and on type and spirituality. Through their business consulting work, Jane gained experience in executive coaching.

Another coincidence turned Jane's interests toward schools and differentiated coaching, an approach that puts personality types at the heart of the coaching process and is described in *Differentiated Coaching: A Framework for Helping Teachers Change* (Kise, 2006). Beth Russell, who was one of the participants in Jane's church class, invited Jane to her school where she was a principal. Jane soon began conducting 90-minute workshops on personality types every week to teach the teachers how to differentiate with their students. From that point on, Jane and Beth continued to work together, so much so that Beth eventually became a coauthor with Jane on *Differentiated School Leadership: Effective Collaboration, Communication, and Change Through Personality Type* (Kise & Russell, 2008).

Jane began to apply her knowledge of personality types—she has become an internationally recognized expert on personality type and is currently president of the Association for Psychological Type International (APTI)—to the way she

(Continued)

(Continued)

coached and led professional learning in schools soon after she began working with the teachers in Beth's school. As Jane says, "it hit me square in the face" that to share knowledge effectively with teachers, she would have to adapt her way of working to meet their learning style needs. For Jane, that adaptation was extra work, because the teachers "really needed different help to change their classroom . . . but it paid off big. Every single one of them changed their classroom and we made major changes in the failure rate of students. And the students saw the differences and started advocating for themselves."

In this chapter on differentiated coaching, Jane makes the case that coaches will reach more teachers if they differentiate their services so that they meet the needs of each individual teacher based on his or her personality type, which in many ways determines learning style as well. Jane provides quick descriptions of the personality types described by the Myers-Briggs Type Indicator (MBTI®). As Jane explains, the well-researched theory behind the MBTI "holds that people take in information and make decisions differently." Her descriptions are fascinating because they prompt some enlightening reflection about our own type and then our friends', family members', and colleagues' types.

Inevitably, after we develop an understanding of personality types, we think about how we might better meet the needs of those around us by taking into account their diverse informational needs. This is where Jane's chapter may be most helpful. She provides a practical four-step framework that we can use to understand and differentiate our coaching for the various personality types. Thus, differentiated coaching follows this process:

- The coach draws a hypothesis about the teacher's natural style.
- The coach identifies teacher beliefs.
- The coach and teacher together identify the problems the teacher wants to solve.
- The coach and teacher develop a coaching plan.

Although differentiated coaching is, of course, the most appropriate approach for coaching teachers to approach instructional differentiation through personality types, Jane's ideas have implications for all approaches to coaching. Differentiated coaching helps us see that just like teachers need to adapt to meet the needs of their students, we need to adapt our way of working to meet teachers where they are. This seems like an important lesson for any coach.

A teacher we'll call Sara volunteered to be coached by me on differentiated instruction, excited to learn about ways to reach more children. She and the others on her team were so enthusiastic to get started that they actually scheduled two afterschool meetings in one week with me—on their own time! So how quickly did Sara adopt the strategies she was eager to learn?

She corrected papers during those meetings. She failed to participate in brainstorming sessions. She ignored even the shortest of suggested readings. She said, "If I'm using the District curriculum, then I'm already differentiating." She irritated her teammates by asking detailed, seemingly irrelevant questions.

Was Sara resistant? Literature on the subject often places teachers on continuums from "innovators" to "laggards" (Tye, 2000) or "key members" to "deadwood" (Evans, 2001). Usually, blame for resistance is placed solidly with the teacher.

Sara, though, was unique. I use a framework called personality type to examine teacher strengths and beliefs. You may have encountered the theory through the Myers-Briggs Type Indicator®. It's a theory about normal differences in how people take in information and make decisions. Coaches can use other theories and frameworks for the same purpose, but data collected over decades by the Center for Applications of Psychological Type show that Sara's personality type is least frequent among teachers— less than 1% of all teachers share her personality type. Staff development is seldom designed with teachers like Sara in mind.

However, Sara was the first on her team to try the new differentiation techniques, *once I differentiated my coaching methods to meet her concerns, beliefs, and learning style.* Then I did the same for the other teachers on the team, and they changed, quickly.

I hadn't done so at first because, after all, they'd chosen to work with me. I'd assumed that a small-group approach, with rich dialogue around lessons from their own curriculum and a proven planning process, would be enough. That coaching practice had worked for me at other schools. But the concerns and beliefs of these teachers made them hesitant to change their classrooms until I changed my coaching plan in ways that produced evidence that countered those beliefs.

RESISTANCE?

Often, information on coaching teachers suggests that we consider differentiating for content areas, grade levels, and years of teaching experience. However, what if the following is true, as I've found in working with countless teachers?

- Teachers form their practices around what they do best.
- Their strengths are related to their own personalities and learning styles.
- Their personalities and learning styles drive their core educational beliefs.
- Changing their teaching practices means changing those core beliefs.

That makes change very, very difficult. As Fullan and Hargreaves (1991) put it, changing teacher beliefs involves changing the person the teacher is.

It also makes the job of a coach more intricate, removing the concept of resistance and substituting the following: *How can I adjust my coaching style to meet the needs of this teacher?* Changing styles goes far beyond choosing from such coaching roles as modeling, coteaching, providing resources, and so on, which mainly focus on delivery methods, although this is part of it. Extensive research (Barger & Kirby, 1995; Clancy, 1997) found the following:

- There are clear differences in the kinds of information people with different personalities and learning styles need, how they process that information, and what makes change most stressful.
- Resistance to change increases when those needs aren't met.
- Leaders in general fail to recognize and deal effectively with those needs.

In differentiated coaching, then, the goal is to identify what information an individual teacher needs during change. That information will be affected by his or her personality type, which in turn influences the teacher's teaching style, beliefs about education, and main concerns during change.

The purpose of using a framework such as personality type isn't to label the teacher, but to *undo* the label of "resistor," to unearth needs that the coach, who most likely has a different personality type, doesn't naturally think of or meet. Let's look at a process for understanding a teacher's personality and beliefs, informational needs, and the coaching strategies that have the best chance of bringing about change.

STEP 1: DRAW A HYPOTHESIS ABOUT THE TEACHER'S NATURAL STYLE

While I use personality type, other learning styles models can also be used to foster strengths-based conversations about teaching and learning. If you use another model, consider whether you can adapt it for the same purposes I describe. Personality type is simply the model with which I am most familiar and can use to provide the richest examples.

Why Personality Type?

Coaches can use other learning styles frameworks for differentiating teacher needs. However, personality type is a strengths-based model that can turn the focus away from "right" and "wrong" to "Which students will this curriculum/teaching strategy/assessment format reach?" This theory holds that people take in information and make decisions differently, two key processes in education. Further, these variations in behavior are quite orderly and consistent. Using a framework such as personality type makes coaching less threatening to a teacher, who after all is teaching from his or her core self.

Personality type is also well researched; search the bibliography at www.capt.org to see over 10,000 studies and articles, including reliability and validity studies, correlations with other learning styles models, connections between type theory and misdiagnosis of conditions such as Attention Deficit Disorder, the overrepresentation of some types in Teacher of the Year awards, the use of type concepts to improve student achievement, and so on.

If you choose a different framework, make sure that it (Kise, 2006)

- Describes teaching and learning in nonjudgmental ways. No one should feel labeled.
- Is strengths based, emphasizing each person's natural teaching and learning style rather than placing limits on what the person can do.
- Describes what learning styles a practice will reach.
- Works for both adults and students, and across cultures, to facilitate conversations about classrooms.

As you read through the information on the preferences, take notes. Which is your *preferred* style? Most people have elements of each, but one is easier and takes less energy. And bring to mind a teacher whom you have struggled to coach. Which preferences might they have? Does this explain any of your coaching struggles?

Extraversion and Introversion

This preference pair describes our source of *energy.* In personality type theory, it is not about gregariousness or shyness; it's even spelled differently. Instead, people who prefer Extraversion are energized by interacting with others and through activities. People who prefer Introversion are energized by time alone for reflection.

Most Extraverted teachers run classrooms that have Extraverted characteristics—lots of activities, interactions, student work and learning aids on display, and so on. Introverted teachers run more Introverted classrooms, usually with less noise, fewer pieces of furniture or artwork, more individual time, and so on.

As you think about your "resistant" teacher, which style fits best? Then, consider whether his or her needs are being met (Kise, 2006) in the coaching process:

Extraversion	*Introversion*
Is there time for productive conversations regarding the changes?	Is information available for reflection before teachers are asked to respond or act?
Are there active roles for those who want them?	Are there one-to-one opportunities for communicating, both to share thoughts and to ask questions?
Is action as well as talk taking place?	Is there time to internalize the meaning of the change before having to act?

Sensing and Intuition

This preference pair describes the kinds of *information* people pay attention to first. Those who prefer Sensing pay attention to *what is*, first attending to facts verifiable by the five senses and to past experiences. Those who prefer Intuition pay attention to *what could be,* first attending to hunches, connections, analogies, and inspirations.

Sensing teachers tend to give structured assignments that can be objectively graded. They often search for what has worked for other teachers and may be content to use curriculum. Some even resist skipping over sections, concerned about missing something vital.

Intuitive teachers tend to prefer open-ended assignments that allow for student individuality and creativity. They love trying new ideas and often treat curriculum as a starting place, adding, subtracting, or innovating as ideas occur to them.

As you think about your "resistant" teacher, might that person be more Sensing or Intuitive? Consider whether his or her needs are being met (Kise, 2006) through the current change or coaching process.

Sensing	*Intuition*
Are real data available to demonstrate why the change needs to be made and why it is better than the present?	Have you provided the big picture—the underlying theories and the long-term vision?
Have specific details been provided regarding schedules, costs, and responsibilities?	Are there options for implementation to allow for creativity and individuality?
Have you made specific connections between the proposed changes, past practices, and other change efforts?	Do teachers have opportunities to influence the change effort design?

Thinking and Feeling

This preference pair describes how we make *decisions.* People who prefer Thinking make decisions through logic and universal principles, objectively considering precedents and consequences. People who prefer Feeling make decisions by stepping into the shoes of those involved to subjectively consider the impact on individuals and community values. Note that both are rational decision-making processes. In educational decisions, the Thinking preference considers data, standards, and benchmarks, while the Feeling preference considers student engagement, motivation, and relationships. Both considerations are vital to student achievement, and the best decisions balance the two decision-making styles.

The classroom of a Thinking teacher might emphasize rigor over relationships. Yes, these teachers will build relationships with their students, but they're motivated first by ensuring that their students are working toward high standards and learning how to reason.

The classroom of a Feeling teacher might emphasize relationships over rigor. Yes, Feeling teachers will hold their students accountable to high standards, but they're motivated first by ensuring that their students are engaged in the learning process and the learning community.

As you think about your "resistant" teacher, consider whether his or her needs are being met (Kise, 2006) during the change or coaching process.

Thinking	Feeling
How clear is the logic of how the change measures were chosen? What about the internal logic of the proposed changes?	Is the change consistent with the values of the organization and people involved?
Has leadership demonstrated competency in implementing change?	Do plans take into account the needs of people?
Has leadership shown the fairness and equity of the proposed changes?	Do those most affected have a voice in the implementation plan?

Judging and Perceiving

This preference pair describes how we *approach life and work.* People who prefer Judging approach life by planning their work and working their plan. People who prefer Perceiving approach life by staying open to more information and leaving room for spontaneity.

Note that almost all schools in the United States—and around the world—have a Judging culture. Bells tell us when learning is to start and end, curriculum maps outline what is to be learned regardless of world or personal events, students are to be ready for the same test on the same day even as we give lip service to individual needs and differences, and so on.

The classrooms of Judging teachers often reflect time management skills and they may engage in lesson planning or curriculum mapping more willingly. Perceiving teachers may be able to change classroom direction more quickly when children's needs or circumstances change. They may dislike making lengthy plans because things always change and children are unpredictable, anyway.

As you think about your "resistant" teacher, consider whether his or her needs are being met (Kise, 2006) during the coaching or change process.

Judging	*Perceiving*
Are there clear goals and time frames for the change process?	Is the plan open-ended enough that goals and time frames can be adjusted as the process unfolds?
Are priorities clear? What will be left undone to implement this program?	How will the change effort stay open to new information?
Are surprises being minimized?	Is there flexibility for how each person implements these changes?

Have you identified your own natural preferences? If you are unsure of one or more, think through a change effort that frustrated you and consider the aforementioned needs during change. Which of your needs weren't met? Consider the information in Table 7.1, Type Preferences and Coaching Implications. Additional references on learning about personality type are listed at the end of the chapter.

Have you hypothesized about the personality type of a teacher who seems resistant? Let's turn to using that hypothesis to come up with a new coaching plan for that teacher.

Table 7.1   Type Preferences and Coaching Implications

Extraverted types *may*	Introverted types *may*
• Need to talk, not listen, to understand • Change their minds as they talk	• Prefer to reflect on materials or experiences in advance • Take on a "deer in the headlights" feeling if the meeting focus changes from what they expect
• Prefer act-reflect-act patterns of learning; for Extraverts, the doing gives them something to think about	• Prefer a reflect-act-reflect pattern of learning, anticipating or reading about what might happen in advance of trying it
• Be stressed by too much lecture/inaction/quiet	• Be stressed by noise, changes without reflective time, being asked to self-disclose too much information
Sensing types *may*	Intuitive types *may*
• Want immediate applications and relevant examples	• Be less interested in isolated skills than in how they fit into overall goals and strategies
• Prefer step-by-step implementation strategies and details to take them from what they know to what you want them to do	• View curriculum or instructional practices as a starting place for innovation *unless* given clear reasons not to deviate from them

- View theory as beside the point; they want to know what will work in *their* classroom
- Be stressed by removal of what is working with no proof that the change will be better

- Respond more to metaphors or theories than to facts

- Be stressed by details, structure, no room for creativity

Thinking types *may*

- Want to know a coach is competent; tout your credentials and experience

- Need logic and the rationale for changes

- Distrust nonspecific praise

- Be stressed by displays of emotion, assumption of a personal relationship, lack of fairness or equity

Feeling types *may*

- Take problems or critiques personally. Start with concrete positive reinforcement.
- Be concerned about the impact of practices on the *whole* person—teachers and students—not just academic achievement
- Want students (and coaches) to like them
- Be stressed by disharmony, not being listened to, or awareness that the needs of some teachers or students are not being met

Judging types *may*

- Find good practices and stick with them.

- Have things planned out and resist coaching interventions that interfere

- Seem rigid without sufficient attention to their informational and timing needs
- Be stressed by changes—they had it all planned!

Perceiving types *may*

- Avoid planning very far ahead—things could change! A coach needs flexibility regarding the whens and whats of interactions.
- Resist deciding quickly about lessons or practices—or may easily change their minds with new information
- Be more likely to over- or underestimate how long activities will take
- Be stressed by closure: something better or more appropriate may be revealed through waiting

SOURCE: Kise, J. A. G. (2006). *Differentiated coaching: A framework for helping teachers change.* Thousand Oaks, CA: Corwin Press. Reproduction authorized only for the local school site or nonprofit organization that has purchased this book.

Perhaps you're thinking, "This is too complicated—eight preferences make sixteen types!" Note that the process can easily be broken down:

- In coaching, Extraversion and Introversion mainly affect how you interact with a teacher. See Table 7.1 for suggestions on what Extraverted and Introverted teachers may need, and take note of how you might need to adjust your style when working with teachers of the opposite preference.

- In coaching, Judging and Perceiving mainly affect a teacher's natural drive for planning and closure. Again, Table 7.1 contains suggestions for adjusting to meet the needs of teachers with the opposite preference.
- This means that the bulk of differentiated coaching involves the remaining four preferences. The essence of what teachers need during change can be described by how they take in information and make decisions—Sensing or Intuition and Thinking or Feeling—resulting in just four different coaching styles.

Think of these styles as shorthand for meeting the teacher's needs during change. Table 7.2 outlines the four styles, the kinds of information and evidence that will be most influential, and the coaching roles and methods teachers with each style are likely to respond to.

The information in Table 7.2 serves as a starting place for conferencing with teachers about how you might best approach them, especially if you're working from a hypothesis of their personality type or other learning style. A conversation about whether your approach will fit their needs usually increases buy-in. However, working through the next two steps will provide even more information to help you coach most effectively. Let's look at some ways to discern if teacher beliefs, often closely tied to their personality type, might be blocking their willingness to change.

STEP 2: IDENTIFYING TEACHER BELIEFS

When I began coaching Sara, I quickly discovered that as a Sensing type, she looked for tried-and-true methods. To her, a standardized curriculum, developed by experts, would certainly meet the needs of her students and she hesitated to add or subtract from it. Especially in their first years of teaching, Sensing types often rely on curriculum or pacing schedules or other "expert" resources.

In Sara's case, this belief that her curriculum must be meeting the needs of her students kept her from examining it closely. When we used the framework of personality type, she quickly learned to identify overstructured activities that demotivated Intuitive students as well as understructured activities that undermined the confidence of Sensing students. We were then able to move forward on making adjustments to the curriculum.

A variety of beliefs can block a teacher from change. Here are some examples:

- *Students don't receive enough home support, so it's inevitable that many won't complete major projects.* Through differentiated coaching, we helped teachers see that their low expectations had kept them from

(Text continues on page 159)

Table 7.2   The Four Coaching Styles

Sensing and Thinking (ST): Coach as Useful Resource

For this style, coaches need strategies and methods—almost a bag of tricks—that they can tailor to meet the specific content area or situation the teacher faces. Buy-in comes through seeing something work or seeing evidence that it worked in a very similar classroom with similar students.

- Provide hands-on, relevant exercises or tips that produce tangible results. These teachers want to test something out to see if it works. If it *does* work, they'll take the time to learn more.
- Provide evidence of effectiveness of these strategies as used by others. The ST does not want to experiment. Further, knowing exactly for whom and where it worked is important information to these teachers.
- Give examples that are easily customized to their jobs. These teachers may discount examples that do not deal with their specific responsibilities.
- Listen carefully to their concerns about new methods or theories. Often their informational needs have not been met.
- Show them it works. These teachers naturally prefer to see results rather than read about theories. Background information is almost irrelevant.

Information and Evidence They Want

- Immediate applications with specific, step-by-step directions.
- Implementation details—their responsibilities, time line, training, trouble-shooting contact.
- Proof that the new is better than their current practices. ST teachers have often modified practices over time and believe they work quite well. Evidence from student work or progress toward meeting objectives may convince them of the need to change what they are doing.

Effective Coaching Roles

- *Modeling.* STs often thrive when using the gradual release of responsibility model. They want to hear about a strategy, watch you use it with their students (or in a classroom like theirs), talk through questions and anticipated problems before they try it themselves, and finally try it while the coach watches so they can ask for help if they need it and receive suggestions afterward. *Keep your schedule open; they may request a second modeling or coteaching session—reflecting their hands-on learning style.*
- *Lesson Planning.* STs may not engage in revising or creating new lesson plans until they have enough evidence of the worthiness of the change. These teachers often like being handed a ready-to-go lesson. If it works, they'll be ready to sit down and plan another one with you.
- *Providing Resources.* These teachers are seldom insulted when coaches hand them relevant curriculum supplements, activities, or project directions. To deepen the coaching relationship, offer to locate what they need.
- *Providing Alternatives.* ST teachers want your ideas and are often demotivated by facilitative questioning designed to draw ideas out of them. They may bluntly say, "If I had an idea, I'd be using it." Instead, start with concrete alternatives, answer all their questions, and then help them choose.

(Continued)

Table 7.2 (Continued)

Sensing and Feeling (SF): Coach as Encouraging Sage

These teachers often thrive when a coach can adopt the traditional mentoring role, providing custom-designed pathways for growth.

- Meet the teacher's needs for encouragement, clear goals, and concrete tasks. They take personally the day-to-day events in their classrooms, assuming that deviations from perfect results or performance are their fault.
- Offer to join them on the job when applicable. Show them what is going right and make concrete suggestions to fix "molehills" that seem like "mountains" because of their desire to serve each student.
- Don't provide too many choices—they may be overwhelmed.
- Model one new strategy at a time and provide methods to document progress. Keep the focus on the overall objective; otherwise, the teacher may get sidetracked by perfectionism over details.

Information and Evidence They Want

- Stories and examples from peers who have used the strategy or technique. They also respond to stories of specific students who experienced growth.
- Specific, step-by-step instructions.
- A clear understanding of what is expected of them. Most SFs are very conscientious. Give them a list of alternatives and they may assume they're expected to try them all.

Effective Coaching Roles

- *Data Coach.* You'll often need data to convince an SF teacher that one of her favorite practices isn't effective, but a high percentage of people with math anxiety prefer Sensing and Feeling. A coach may need to compare test scores, disaggregate data, and engage in more of the data analysis, presenting conclusions for discussion with the teacher. The teacher may gradually take over more of the tasks after seeing how it's done and why the process was valuable.
- *Modeling.* SF teachers often gain confidence by watching and also respond to the gradual release of responsibility model. Often, once they've seen a coach model a practice, they easily come up with suggestions for improving it for their particular students.
- *Coteaching.* SF teachers like to work with people, so coteaching is a great coaching activity. They often need immediate feedback as to whether they've done something correctly. Also, being present allows a coach to point out what is working well. Things seldom go smoothly when students are introduced to something for the first time, and the SF teacher may need an objective voice before he or she is willing to try it again.
- *Coplanning.* SF teachers often enjoy brainstorming ideas with others. They may not see themselves as inherently creative, but a suggestion, or an example of what worked for another teacher, often jump-starts their ability to innovate. Also, coplanning provides a vehicle for answering the teacher's questions immediately.

Intuition and Feeling (NF): Coach as Collegial Mentor

These teachers march to their own beat, and coaches need to keep this in mind. They love new ideas but then need to make them their own. Provide space for their creativity and they can become staunch supporters of any strategy.

- Engage in conversations to help these teachers use their creativity. Let them generate their own ideas for critique rather than work only from a coach's suggestions.
- Show them how to communicate with concrete examples of abstract concepts and techniques, providing demonstrations and directions for each technique.
- Demonstrate how to provide structure while still allowing for student creativity. Provide examples of rubrics or objectives that give clear direction yet avoid the overstructuring that NF's hate.
- Let them talk through several scenarios before deciding on strategies.

Information and Evidence They Want

- *The Big Picture.* These teachers are motivated by improving student motivation, opportunities in life, self-esteem, and altruism, not by improving test scores, even though they're well aware of the importance of measurable student achievement.
- *A Vision of How Each Student Will Be Affected.* They may filter new ideas through their potential impact on students at both extremes of the achievement spectrum, those from every culture, past key students they succeeded or failed to reach, and so on. Objective data leaves them cold unless it's accompanied by qualitative evidence that students will also grow personally.
- *Stories of Systemic Change.* They'll often pursue in-depth knowledge of a model or theory if it's presented with case studies of how a school changed or how a targeted group of students embraced academics.

Effective Coaching Roles

- *Study Groups.* NF teachers often like to read about and discuss new ideas. If they prefer Introversion, their best route to change is independent study. They enjoy trying things in their classrooms and then sharing results and student work.
- *Collegial Observations.* NF teachers may appreciate specific feedback when implementing classroom changes. Use a preobservation conference to identify the information they'd like to receive from you. They are less open to modeling and coteaching, unless a new strategy is out of their comfort zone. For example, one NF teacher asked for modeling only when she agreed to implement a strategy for helping students plan out how to complete projects. She knew she struggled with the same planning skills and welcomed the opportunity to learn with her students.
- *Consultant.* NF teachers often prefer to proceed independently with a new idea until they need additional input. Instead of working with them in the early stages of lesson planning or strategy implementation, ask if they'd like to outline their ideas and then run them by you.
- *Troubleshooter.* Advertise coaching as a way to receive help with the most reluctant learner, the class that's most difficult to settle down, the subject they least prefer to teach, and so on.

(Continued)

Table 7.2 (Continued)

Intuition and Thinking (NT): Coach as Expert

When coaching these teachers, prepare to be challenged—not intentionally, but because NT teachers learn by comparing any new instructional strategy or change to the models and schemas they've developed about how students learn. That comparison can come across as confrontational if the coach isn't prepared. The coach can't take things personally.

- Provide credentials and references to establish trust in your expertise. They expect a coach to answer any question to satisfy their informational needs.
- Provide instructional methods for balancing theory and creativity with hands-on experimentation and structure. NTs can assume that everyone is as interested in models as they are.
- Allow them to probe suggestions, fit them into their own mental models, and then improve on them. A response of "That's plausible" to your most brilliant idea is *high praise* from these teachers. Often, people with this learning style are viewed as contrary, resistant, or abrasive rather than the deep thinkers they are.
- Meet their needs for evidence and data. If they embrace a change as valid and important, they often become enthusiastic.

Information and Evidence They Want

- *Depth of Knowledge.* If a coach can't answer an NT's questions, he or she might recommend Web sites, books, articles, and other resources to satisfy the teacher's need to know.
- *Data and Statistical Studies.* This is the one group of teachers who are very interested in objective research studies.
- *Logical Theories and Models.* NTs need to know how and why things work.

Effective Coaching Roles

- *Coleadership.* NT teachers thrive when they have a say in implementation planning. Carefully considering their critiques often increases buy-in. Ask about areas where they feel competent enough to coach other teachers or perhaps lead a study group.
- *Observation.* NT teachers are generally interested in making improvements and appreciate the preconference/observation/postconference model.
- *Study Groups.* Group discussions allow NT teachers to formulate ideas and receive feedback. They may prefer a more in-depth approach—research or theory-based books or more than one meeting on the same topic—than other teachers.
- *Collaborative Conversations.* Ask these teachers about the problems they want to solve in their classroom. Offer a hypothesis of the root source of the problem and a few alternatives. Then provide time for an extended conversation (perhaps via e-mail if the teacher also prefers Introversion). Expect to discuss alternative hypotheses, the pros and cons of each alternative, other alternatives, and the difficulties of implementation.

SOURCE: Kise, J. A. G. (2006). *Differentiated coaching: A framework for helping teachers change.* Thousand Oaks, CA: Corwin Press. Reproduction authorized only for the local school site or nonprofit organization that has purchased this book.

(Text continued from page 154)

> believing that assignments can be structured for success. When they added those structures, the completion rate rose from 70%–75% to 95%–100% (Kise, 2005).

- *Basic skills need to come first.* Intuitive students balk at skills practice if they don't have the big picture of how those skills are worthwhile. Teachers saw student engagement skyrocket when they helped to provide that big picture.
- *All-class instruction lets me make sure all students are grasping concepts.* With modeling and support, this teacher learned that independent learning activities allowed her to target struggling students while those who understood what to do could keep moving forward.

The list is endless—assumptions that arise based on a teacher's own learning experiences, stereotypes about groups of students, inherent difficulties with a teaching strategy that's out of the teacher's style and therefore isn't implemented with fidelity, and so on. Often, the dissonance is so great that these beliefs block the individual from hearing a coach's advice or evidence of a strategy's research-based effectiveness.

How do you unearth these beliefs? First, assume that the teacher is resisting the change for a rational reason and not because of laziness or anger or other negative emotion.

Second, look for clues. For example, if a teacher has folders filled with tried-and-true lesson plans, is he or she going to be enthusiastic about jettisoning all of it for a new curriculum? Combine Sensing with Judging and you'll have teachers who've found proven methods and may be suspicious of alternatives. One told me, "I will not experiment on my students!" Or, is the classroom uncluttered and class time filled with listening activities or seatwork? This teacher, who may prefer Introversion, may struggle to implement any kind of group work, perhaps even interpreting student difficulties in working together as a sign of their disinterest or immaturity rather than a lack of collaboration skills that can be taught.

Third, ask questions. Much is written about the power of establishing trust with teachers. In differentiated coaching, part of that trust comes from using the right coaching style (Table 7.2) so the teacher feels free to express his or her concerns and struggles. Questions that usually let them speak freely, and from their strengths, include the following:

- If you could wave a magic wand, what is one thing you would change about your school (or classroom)?
- Give me a specific example of a time when you felt successful helping a student (or colleague).
- If you could get all of your colleagues (teachers) to be consistent in one thing, what would it be?
- Describe your ideal classroom.
- What kind of situation causes you the most frustration?
- What do you think all students need to learn?

You'll develop new questions that work with your own style, but these are a good starting place. Record your beliefs about the teacher's beliefs in Table 7.3. You'll use them later to determine the kinds of *evidence* that you'll need to provide to change those change-blocking beliefs.

STEP 3: IDENTIFYING THE PROBLEMS THE TEACHER WANTS TO SOLVE

The third step in differentiated coaching recognizes the reality that even in schools with the best possible leadership, a classroom teacher may be preoccupied with different concerns than those addressed in the strategic plan or through the initiatives in which you are engaged as a coach.

With some of the urban teachers I've coached, maintaining classroom control is their biggest concern. If they believe that a new teaching strategy could result in losing that control—even temporarily—the coaching plan needs to ensure that this doesn't happen. Other examples include the following: "I've got to get students to turn in more homework," "These students don't trust me," "Parents don't like our new report cards," and "I spend too much time correcting papers and can't seem to get ahead on lesson planning."

The best way to find out the problems the teachers want to solve is to ask. At one high-poverty school, even though the teachers gave lip service to the initial goal of increasing student engagement, the teachers finally admitted, "We're so stressed by all the things our students need that we're losing sleep!" We worked on stress management before any other initiative.

This doesn't mean that you focus on whatever the teachers feel like focusing on. Instead, work to solve their most pressing problem in a way that builds buy-in for the change you do want them to make. Show them how the proposed change is relevant to their biggest needs. For example, our work on stress management included prioritizing all of the things they hoped to accomplish. That allowed me to reinforce the school's priorities as they admitted it couldn't all happen at once.

Once you've identified the presenting problem, ask yourself the following:

- Is the problem defined correctly or are there other possibilities? Often we leap to problem solving before completing this step, which is dangerous since different problems bring to mind different solutions.
- What evidence can be produced in solving the problem that will influence the teacher's beliefs and therefore motivate them to change?

For example, a math teacher told me that students didn't care about math. No matter what he did, they refused to engage in learning activities.

Table 7.3   Information-Gathering Sheet

Communication				
Your coaching style is:	ST	SF	NF	NT
Teacher's preferred style is:	ST	SF	NF	NT

Style adjustments to keep in mind, including Extraversion and Introversion, Judging and Perceiving (Tables 7.1 and 7.2):

Teacher Beliefs	Evidence of Success
Which of the teacher's habits or beliefs work against success? (Examples: All students like ___; All teachers should ___; Learning can only happen if ___; Our students can't ____.)	**What evidence would persuade the teacher of the value of a new approach?** (See Table 7.2, The Four Coaching Styles.)
Which strengths can you build on?	
Goals	**Roles**
Teacher's main concern or presenting problem: (Examples: Need to have authority acknowledged; Student engagement)	**Coach's Role: What kind of support would the teacher like?** (See Table 7.2, The Four Coaching Styles.)
School's requirements or initiative needs:	**Teacher's Role: What first step might the teacher be comfortable taking?** (Examples: Trying a specific, ready-to-go strategy; reading about a theory; looking at data.)
What teacher interests could be "hooks" for change?	

He told me, "At the last test, only 7 of the 25 students even tried. The rest put their names on the top and just sat there." What was his solution? Keep marching through the curriculum to reach the seven engaged students. He felt he'd tried everything humanly possible.

I watched the classroom and formulated a different problem: The students didn't know *how* to learn math. If they didn't care, I thought I'd see more misbehavior. My solution set involved explicitly teaching how to be mathematicians and active learners. However, the math teacher needed evidence that his students didn't know how to learn math, evidence to change his initial definition of the problem and motivate him to change. In this case, I suggested, and he agreed, to have students write down what came to mind when they thought of math and what they need to do to learn math.

The students described math as hard, boring, difficult to understand, and confusing. One student wrote, "Huh? Why? What? Too many numbers." As for what they needed to do, all but one student listed *passive* roles such as listening to the teacher, having a teacher who explained more, bringing a pencil. One student wrote, "I don't know how to do math. I don't learn. I watch." Only a handful of students—perhaps the seven who took the test?—listed active strategies such as practicing math facts, asking for homework help, or asking for more examples. Once the teacher saw this evidence, he was ready to try strategies designed to help students learn to ask questions, engage in problem solving rather than waiting for solutions, and take responsibility for their own learning.

Should the teacher be involved in defining the problems and looking for alternatives, as the Cognitive Coaching model advocates? Yes, but with "resistant" teachers, I've found that the alternatives are often so far removed from their natural teaching style that they don't seem like viable alternatives. The coach's role becomes more directive while keeping in mind the teacher's concerns, beliefs, and learning style.

STEP 4: DEVELOPING A COACHING PLAN

At this point, the coach is ready to take all the information about the teacher's natural strengths, beliefs, and major concerns and wrap it together into a coaching plan. Another way to describe the process is as follows:

- Choose the coaching style and strategies that best meet the learning style and informational needs of the teacher, whether you use personality type or another framework.
- Identify teacher beliefs that might block change.
- Talk with the teacher about the biggest problem he or she would like to solve.
- Reframe or redefine that problem if necessary. Involve the teacher in this process unless he or she believes the problem is hopeless or the

teacher seems resistant, perhaps because proposed solutions are so foreign to his or her natural style.

• Develop alternatives, evaluate them, and choose one that will produce evidence that can influence the beliefs that are blocking this teacher from change.

Table 7.3 can help you organize your thoughts. Filling it out is seldom a linear process. Instead, one insight may provide new information for other elements of your draft plan. You might first discover a "hook"—the teacher reveals a vibrant interest in teaching a new novel or in developing a lesson that effectively uses an interactive whiteboard—that you know you can use to help the teacher implement the new strategy the principal wants adopted.

If this sounds complicated, remember that some teachers have the same style as yours. You can coach them as you would like to be coached. Many, many others share part of your style. In personality type terms, you might share Feeling, but then be opposite on Sensing and Intuition. Much of your natural style will work for these teachers. Those with the opposite style require the most work, but without that extra effort they're the ones least likely to accept what you have to offer as a coach. They may be your "resistors." It's worth the effort.

Sara, for example, was my total opposite. The coaching style she responded to—having me hand her a complete lesson plan to try, for example—would have been *insulting* to me. Yet once she'd experienced that complete plan with her students, she quickly developed others on her own.

Thus, what seems to be a complicated coaching process often becomes the most direct route to change. Guskey (2002) wrote as follows:

> The crucial point is that it is not the professional development *per se*, but the experience of successful implementation that changes teachers' attitudes and beliefs. They believe it works because they have seen it work, and that experience shapes their attitudes and beliefs . . . the key element in significant change in teachers' attitudes and beliefs is clear evidence of improvement in the learning outcomes of their students. (p. 384)

Differentiated coaching acknowledges that teachers need different experiences and evidence to change those beliefs and thus makes it possible for more teachers to embrace change. Does it work? Here's what one teacher leader had to say about his first attempt:

> Teacher Y was having difficulty in her class. By the end of the first term she was considering . . . quitting teaching in general. I knew she was working hard and I knew she knew her math. Initially,

when I was trying to help her with her classroom issues, I was very direct with her. I would give her a detailed list of teaching practices she should implement to better instruct her class. Then, when I would observe her class again, I would see the same issues. She was not being an effective teacher, I was not being an effective coach, and worst of all, the students were not learning. Things were bad and getting worse.

Then we, the teacher and I, discussed her type. It turns out she prefers Feeling and I was coaching her as if she preferred Thinking. After this conversation, I dramatically changed my coaching approach. I stopped handing her lists of practices to implement. I started listening instead of talking. I would ask her how she felt about the class and what she thought could be done to improve the class. I listened to her ideas, empathized and validated her feelings, and made suggestions on how to implement them in the class. She had many great ideas and her class started improving almost immediately. By utilizing the notion of type I was able to help Teacher Y help herself. Now Teacher Y is one of the strongest teachers in the department and I look forward to her return in the fall.

Differentiated coaching provides teachers with the best kind of freedom—not freedom to do as they please, but the freedom to recognize, embrace, and move toward their full potential as educators.

RESOURCES FOR USING DIFFERENTIATED COACHING

Practice case studies are available for downloading at www.edcoaching .com. These can be used by individuals or for group discussion and contain descriptions of the teachers' styles, information from interviews, and a sample coaching plan.

Fairchild, A. M., & Fairchild, L. L. (1995). *Effective teaching, effective learning: Making the personality connection in your classroom.* Mountain View, CA: Davies-Black.

Kise, J. A. G. (2006). *Differentiated coaching: A framework for helping teachers change.* Thousand Oaks, CA: Corwin Press.

Kise, J. A. G. (2007). *Differentiation through personality types: A framework for instruction, assessment, and classroom management.* Thousand Oaks, CA: Corwin Press.

Lawrence, G. (1993). *People types and tiger stripes* (3rd ed.). Gainesville, FL: Center for Applications of Psychological Type.

Murphy, E. (1992). *The developing child: Using Jungian type to understand children.* Palo Alto, CA: CPP.

Pajak, E. (2003). *Honoring diverse teaching styles: A guide for supervisors.* Alexandria, VA: Association for Supervision and Curriculum Development.

REFERENCES

Barger, N. J., & Kirby, L. K. (1995). *The challenge of change in organizations: Helping employees thrive in the new frontier.* Palo Alto, CA: CPP.

Clancy, S. G. (1997). STJs and change: Resistance, reaction, or misunderstanding? In C. Fitzgerald & L. K. Kirby (Eds.), *Developing leaders: Research and applications in psychological type and leadership development* (pp. 415–438). Palo Alto, CA: CPP.

Evans, R. (2001). *The human side of school change: Reform, resistance and the real-life problems of innovation.* San Francisco: Jossey-Bass.

Fullan, M., & Hargreaves, A. (1991). *What's worth fighting for in your school.* Toronto: Ontario Public School Teachers' Federation.

Guskey, T. R. (2002). Professional development and teacher change. *Teachers and teaching: Theory and practice, 8,* 380–391.

Kise, J. A. G. (2005). Coaching teachers for change: Using the concepts of psychological type to reframe teacher resistance. *Journal of Psychological Type, 65*(6), 47–58.

Kise, J. A. G. (2006). *Differentiated coaching: A framework for helping teachers change.* Thousand Oaks, CA: Corwin Press.

Kise, J. A. G., & Russell, B. (2008). *Differentiated school leadership: Effective collaboration, communication, and change through personality type.* Thousand Oaks, CA: Corwin Press.

Tye, B. B. (2000). *Hard truths: Uncovering the deep structure of schooling.* New York: Teachers College Press.

8

Leadership Coaching

Karla Reiss

INTRODUCTION

Karla Reiss provides us with another approach, leadership coaching, which she describes in more detail in her book *Leadership Coaching for Educators: Bringing Out the Best in School Administrators* (2006). Karla's interest in coaching blossomed in what might be the most natural way, by being coached. In conversation with me, Karla explained that "it honestly wasn't until I had an opportunity to work with a coach that I saw the potential. Being on the receiving end was a real eye-opener."

Karla's experiences being coached began when she was coordinator of staff development for a large region. Not only did she find coaching to be valuable, but she began to think about how helpful coaching could be for administrators. Traditional professional development, where administrators went to sessions and then back to their jobs, did not seem to meet leaders' needs. Karla quickly realized that coaching could be "a big missing piece for administrators."

Coaching offered professional learning that addressed the practical needs of each unique leader. As Karla explained to me, "most administrators are too busy, too overwhelmed with different challenges and just going to a training and coming

---

AUTHOR'S NOTE: The following chapter contains content reprinted with permission from the book *Leadership Coaching for Educators: Bringing Out the Best in School Administrators* (Reiss, 2006).

back wasn't a model for them. I saw that coaching was a great model that was customized, designed for the leader, and focused on specific challenges each leader faces."

To develop as a coach, Karla became involved with the International Coaching Federation, and she learned about the competencies and skills of effective coaches through certification training programs at two nationally known coach training schools. During this process, she realized that becoming an effective coach requires effective training. "We should not underestimate the intensity of the training that it takes. That means guided practice, with people-focused work that is all about making transformational change from the inside out."

In her chapter, Karla asserts that coaching should be an important component of any educational leader's professional development. Karla elaborates on the International Coaching Federation's definition of coaching, offering a description of leadership coaching in action. Karla also explains that leadership coaching is a service leaders can receive and that administrators who adopt a coaching approach to leadership can be more effective while having a positive impact on school culture.

Karla's chapter also includes many features that could be helpful to other coaches utilizing other approaches. For example, she paints a vivid picture of a coach and administrator coaching relationship, which nicely shows the potential that coaching has for promoting growth and providing support. Karla also explains how recent brain research shows that coaching provides the kind of support that is necessary for lasting change. Finally, throughout the chapter, Karla lists many skills that are important for coaches.

There is a subtext woven throughout this chapter, and that is that coaching is not just something that is done to leaders. Coaching is a process that should be a part of the makeup of schools. In our conversation, Karla explained that she believes growth and empowerment need to be shared across schools. "I think it is important for educators to start seeing coaching as a whole-school strategy. Coaching could be so much more. Leaders could not only receive the services of a coach but learn how to coach others. Teachers could coach students. Coaching is a really untapped strategy that can really make a difference." Her point seems important no matter what approach or approaches to coaching we might adopt.

You will never maximize your potential in any area without coaching. It is impossible. You may be good. You may even be better than everyone else. But without outside input you will never be as good as you could be.

—Andy Stanley (2006)

"You don't need coaching for ordinary results" is a powerful quote from Robert Hargrove, author of *Masterful Coaching Fieldbook* (2000). Making minimal change is not the challenge schools are facing. Making major change has long been the challenge for schools and their leaders, and coaching is a significant strategy that supports transformational change.

The initial notion of leadership coaching came to me five years ago from a number of paths. I had been intrigued by the coaching concept in the late 1990s, first as a result of a peer coaching model for teachers I was implementing in the region in which I lived. I thought, "Coaching appears to be a great process." It appeared to be a solution and perfect design for professional growth and the continuous improvement of not only teachers but of leaders for accomplishing challenging goals. It had all the elements of high-quality professional development, and I envisioned a broader use of coaching beyond the classroom. I saw how the benefits can empower leaders, as well as teachers, to become high-performing, more confident leaders. Not only does coaching deserve its place as an effective strategy for school-based, instructional coaching as a model for supporting teachers in the classroom, but it is highly effective for assuring the development and success of every school leader.

I began the quest to learn more. First, I became a client of a well-known coach. For six months, I experienced the possibilities coaching had for both personal and professional transformation. I received weekly coaching via telephone. I was hooked on coaching. My assumptions were confirmed that the coaching process can have a great impact on school leaders and the districts they serve. I made a life- and career-changing decision and decided to obtain my professional coach credentials and explore ways of bringing greater awareness and opportunities for leadership coaching to schools.

The field of coaching, as its own profession, is rapidly growing. People are refocusing their career paths in droves. However, coaching as a process, leadership style, and continuous improvement strategy is one that needs to be seriously considered to achieve the challenging results faced by school leaders across the country and around the world.

In this chapter, I refer to leadership coaching in a similar manner to executive coaching and how it is utilized in the business world: school leaders (from department chairpersons, principals, central office administrators, and superintendents) working with a trained professional coach on an ongoing basis, to discuss and strategize their goals and challenges to achieve results for their organization. School leaders and a coach are strategic partners who meet on a weekly (or other agreed-upon schedule) basis. Together they explore the current challenges and devise means and tactics for successfully moving forward, managing or overcoming resistance and obstacles that may impede success. School leaders engage in one-on-one, confidential coaching on a regular basis. While coaching focuses on the individual, the goals discussed are aligned with the organization. Benefits of coaching include the following: achievement of the organizations' objectives, leader retention, increase in job satisfaction, increase in decision making, improvement in working relationships, reduction in stress, and increase in motivation.

This chapter also focuses on school leaders adopting a coaching style of leadership, to coach others within the organization. The traditional management style of top-down, "command and control" is no longer seen as the optimal leadership style. School leaders can shift from a management approach to a coaching approach, one in which they challenge and support people in achieving the school's goals while acknowledging individuals and their desire to contribute meaningfully to their work. In a coaching approach, leaders bring out the best in others by using coaching skills, techniques, and processes to develop awareness and creative choices in forwarding action toward the individual's and school's professional goals.

LEADERSHIP COACHING MAKES A DIFFERENCE

As a fairly new strategy being used by school systems, research on leadership coaching in schools and evidence of student achievement gains is sorely needed. However, we can learn a great deal from the data uncovered by two significant studies that describe the benefits and results of leadership coaching in the business and nonprofit sectors.

In 2001, Manchester, Inc. conducted a study of 100 *Fortune* 1000 business executives who received individual executive coaching for one year. The study includes data on executive behavior change, organizational improvements, and the return on investment from customized executive coaching. The following results were reported:

- Improved organizational strength
- Increased executive retention
- Increased productivity
- Improved job satisfaction
- Richer learning environments
- Improved decision making
- Improved working relationships
- Improved team performance
- Improved employee motivation
- Increased benefits for both individuals and the organization

In addition, the study showed a 529% return on investment and a 788% overall return when factoring employee retention. Seventy-seven percent of those studied reported that coaching had a significant or very significant impact on their results and success as a leader.

In a study by CompassPoint Non-Profit Services (2003) of executive directors of nonprofit organizations who received executive coaching, six main areas were identified where coaching had a positive impact on the leader and the organization:

1. Leadership, management, and technical skills
   a. Exercised greater leadership on a daily basis
   b. Exercised greater leadership in the face of challenges and obstacles
   c. Gained the ability to move the organization toward achieving its goals

2. Organizational structure and capacity
   a. Increased financial stability
   b. Improved internal communication
   c. Improved ability to fulfill the organization's mission and vision
   d. Increased direct communication among coaches, staff, and the board of directors

3. Attitudes and beliefs about coaching
   a. Coaching met or exceeded their expectations
   b. Coaching provided an ongoing relationship that fosters confidence, trust, and deep dialogue
   c. Satisfaction with coaching scored 4.6 on a scale of 1 to 5

4. Personal lives
   a. Increased balance between personal life and work
   b. Increased opportunities for physical exercise
   c. Increased development of creative outlets

5. Job satisfaction
   a. Increased ability to exercise more authority and be more assertive
   b. Reduced job stress
   c. Increased confidence

6. Tenure
   a. Increased the length of time that leaders remain at their organization
   b. Improved the fit between the leader and organization
   c. Increased ability to exercise leadership in the face of challenges and obstacles
   d. Increased ability to move the organization toward achieving its goals
   e. Increased ability to connect with the organization's vision and increased confidence in leading the organization toward fulfilling that vision

According to the study, coaching was reported to be a relatively inexpensive, high-impact way to develop the leadership of executive directors. One participant stated, "Coaching more than exceeded my expectations because I doubt I'd still be here. In the face of really difficult changes, I get regular, reliable feedback on how I was doing during this period of change. It made me feel I was on the right track. I doubted myself and was hard on myself. Now I feel successful."

"We have a lot of people who were trained to be superb managers but now have horrendous leadership challenges thrown at them. . . . Coaching is aimed at trying to help people develop skills and actions that are different from what they grew up with," states John Kotter (2000), professor of leadership, Harvard Business School. And Robert J. Grossman (1999) in *HR Magazine* stated, "Forty percent of newly appointed leaders fail in the first 18 months, according to a study. Executive failures can be traced back to a flawed selection process; in other cases, new hires are not given adequate coaching and feedback to help them adapt and succeed."

School systems cannot afford their leaders to fail. High turnover can be avoided and successful longevity enhanced by providing coaching support to administrators.

COACHING—IT'S NOT A BUZZWORD

"Greetings, Ms. Jones. I'm your coach. I'm here to support you."

Ms. Jones is the principal of a school that has not met Adequate Yearly Progress (AYP) for the past two years. The coach was assigned to coach Ms. Jones. So what does Ms. Jones think? If she's never been on the receiving end of this new profession called *coaching,* she is likely to be defensive and think she must need a coach because she isn't a very good leader.

And Ms. Jones is likely to be wrong.

As a principal of a struggling school, there are numerous issues impacting the school and its progress. A leadership coach can support Ms. Jones in becoming an ever-better leader of a staff under pressure. There should be no assumption that a leader of a below-par school or district is defective or a poor leader. Yet many assume this.

Let us acknowledge the challenges school leaders face in schools under similar pressure. Morale may be low, frustration levels and achievement goals high.

Let us also acknowledge that *every* principal or district leader can flourish with the gift of coaching. Great leaders can partner with a leadership coach to strategize and discuss challenges as they arise or deal with daily challenging staff or community issues. Good leaders can become great ones. New leaders or mediocre ones can grow in their roles when part of a productive coaching relationship.

Ideally, the principal would choose to have a coach and one would be available. There would be a choice of coaches to assure a positive relationship and a good match. Ideally, Ms. Jones would realize that she, like thousands of leaders, can benefit greatly by having a coach by her side, as her partner in success.

The term *coach* has been tossed around like a Ping-Pong ball and has become a hot new buzzword that infers some form of assistance to reach a big goal. As coaching has begun to find its way into schools, classrooms, and the central office, it is imperative that districts and boards investing precious resources into this highly effective strategy have a common understanding of what "coach" and "coaching" mean.

The International Coach Federation (ICF, 2005), the organization that has created standards and competencies for professional coaches, defines coaching as

> . . . an ongoing relationship which focuses on coachees taking action toward the realization of their visions, goals or desires. Coaching uses a process of inquiry and personal discovery to build the coachee's level of awareness and responsibility and provides the coachee with structure, support and feedback. The coaching process helps coachees both define and achieve professional and personal goals faster and with more ease than would be possible otherwise.

There is much to be understood about the work and process of coaching *before* it is implemented. While the term *coach* is common, it is far from common that individuals, leaders, and decision makers of schools, districts, or any organization have yet to experience a coaching relationship, and thus, the profound benefits it can have for them. Coaching is far from mainstream, yet it holds enormous promise for assuring strong leaders in every school. Up-front planning and deep learning about the coaching process is strongly recommended prior to implementing a district coaching program.

As of this writing, the ICF reports that there are more than 11,000 certified coaches worldwide and 30,000 practicing coaches, including those without a professional coaching credential. Many coaches work within large corporations. Many are independent and work with several companies, organizations, or individuals. Few work with schools. That must change.

It is high time that school boards and leaders themselves realize that coaching helps one be and become a better leader. Every district and every leader is different, with varied experiences and challenges. Therefore, solutions that may be effective for one school, district, or leader may not work for another.

Coaching provides the missing piece—the person—in the form of a leadership coach—with whom one can dialogue about the challenges that are faced. While the client does not receive specific solutions from a coach, he or she does receive a confidential relationship that is focused on boosting results and enhancing performance of the leader.

Leaders will achieve success aligned with how they perceive themselves. Coaching taps into the mind of the leader and explores the thoughts and beliefs that lead to actions, behaviors, or lack of each.

Ms. Jones might see herself as confident and effective with students, but less so with certain teachers, especially those she perceives as resisting school efforts. She might blame resistant teachers for thwarting her efforts. A good coach will help her see it is *she* who is the solution to the challenges she faces. Ms. Jones has to interact differently with the teacher to obtain a different result. Keeping the focus on the teacher doesn't help Ms. Jones create a solution. Although she might need to vent a bit to air her frustration, a good coach will bring the coaching conversation back to Ms. Jones and what she might do to improve the situation.

WHAT IS COACHING?

Coaching is a rapidly growing profession with specific skill sets and techniques that support people in making important changes. It is not a vague kind of help.

Coaching is

- An ongoing process.
- A set of specific skills and competencies, tools and techniques.
- A process that leads to transformation for people and, in turn, the organization they serve. Transformation occurs when people shift how they see themselves, their thoughts and beliefs, and what they do to take action toward their personal, professional, or organization's goals.
- A mindset; an outlook of hope and possibility.
- A productive, results-focused conversation giving leaders the rare opportunity to step back and strategize their challenges.
- A unique relationship; a success partnership.
- A rapidly growing profession.

The figure on page 174 offers a look at a coaching relationship.

EVERY GREAT LEADER NEEDS
TO COACH AND BE COACHED

Leaders orchestrate others to action—like a conductor of a symphony or a movie director. A wise one knows when to step in or when to back off. A great leader holds the organization's vision and mission and leads

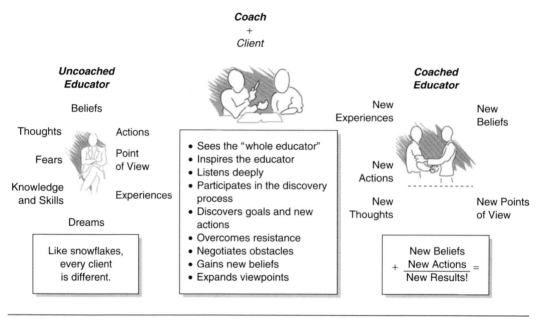

SOURCE: Reiss (2006).

other people to get onboard and stay on track toward the realization of that vision and mission.

However, in reality, straying from the path often occurs.

Every leader knows the game can change quickly. New initiatives from federal or state governments or other sources impose new directions for schools. Urgencies and emergencies often arise, leaving leaders in reactive mode. Staff turnover—new leaders, teachers, and board members—can create a shift in culture or direction. Dealing with an abundance of constant change can challenge the best of leaders.

Coaching should be seriously considered a must-have strategy for school improvement, not only for instructional coaches at the classroom level. Every leader can benefit from working with a coach. And every leader can learn to coach others. With a coaching approach to their leadership style, leaders will create positive, results-focused, action-oriented relationships and boost results for their school or district.

So what would leadership coaching look like? Although scheduled coaching sessions can vary in length and frequency, it is typical for coaching to be weekly meetings of about 45–60 minutes. Short- and long-terms goal would be discussed and agreed on. During each confidential session, the leader would discuss progress toward the school's goals or challenges and perceived obstacles that appear to get in the way. Together, the coach and leader would identify ways to move forward. Coaching sessions can occur on the telephone, a method most leaders find convenient and easy to incorporate into their busy day. In circumstances where the coach is local, a personal meeting could allow the coach the chance to observe the leader and provide feedback. However, this is not necessary, as successful coaching can be effectively conducted on the telephone. It is convenient and cost-effective to do so. Because good coaches are highly skilled at listening and questioning techniques, it is easy for them to gather the information needed to learn all they need to know about a client's situation.

Coaching is not a passing fad. It has demonstrated proven results. Coaching is focused on success, flexibility, and respect for the individual. Becoming a more effective leader is best learned in real time, with real issues facing the leader than off-site canned workshops. School leaders appreciate the safe space of a coaching relationship to dialogue and design individual responses to their challenges. A leadership coach is a facilitator of continuous learning, allowing the leader to modify and apply suitable approaches to challenges.

COACHING MYTHS

- Coaching is for leaders who are underperforming.
- Anyone can be an effective coach.
- You need to have experience in the leaders' role to coach them.
- Coaching has to be done in person.
- Asking questions and listening is all it takes to coach someone.

A lack of understanding might exist about the benefits for coaching among people who have yet to experience it. I have found many surprising and "aha" moments when people experience a coaching conversation for the first time. Coaching is effective for already-successful leaders, experienced leaders in a new role, novice leaders, and those new to an organization. It is a useful strategy for gaining new skills and improving performance, relationships, confidence, competence, and results.

A professionally trained coach usually has a minimum of 125 hours (ICF minimum for attaining the Professional Certified Coach credential) of training and practice in which he or she learns and practices coaching skills and techniques with numerous people. It takes a great deal of expertise and confidence to partner with those who wish to create meaningful change for themselves or their organization.

What does coaching sound like? A coaching conversation is a different conversation. It is one that is empowering, in which the coach is deeply listening to the client, often beyond what is being said. Coaches listen for what is beneath the words and explore the client's thoughts and beliefs.

Here's a brief example:

Client: I have so much on my plate. I don't have time to do it all. I am in my office late every day and can't get to my son's soccer games, ever.

Coach: I hear you are overwhelmed. It sounds like going to your son's games is a high priority to you. Let's take a look at all those priorities. Which would you say are the three most important to focus on now?

Client: Hmm. Well, as a principal, I do have a lot of priorities. And as a mom, I have to say my son is my highest priority; it's number 1.

Coach: That's great.

Client: And at work, I want to refocus our staff meetings so they become more productive, and I want to spend more time in classrooms.

Coach: Let's take a look at this week. When is your son's game, and what time must you leave to get there?

Client: Wednesday at 5. I'd have to leave no later than 4:30.

Coach: Since that is priority number 1, will you commit to leaving at 4:30?

Client: It will be difficult, but yes.

Coach: It was difficult in the past. Now that you're clear about your priorities, it will be easier. Walt Disney once said, "When your values are clear, your decisions are easy." So, let's write that down as a commitment you'll make this week, OK?

Client: Sure. I feel better already.

Coach: Now let's look at your work priorities. You know we all have 24 hours in a day, and you get to choose how you use every one of them. That might be a new concept. I know how important it is to you to be effective and make a difference in your school. You are so dedicated. However, no one can do it all, every day, without draining the precious energy you need to keep going. So you must learn to set boundaries, say "no" more often, and schedule your day to include your highest priorities or most important goals. What would you have to start saying "no" to in order to make more classroom visits?

Client: Good question. There are so many little things that crop up during the day that sidetrack me. I'd have to say "no" to inter-ruptions, phone calls, and e-mail for at least one hour per day.

Coach: Now we're getting somewhere! What time of day will you allocate as classroom visit time?

Client: Best time is 9–10 a.m.

Coach: How many days a week do you wish to do that?

Client: At least two; more would be better.

Coach: How about three?

Client: OK. I really do want to see what is happening in every classroom. Monday, Wednesday, and Friday, from 9–10 a.m., that's where I'll be.

Coach: OK, great. We have a plan. Next week, we'll discuss how it went.

Client: Thank you. I feel better and can see this is really doable, once I focus.

Coach: OK, see you next week. I'll be thinking of you Monday morning at 9.

You will notice in the example, the coach led the client to identify and prioritize her goals, and find a way to make them happen. The coach did not prescribe a solution, but rather guided her through the coaching conversation to find what would work for her.

ADOPTING A COACHING STYLE OF LEADERSHIP

Coaching isn't often taught or required in certification programs for school leaders, in most cases. I predict that will change. Receiving coaching is a different strategy than learning to coach others. Being on the receiving end of coaching is like receiving a potentially fruitful gift, the gift of personal and professional growth. It is an opportunity for leaders to reflect on what they do and why they do it in a certain way, to grow into more successful leaders.

Learning to coach others presents a different opportunity for schools and for every person with whom the leader interacts. Shifting to a coaching style of leadership will result in movement toward a more positive culture among staff and community. When principals, department leaders, and central office leaders learn and use coaching skills, students, teachers, and other staff will feel acknowledged, hopeful, and positive. They will be heard and respected as they observe their own performance and results on the job and explore ways to improve them.

Given the ever-present challenge of creating change and managing people, school leaders can gain the skills needed to transform people and, in turn, transform schools. Becoming a coaching leader will provide new ways of communicating with staff, students, and the community. It will help them reshape their ways of thinking, acting, and being. It will support them in bringing out higher levels of performance by challenging the current thinking and reality of those they are coaching. Leaders who coach represent a transformed way of leading. Learning to coach involves a deep learning process that embodies new skills and capabilities for leading people to success. The coaching process enables people to achieve results and take action toward areas in which they might have been stuck or ineffective. It opens up new possibilities for managing people and new hope for managing resistance.

Learning to coach is a lot more than learning to ask good questions. Good coaching takes time to learn and practice new skills, for the purpose of helping people create new results. Great coaches adopt a mindset and way of viewing people and change. Great coaching versus good coaching is like comparing recipes for an adequate meal and a great, gourmet meal. A great meal is memorable. It is a combination of great ingredients in just the right setting, with just the right ambience. Great coaching combines skills, attitudes, and processes with a trusting relationship to achieve memorable results.

Coaching is a process for both improving current performance and developing future leaders. If one thinks that coaching is just about identifying gaps in skills a leader may have, we will have missed the mark, because coaching is a learning process. Coaches engage individuals in learning about their strengths, their lifelong goals, and the future they want to create. Coaching is not a model that says, "You're broken. I'm here to fix you," but more a process for igniting what is already within and intentionally creating one's future. Imagine how a staff member will respond. Most I've encountered feel supported, respected, and excited about participating in a coaching relationship. A coaching leader empowers others, brings out their strengths, and aligns them with their work.

Coaching provides a methodology and skills for confronting resistance, a thorn in the side of leaders everywhere. The coaching process, done well, reveals what lies beneath resistance. In a trusting coaching relationship, a client feels free to divulge his or her inner thoughts, doubts, or fears. There can be numerous reasons for someone to resist a change imposed by the organization. And most often the person keeps that reason inside or gripes to a colleague. With a coaching style of leadership, one that is nonjudgmental, the client will feel safe enough to disclose his or her inner thoughts without fear of judgment. Every coaching conversation is a dialogue focused on the success and results the client wishes to achieve. Every school leader can incorporate a coaching conversation with every staff member that supports them in taking new action toward the school's results, while honoring and respecting their individual differences.

Having had the opportunity to coach many school leaders at all levels, the most common challenges brought to our coaching work are interpersonal:

- Strained relationships with school board members, staff, or community members
- Passive resistance to school improvement efforts
- Discomfort confronting people

Here's an example: Dave, a coaching client, was greatly disturbed by Jim, who threatened to abandon a significant school improvement effort my client worked on for many years. Dave's heart was in it, and he had observed great success. He expressed that he felt deep grief over the looming loss of the program. Jim had a different agenda and a very different personality. Jim had numerous outbursts, causing Dave to resist confronting him. In our coaching session, Dave first considered leaving the district rather than face the discomfort of confrontation. Over the course of several weeks, he instead chose to gather his courage and speak his mind. Dave began to incorporate what he learned in our coaching sessions and applied them to his everyday conversations with Jim, achieving what he described as "breakthroughs" in their relationship and the direction they were going.

All school leaders can gain these skills, and districts will benefit greatly by hiring leaders with coaching skills or providing opportunities for learning a coaching style of leadership. It is an invaluable process for achieving positive relationships, a positive culture, and challenging goals. It is important to point out that coaching skills and competency that are aligned with the coaching profession, and ICF Professional Coaching Competencies, can be successfully applied to coaching leaders, teachers, students, anyone.

The significant difference between coaching for the teacher and coaching for a leader is the nature of the goals on which the coach and client focus. Coaching for leaders focuses on achieving the school's and district's goals by looking deeply at the leader's strengths and areas for their professional growth that better enable him or her to be a high-performing leader, with the ultimate goal of achieving the organization's goals. Leadership coaching often includes the use of assessments to identify leadership strengths and areas for growth. The coaching process, skills, and techniques used can be the same as those used for coaching teachers. Instructional coaching often includes combining the multiples roles of mentor, data gatherer, facilitator, and consultant with coaching and uses the appropriate role with a specific situation.

WHAT IT TAKES FOR SUCCESSFUL COACHING

More than learning a few dozen skills and techniques, success in coaching can hinge on first developing a deep understanding of people and transformation. Adopting certain attributes can ensure coaching success. A successful coach is

- An active listener
- A possibility thinker
- Compassionate
- Nonjudgmental
- Focused on results
- Courageous
- Focused on action
- A continuous learner
- An inspirational thinker
- Curious

These and other personal qualities help future coaches think like a coach and develop beliefs about people that will support them in achieving change with clients. Each attribute in the list contributes greatly to the success of the coach.

Here's an example: At a recent training session, a future coach presented a challenge with the person she was coaching. She was brand new in the coach role and was just starting leadership coach training. She was assigned to a principal of a school not meeting AYP. The principal had "had it" with her job and wanted out. She wanted to move up to a central office position. The new coach-in-training said to me, "Jobs are tough to come by in this state and she won't get one." Ouch. That new coach isn't likely to help the client obtain a new position if she herself doesn't see it as possible. Coaches believe anything's possible. Shifting to possibility thinking opens up the dialogue and exploration of what is possible and offers hope to the client. Asking empowering questions reveals why the client wants to leave. Is she running away from something or running to something? The new leadership coach had to change first and shift to being more of a possibility thinker to be helpful to the principal. A coach holds the goal of the client as achievable and helps the client design a plan to achieve it.

CAN SUPERVISORS COACH?

People frequently ask me to clarify the leader-as-coach role versus leader-as-supervisor. Is it possible for a principal or other leader to coach the person they supervise? It's a great and important question.

My best answer is, yes and no. Districts need to discuss policies for how they will integrate coaching as a strategy. They need to decide who can and will coach whom. The answer to the question lies there. District leaders need to deeply understand the coaching strategy and process to best design an effective and successful program.

Why Yes?

School leaders can most definitely be an effective coach to someone they supervise when certain conditions are present. When a leader is also the supervisor of the client, it is typically not possible for the relationship to become a 100% pure coach-client relationship, unless there is an agreement that coaching conversations remain confidential and there will be no retaliation based on those conversations. Successful coaching requires both confidentiality and an agreed promise that coaching conversations will not be reflected in the client's supervisory process. If that is not present, a third person can and should be the coach. A district with several trained coaches might wish to consider a model where the client has a choice of coach and the coach-client relationship remains confidential.

Another approach is for leaders to adopt a coaching style of leadership and use it in their daily conversations with the people they supervise. A coaching style of conversation will be open, honest, trusting, and goal oriented. The dialogue would sound like one full of possibility, acknowledgment, and action toward teachers' goals. Teachers and other staff will feel heard and respected for their viewpoints.

Why No?

In a district or environment where trust is not established, or the coaching conversation is not confidential, or there are unclear boundaries between coaching and supervising, coaching by the supervisor-leader should not take place. Because coaching should always be a confidential process, if a principal or other supervisor cannot promise that, he or she should not be the coach. However, someone else can.

So the distinction here is to clarify if a leader provides one-on-one, confidential coaching, and to whom, or instead, can adopt a "coaching style of leadership." A coaching style of leadership is a compromise and represents a shift in the leader's communication style without engaging in a formal coaching relationship. It's a middle ground that I recommend for supervisors and enhances communication, results, and relationships. A coaching approach is one that focuses on achieving professional and personal goals by

- Identifying goals for improvement.
- Identifying action steps.
- Discussing possible obstacles.
- Listening more intently.
- Asking more questions.
- Being nonjudgmental.
- Refraining from telling solutions.

A coaching style of leadership can have a powerful effect on the client and represent more open and accepting conversations, positively affecting the culture of the entire organization, especially when coaching is spread throughout the district.

Best-Case Scenario

Forward-thinking districts who embrace the coaching concept will provide access to several, competent coaches. In the best-case scenario, a district will have several well-trained, confident, experienced coaches available to provide coaching services throughout the district. Coaches aren't assigned, but rather interested clients can access one to choose their best match. Coaches won't be coaching those they supervise. Keeping it clean and clear without obscuring the boundaries between coaching and supervising will ensure success.

CURRENT PROJECTS

There is growing interest in leadership coaching across the country and overseas. In the United States, leadership coaching projects are beginning or under way in Pennsylvania, Virginia, Michigan, Texas, and other states. The challenge for school districts is finding funding and assuring quality, depth, and breadth of training and practical experience.

Overseas, a study by the Australian Department of Education, Science and Training, found that most teacher professional development programs had a fundamental flaw. Few provided coaching and feedback in the workplace for teachers—despite its being essential to learning new skills. According to Graham Hoult (2005), an executive coach in Australia, teachers and administrators are becoming more and more aware of coaching in the workplace. More and more educators have either been coached by a coach or have learned about coaching from a coach. Coaching is being used in a variety of models, including the following:

- External coaches work with administrators, typically regarding leadership issues.
- Networks of schools engage coaches with a range of foci including peer coaching and Cognitive Coaching.

- Principals in different schools coach each other.
- Teachers in schools coach each other in structured programs and informally.
- Educators coach students and parents.

ACHIEVING BALANCE BETWEEN CHALLENGING WORK AND A MEANINGFUL LIFE

A recent coaching client, Janet, contacted me to begin leadership coaching. Initially, she was intrigued by the coaching concept and considered doing her doctoral dissertation on coaching school leaders, and she thought she would experience it herself first. She was a high-level, central office administrator in a large, rapidly growing suburb, toying with the idea of becoming a superintendent in the near future. She was also struggling with how to be a successful leader, while also integrating other parts of life important to her.

Janet arrived at the office early every day and left after almost-daily late meetings. She felt a growing sense of not only frustration but exhaustion. She literally could find no time, morning or evening, to squeeze in a run with her husband, do yoga, or spend time with her family. She was running out of steam and wondered how school leaders can balance it all and be successful.

As we began our coaching relationship, Janet's initial goals were to feel successful as a leader and still have a life she enjoyed. Janet had left her job as principal three years earlier to take on a high-level district position along with a new superintendent she'd known. She felt they could do great things together. Janet had loved her job as principal. She left, initially, to do more, for more people. Three years down the road, the superintendent was let go and things changed. Janet felt a growing sense of discontent.

In our first coaching session, she began to think deeply about the source of her discontent. She noticed she was less happy than in her prior position. (Remember, she contacted me to clarify coaching, not because she initially felt unhappy.) She began to realize a few things that ultimately caused a huge shift in her life:

- She recognized how much she disliked the politics present in the central office.
- She sorely missed the sense of community she felt as a principal.
- She was experiencing the "empty nest" syndrome as her oldest child left home.
- She couldn't find time to do things she loved outside of work.

In our first session together, Janet's tears began flowing as she noticed a connection between the empty nest she was experiencing and how much she missed being in a community at work. It was a profound moment for her and an unexpected one.

Janet began to shift from her initial goal of pursuing a superintendent position to a return to what she loved with a passion—her work as a principal. Our goals for coaching changed too. In the early weeks of our coaching relationship, she considered the option of returning to a principal role. It was almost as if she were in shock and needed some time to carefully and thoughtfully process her thoughts and make this good decision. So, our goals for coaching became as follows:

- Find a position as a principal, with a preference in a struggling school.
- Return to running and yoga.
- Clarify a doctoral dissertation topic.

Week after week I held both her professional and personal goals at the forefront. We collaborated to create time for her workouts and often looked at each day of the week and considered possibilities for fitting them in. Doing so gave her a sense of hope that it is in fact possible for school leaders to have balance in their lives—to feel fulfilled at work and at home. To accomplish that, she had to make specific changes: awaken earlier to hop on the treadmill, carve out time in the evening for yoga, commit to leaving the office at a specified time, learn to say "No" to things that would prohibit her from keeping her coaching commitments.

When Janet made the choice to pursue a principal position, she did so with such clarity that she was offered the first job she applied for, in the school of her choice. She was absolutely clear what she wanted to do and why. She was what I call in coaching *aligned.* Her inner goals and passion were aligned with her work. She made the decision, and the move, with peace, ease, and certainty.

I have yet to work with a school leader in a coaching relationship where we have not integrated goals that would help them enjoy both their professional and personal sides of life. Sometimes they feel torn, feeling an obligation to stay focused only on district issues, but the resulting surge of energy clients feel when including both professional *and* personal goals keeps them in the coaching plan. The desire to focus on some personal development goals assures that coaching meets their needs. Among the personal goals many clients include in their coaching plan are balancing personal life and work, finding time for exercise, developing creative outlets, reducing stress, and living life more joyously.

To be an effective leader takes a great deal of positive energy to create the teams willing to do what it takes to reach their school's or district's goals. One can easily become drained of positive energy and go into neutral or negative. The last thing districts need is a leader reeking of negative energy.

Staying positive can be a monumental challenge that requires daily or hourly attention. Leadership coaches help leaders stay focused on goals with a "can do" attitude, managing any obstacles that emerge. They also help them bring into their lives other things that create happiness for them. It's too easy to let go of things we enjoy and say yes to all the obligations. Most leaders are very responsible and might just be saying yes to too many things, preventing them from doing those activities that energize and fuel them.

In another instance, a superintendent client, weeks into our coaching relationship, brought up how she wished she arrived at work Monday morning happy and full of energy, as did one of the directors. That one comment brought to the surface an issue we hadn't yet discussed—her social life. I cannot underestimate the importance of looking at one's entire life as it relates to one's leadership role. In this particular case, it was after two months of weekly coaching that she decided to pay attention to that part of her life. It is nearly impossible to be the happy, positive energy force an effective leader needs to be and be unhappy or feel numb on the personal side of life. When the client is ready, or when the coach notices what is draining him or her, focusing on one's personal life can be extremely helpful to the leader and his or her ultimate success.

Good coaching takes into consideration individual needs for acquiring behaviors consistent with success for the organization. Coaches see the client as an individual and a member or leader of an organizational team. We see clients as whole, with their work life a part of their entire life. We look at how it all fits together. Leader as workaholic is a recipe for disaster, burn-out, and represents old thinking.

In working with clients, leadership coaches often explore and integrate all parts of their lives that need attention at the time, when clients are willing to address them:

- Work and career
- Family life
- Social life
- Physical environment
- Love and relationships
- Money and finances

While this may appear to be unrelated to a school or district goal, leadership coaches can identify those factors that might be draining the energy from the leader's life. By dealing with them, we help leaders eliminate or reduce the "drains" and free up energy that we can direct toward achieving performance goals.

HOW COACHING SUPPORTS BRAIN FUNCTION AND CREATES LASTING CHANGE

Almost everyone I've ever encountered supports the long-held belief that change is hard, both personal and organizational change. Many educators lament over the challenge of creating change in their school or district.

I bet you can name dozens of change efforts that have come and gone. I bet every New Year's Eve you create a new list of resolutions. It's almost acceptable to go along with the belief that meaningful change is hard to come by.

I say no.

I say change is doable and easier to achieve than we've been led to believe. I believe successful change requires a number of factors:

- Passionate commitment to a goal
- Attention and focus
- A clear picture of the goal, accomplished
- Awareness of limiting beliefs
- A willingness to let go of thoughts and actions that deter from the goal
- Consistent action steps to achieve it
- A team of support
- Challenging one's assumptions

It is crucial that school leaders gain a new perspective on change, and people's capacity to create it. We used to think all it took was motivation, that if people would just fix the broken parts, their attitude and resistance to the change, all would be well.

From recent findings about how our brain works, we now know it takes more than that. It takes new thoughts, focus, and attention on the desired result and action. Our brain can learn anything. We can choose thoughts the same way we choose what to order in a restaurant. Just choose!

Dr. Jeffrey M. Schwartz, neuroscientist and author of *The Mind and the Brain* (2002), conducted studies about people with Obsessive Compulsive Disorder (OCD). People with OCD tend to believe that they can't change their behavior or actions that cause distress in their lives. However, he showed that choices change brain function, that we can actually choose different thoughts, and in doing so, create new pathways in our brain. He also showed that we must act quickly on those thoughts for new behavior to occur.

According to Dr. Schwartz (2002), when our brain is doing the work of creating new circuits, it takes more energy to do that. We go slower and have to expend more energy. It takes focused attention (energy) and action (acts) to create changed behavior. This can appear as defiance or resistance to change efforts.

Coaching works on a brain level, by developing new circuits that help clients stay focused and attentive on the goal. When coaching is self-directed and focused on solutions and results, it works to create the changes the client or organization seeks. More specifically, Dr. Schwartz (2002) identified four main areas of brain function that also serve as a useful explanation of why the coaching process works:

- Attention
- Reflection
- Insight
- Action

Attention

In an article, "The Neuroscience of Leadership," Rock and Schwartz (2006) state the following: "The mental act of focusing attention stabilizes the associated brain circuits. . . . Over time, paying enough attention to any specific brain connection keeps the relevant circuitry open and dynamically alive. . . . The power is in the focus." In other words, what you think about, you create more of. Coaching, as a results- and action-focused process, steers the client to what he or she wants to do or create versus dwelling on the problem. By focusing attention on something new, physical changes in the brain occur. Coaches ask questions to encourage clients to think differently, therefore creating new connections in the brain. Coaches know that focusing on solutions actually creates solutions. Coaching conversations shift the direction away from the problem to ways in which the client can take actions to solve it.

Reflection

Educators know and use reflection techniques as part of good staff development and instruction. The same is true for coaches. We look for and celebrate moments of silence in coaching sessions. We know that when a client gets quiet, he or she is deep in thought. The client has accessed different parts of the brain and becomes more relaxed. He or she moves away from the left, logical-thinking, problem-solving part of the brain to the right side, where emotions, hopes, dreams, and possibilities lie.

Insight

When we acknowledge that there's a problem to be solved between the client and others, or the organization, or that there is a conflict, the first step is awareness. Facial expressions may change to a puzzled look. Coach and client explore, through conversations, the dilemma between what is perceived as a problem and how the client views it. Insights are learning moments and significant moments in coaching. True insights result in a "rush" of energy and readiness for action.

Action

When a moment of insight occurs, action steps must be taken immediately afterward to assure that a new idea or goal becomes real. Too often the excitement fades and no new learning or movement occurs. The coaching process focuses on the client agreeing to take specific actions between each session, assuring that he or she is "doing" something toward the goal. The action steps, according to Dr. Schwartz (2002), cement the new circuits and, over time, cause new habits (and change) to occur.

In *The New Brain: How the Modern Age Is Rewiring Your Mind,* Restak (2003) refutes what we've been led to believe—that multitasking is a beneficial skill. Not so, according to what we have learned about brain function. Doing more than one thing at a time or switching back and forth from one task to another involves time-consuming shifts in brain processing and reduces effectiveness at accomplishing either task. When you try to do two things at once, your attention at any given moment is directed to one activity or the other rather than to both at once. These shifts decrease rather than increase efficiency; they are time and energy depleting.

Brain research supports and validates the work of coaches and explains why coaching is effective. It provides us with a greater understanding of how we learn new behaviors that lead to results. It can help us better understand change management for schools and guide leaders to focus on what they want to create instead of what is wrong.

There is consistency between what coaches guide clients to do and recent findings about the brain. What coaches do actually helps improve the brain function of the client. Coaches partner with clients to help them "see" their thoughts and choose new ones. They work together to maintain their focus on the chosen goals and to take immediate action toward them.

What coaches do when working with clients is precisely what research has shown to be effective in adopting new habits and creating changed behavior and changed results. Leadership coaches help clients notice and shift their thoughts and take new actions toward the achievement of their professional goals. While more specific research is needed in this new area of coaching school leaders, the feedback from science and new revelations on brain function and coaching is promising.

COACHING AS A STRATEGY FOR SUCCESSFUL LEADERSHIP TRANSITIONS

"I will be leaving the district by the end of the school year," says the current superintendent. These words are heard often, too often, and can create havoc, unrest, feelings of stagnation among staff, or cause initiatives to come to a screeching halt. Does this sound familiar? Not only is the cost of searching for a new leader a great one, there is also the cost of lost energy and momentum to be considered. If you were to put a dollar cost on that loss, it would likely be staggering.

A superintendent, principal, or other leader might choose to leave to achieve a new goal. He or she might move to a new location or larger district, creating anxiety, confusion, or stagnation among staff. However, transitions can also be exciting and potentially energize a district. A leadership coach helps a district create a smooth transition between the arrival of a new leader and the departure of a current one. A leadership coach can help a leader orient to a new role seamlessly. An external coach has no personal agenda other than the success of the leader in his or her new role. A coach can help the new leader navigate political issues and can also raise concerns and questions and provide honest, sometimes ruthless feedback.

If an outgoing leader leaves behind an upset, stressed staff, or leaves under difficult circumstances, the incoming leader has cultural issues to manage in addition to the conveyance of his or her future vision. Leadership coaching can better assure that the incoming leader gets off to a good start, building and leading a high-performing collaborative team.

Top leadership change provides a critical and significant shift within a district. Leadership coaching for the incoming leader enables the opportunity for a smooth, positive transition and ultimately the ability to make the impact that is desired.

On the flip side, it is worth considering that leadership coaching can lead to retention of the leader and greater stability for the district. Often leaders decide to leave and escape the difficult challenges they face, when they can constructively deal with them instead by strategizing with a coach. For example, a recent coaching client struggled with the volatile personality of another leader who claimed to "make her life miserable" on a daily basis. Instinct told my client to leave, and she was preparing her resume. However, through our coaching sessions, she began to recognize that she would be running away from the discomfort of conflict. Learning to deal with challenging people and have difficult conversations was part of her learning curve and involved important professional growth for her. She realized that it was her inner lack of confidence to confront the behavior and attempt change that was the culprit. She would likely find challenging behaviors and people in another district too. She decided to stay and do the hard work of personal change in managing difficult people.

In a study of the superintendency (Colorado Association of School Executives, 2003), it was reported that only 29% of superintendents felt they were "somewhat prepared" for the role. Given that the cost of super-intendent searches can range from $5,000 to $100,000, it makes smart sense for districts to protect their investments by providing a coaching strategy that leads to leader retention and success.

SUMMARY

Leadership coaching is an idea whose time has finally come. The benefits of coaching have been well reported and demonstrated among business and nonprofit leaders. School districts, as complex organizations with very challenging goals, benefit by providing and implementing programs for their district leaders that offer one-on-one coaching and means for leaders to adopt a coaching style of leadership.

School systems will be wise to consider providing leaders with both training in coaching skills and the resources to obtain coaching for themselves. Coaching is becoming more common in classrooms and boardrooms. It is a specific skill set, a possibility-thinking mindset, a highly supportive and result-focused relationship, and both an individual and organizational strategy. We are just beginning to witness the results in our schools.

School leaders benefit from both receiving and participating in an individual leadership coaching relationship. They need and welcome the privacy and safety of a confidential, results-focused relationship to better assure their success and that of their school or district. Leaders can also embrace a coaching style of leadership by learning to coach others. Doing so will create a highly positive culture and boost the leaders' skills in creating change and managing resistance among staff and community.

Coaching is all about change, achieving extraordinary results, and accomplishing far-reaching goals. It requires new mindsets and skill sets for school leaders to interact with teachers, students, and the entire school community in a highly positive, productive manner. Recent research about brain function further validates the coaching process. When integrated throughout a system, coaching has the potential to strengthen the professional performance of school leaders, accomplish far-reaching goals, and create lasting change for teachers, students, and communities.

REFERENCES

Colorado Association of School Executives. (2003). *The view from the inside: A candid look at today's school superintendent.* Englewood, CO: Author.

CompassPoint Non-Profit Services. (2003). *Executive coaching project, executive summary.* Retrieved June 18, 2008, from http://www.compasspoint.org/assets/2_cpcoachingexecsumm.pdf

Grossman, R. J. (1999, July 1). Ensuring a fast start. *HR Magazine, 44,* 32.

Hargrove, R. (2000). *Masterful coaching fieldbook.* San Francisco: Jossey-Bass/Pfeiffer.

Hoult, G. (2005). *Investigating the links between teacher professional development and student learning outcomes.* Retrieved October 29, 2007, from http://www.dest.gov.au/sectors/school_education/publications_resources/profiles/teacher_prof_development_student_learning_outcomes.htm

International Coach Federation. (2005). *The ICF code of ethics.* Retrieved June 18, 2008, from http://www.coachfederation.org/ICF/For+Current+Members/Ethical+Guidelines/Code+of+Ethics

Kotter, J. (2000, February 21). So you're a player. Do you need a coach? *Fortune, 141*(4), 144–154.

Manchester, Inc. (2001). Maximizing the impact of executive coaching. *The Manchester Review, 6*(1), 1–9.

Reiss, K. (2006). *Leadership coaching for educators: Bringing out the best in school administrators.* Thousand Oaks, CA: Corwin Press.

Restak, R. (2003). *The new brain: How the modern age is rewiring your mind.* Emmaus, PA: Rodale Press, Inc.

Rock, D., & Schwartz, J. M. (2006). *The neuroscience of leadership.* Retrieved June 20, 2008, from http://www.strategy-business.com/press/freearticle/06207?pg=8

Schwartz, J. M., & Begley, S. (2002). *The mind and the brain.* New York: HarperCollins.

Stanley, A. (2006). *The next generation leader.* New York: Doubleday Religious Publishing Group.

9

Research on Coaching

Jake Cornett and Jim Knight

INTRODUCTION

Educators and policymakers naturally want to know what research says about coaching. Unfortunately, the quickest answer to that question is, not enough. Although we have uncovered more than 200 publications describing some form of research relevant to coaching, most of those studies are preliminary, including some work on instructional coaching conducted at the Center for Research on Learning, and do not meet the standards of rigorous research.

There are at least two reasons why this is the case. First, research on professional learning does not have the same outlets for publication that exist for other forms of educational research. At the time of this writing, for example, there is no *Journal of Research of Professional Learning*, although we hope to see such a publication flourishing in the near future. Second, many forms of coaching are newly developed approaches. These approaches began with people developing theories and practices, conducting exploratory research, and refining those theories and practices through experimentation, implementation, reflection, and revision.

This work, despite some limitations, does shed light on what is being learned about coaching and also suggests where researchers need to study further. Indeed, Jake and I wrote this chapter as an outgrowth of our work writing proposals, because while conducting literature searches, we found (and Jake did the lion's share of this research) that over the past 25 years, many before us, especially Bruce Joyce

---

AUTHORS' NOTE: Cognitive Coaching^{SM} is a service-marked term, but for literary purposes, the service mark will not appear throughout the reminder of this chapter.

and Jenny Edwards, had done a lot of important foundational work studying coaching. We felt this information needed to be summarized and shared. This chapter has become our way of accomplishing that goal.

There is an additional issue that must be surfaced. One major challenge any discussion of coaching research faces is the multiplicity of ways in which the term has been used. In truth, to say that "research shows that coaching works" is a bit like saying "research shows that teaching works." As this book is intended to clarify, there are different ways in which coaching can be implemented in schools and different potential outcomes.

Of course, there are many similarities between the various approaches to coaching, including deep respect for the professionalism of teachers, a partnership orientation, focus on listening before talking, emphasis on dialogical conversation, and recognition of the primacy of student learning. However, there are also differences between the various approaches. Cognitive Coaching[SM] puts thinking at the heart of the coaching relationship. Content coaching emphasizes lesson design and empowering teachers, largely through questioning, to attain a deep, rich understanding of the content they teach. Instructional coaching focuses on providing appropriate, sufficient supports to teachers so that they are able to implement scientifically proven teaching practices. Literacy coaching emphasizes the development of students' reading and writing abilities. Each of these approaches may be more or less appropriate in various scenarios, but clearly they are not synonymous.

When we choose to talk about coaching, we need to understand that what happens when we use one form of coaching isn't necessarily going to occur when we adopt a different approach. For that reason, our chapter describes both some common findings that have implications for all approaches to coaching and more specific findings that relate directly to the four most frequently described approaches to coaching: peer coaching, Cognitive Coaching, literacy coaching, and instructional coaching.

What does the research say about coaching? Is there proof that coaching leads teachers to implement scientifically proven practices? Is there a link between coaching and growth in student achievement? Does coaching have an impact on teacher efficacy? What is coaching? How should it be done? What do teachers think about coaching? Is coaching worth the investment?

Questions like these are suddenly, and rightly, being raised by educators as interest in coaching grows across the nation. This review of the research can only begin to answer some of these questions. Many aspects of coaching are newly developed. Indeed, professional learning in general has only recently received the rigorous scientific study usually reserved for other aspects of school improvement. However, we hope that this review of the current research on coaching will inform conversations around these questions, perhaps moving the conversations to a higher level. We also hope to point the way to areas of research that hold great promise for researchers interested in the scientific study of coaching.

The publications reviewed for this chapter were drawn from a search of ERIC, PsychInfo, and Dissertation Abstracts International (Proquest/UMI) using terms and descriptors of "educational coach/ing," "professional development," "teacher support," "teacher training," "collaborative learning," "instructional coach/ing," "cognitive coach/ing," "peer coach/ing," "literacy coach/ing," and "reading coach/ing."

Since educational coaching is a relatively new field and the *Journal of Research of Professional Development* no longer is published, we expanded our collection of documents by drawing on nontraditional sources of publication and dissemination, including the Literacy Coaching Clearinghouse (www.literacycoachingonline.org), Center for Cognitive Coaching (www.cognitivecoaching.com), University of Kansas Center for Research on Learning Instructional Coaching (www.instructionalcoach.org), and conversations with several leaders in the field, including Bruce Joyce, Director of Booksend Laboratories, and Jenny Edwards of the Center for Cognitive Coaching and the Fielding Graduate University. Also, we examined references cited in other articles on the topic of coaching (i.e., "backwards search" procedures). Ultimately, this document search yielded 254 research articles, books, book chapters, technical reports, position papers, dissertations, and presentations related to coaching or school-based ongoing professional development. We reviewed all 254 documents, and we discuss several of them here.

We did not set out to conduct a meta-analysis of the effects of coaching but rather a narrative review with the purpose of presenting a comprehensive yet reader-friendly discussion in one unified chapter. With that goal in mind, we discuss the following topics: (a) the necessity of coaching, (b) peer coaching research, (c) Cognitive Coaching research, (d) literacy coaching research, (e) instructional coaching research, and (f) conclusions and future directions.

WHY IS COACHING NECESSARY?

School systems introduce coaching programs because they assume that high-quality professional learning that improves teaching practices will increase student achievement. But is this really the case? Two major reports suggest that there is a clear link between teacher quality and student achievement.

Wenglinsky's (2000) analysis of National Assessment of Educational Progress (NAEP) data, summarized in his report, *How Teaching Matters: Bringing the Classroom Back Into Discussions of Teacher Quality*, provides evidence of the importance of professional development for teachers. Wenglinsky studied data gathered from more than 15,000 eighth-grade mathematics and science students to see if teacher inputs (e.g., number of years teaching, academic degree, and similarity between college major and subject being taught), professional development, or classroom practices influenced student performance. Wenglinsky employed multilevel structural equation modeling, a statistical analysis methodology that allowed him to "isolate the influence of any given factor on an outcome, taking into account the other potential influences" (p. 6).

Wenglinsky's (2000) study uncovered that professional development is an important factor in predicting higher student achievement. For example, students in math classes that were taught by teachers who received professional development in working with different student populations outperformed their peers by 107% on the NAEP. In comparison, mathematics students taught by teachers who majored or minored in mathematics, another important factor, outperformed their peers by 39%. These findings support Wenglinsky's claim that "changing the nature of teaching and learning in the classroom may be the most direct way to improve student outcomes" (p. 11).

Further evidence supporting the link between instructional effectiveness and student achievement is provided by Sanders and Rivers' (1996) landmark study of two major Tennessee school districts. Researchers used the Tennessee Value-Added Assessment System (TVAAS) to determine whether teacher effectiveness impacts student achievement. The TVAAS provides individual student data in several disciplines over several years, allowing the long-term impact of effective or ineffective teachers to be measured and evaluated.

To conduct their study, Sanders and Rivers (1996) divided teachers from two large Tennessee districts into five quintiles, with the first quintile (Q1) representing the least effective teachers and the fifth quintile (Q5) representing the most effective teachers. The researchers then reviewed third-, fourth-, and fifth-grade mathematics achievement data on the Tennessee Comprehensive Achievement Test for students who received three consecutive years of instruction from three Q1 teachers—which the authors refer to as Low-Low-Low instruction—and three consecutive years of instruction from three Q5 teachers—referred to as High-High-High instruction.

The findings are, as the authors say, "dramatic" (see Figure 9.1). Students who received three years of instruction from three Q5 teachers (High-High-High) in school district A achieved a mean score of 784.9 (96th percentile), while students who received three years of instruction from three Q1 teachers (Low-Low-Low) received a mean score of 720.2 (44th percentile). Similarly, in school district B, the mean score for High-High-High instruction was 758.9 (83rd percentile), whereas the mean score for Low-Low-Low instruction was 704.4 (29th percentile). In both school systems, students starting at the same level of achievement (50th percentile) three years later had differences in mean percentile achievement scores of more than 50 percentile points. Teacher quality accounted for a 50% spread on

Figure 9.1   Student Tennessee Value-Added Assessment System Score by
Teacher Quintile

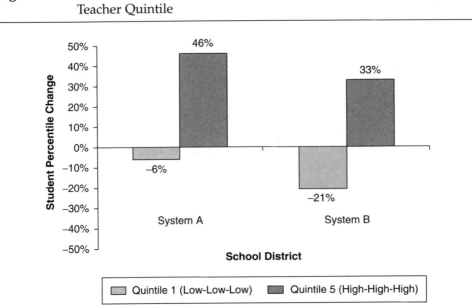

SOURCE: Sanders & Rivers (1996).

student achievement. Differences reported were "very highly significant" (Sanders & Rivers, 1996, p. 3). Commenting on the implications of these findings, the authors conclude that "the single most dominating factor affecting student academic gain is teacher effect" (Sanders & Rivers, 1996, p. 6).

Taken together, the Wenglinsky (2000) and Sanders and Rivers (1996) studies suggest that improving teaching practice is an important way to improve student achievement. Whether or not coaching improves teaching practice is discussed in the remainder of this chapter.

RESEARCH ON THE APPROACHES TO COACHING

Four approaches to educational coaching are most frequently mentioned in the literature: peer coaching, Cognitive Coaching, literacy coaching, and instructional coaching. What follows is a discussion of the research conducted using each of these four coaching models. They are discussed in order from the oldest to the most recent forms of coaching.

Peer Coaching

Does Coaching Increase the Rate and Transfer of New Skills?

Bush (1984) presented findings from a five-year longitudinal study beginning in 1979 and concluding in 1983 focusing on staff development in California. Bush's research team, working in approximately 80 schools spread over 20 districts, examined whether peer coaching increased teachers' implementation of new skills (see Figure 9.2). The research team found that when teachers were given only a description of new instructional skills, only 10% used the skill in the classroom. When each of the next three components of peer coaching—modeling, practice, and feedback—were added to the training, teachers' implementation of the teaching skill increased by 2% to 3% each time a new component was added to the training process. Description, modeling, practice, and feedback resulted in a 16% to 19% transfer of skill to classroom use. However, when coaching was added to the staff development, approximately 95% of the teachers implemented the new skills in their classrooms.

Showers (1982) also found that training followed up with peer coaching was much more effective at enabling teachers' use of new practices than without peer coaching. In an early study of the impact of peer coaching, Showers provided 17 teachers with a workshop on three models of teaching. Then, 9 of the 17 teachers were randomly assigned to work with a coach for six weeks, whereas the other 8 were not coached. Teacher observations revealed that noncoached teachers were much less likely to use the new teaching practices presented at the professional development sessions compared with coached teachers.

Showers (1982) also investigated the scores on recall and essay tests for 256 students taught by the 17 teachers in her study. She found that students of teachers having high implementation rates performed better on recall tests than students of teachers having low implementation rates. These

Figure 9.2 Rate of Transfer Into Classroom Practice Following Peer Coaching Professional Development

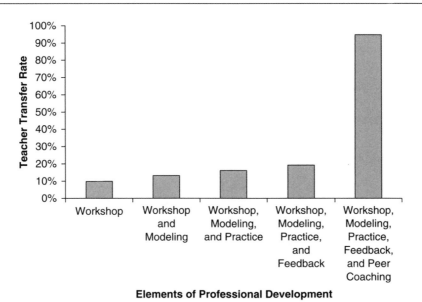

SOURCE: Sanders & Rivers (1996).

findings were significant. There were no significant differences on essay test performance. Further, when closely examining the two groups of teachers at the summation of the study, there were no "high-transfer teachers" in the noncoached group. This study suggests that coaching is prerequisite to high rates of implementation for some new teaching practices.

To better understand the impact of coaching on student achievement, Showers (1984) conducted a follow-up study with 21 teachers and 138 students. Like Showers's earlier study (1982), teachers were randomly assigned to either work with a peer coach or not. After the presentation of a new teaching practice to all three groups, 10 teachers received coaching from six peer coaches, four teachers received partial coaching, and five were not coached. Two important findings emerged. First, coached teachers were more likely than noncoached peers to transfer newly acquired teaching practices into classroom use. Second, coaching contributed significantly to higher student achievement scores as measured by a concept attainment measure.

Truesdale (2003) conducted a 15-week study also examining the transfer of professional development to classroom practice under coached and noncoached conditions. In this study, teachers from two schools attended a workshop. Ten teachers at one school volunteered for coaching, and no teachers at the other school received coaching. Truesdale compared the results of the 10 volunteers (five teams of two peers) at school A and five randomly selected teachers from school B. Truesdale gave the same professional development session to both schools; however, volunteers in school A also received training on how to be peer coaches. Truesdale found that coaching increased transfer of training over 15 weeks. By contrast, teachers in the control condition lost interest in the skills presented at the workshop and stopped using them. Simply put, the traditional workshop without coaching did not have an impact on teachers' practices or interest.

Bush, Showers, and Truesdale's studies suggest that peer coaching supports knowledge transfer, but what about the long-term continued use of new skills following peer coaching? To answer that question, Baker (1983) conducted a six-month follow-up study of Showers's (1982) teacher participants to examine rates of implementation after six months had passed without peer coaching. Baker found that higher rates of implementation and continued use persisted for coached teachers. This was not the case for teachers who did not participate in coaching.

Drawing from these and other randomized control-style studies, Showers (1983) succinctly concluded that 75% of teachers who received peer coaching transferred the skill presented at the initial professional development session to classroom practice and used it with fidelity (see Figure 9.3). In contrast, only 15% of teachers who did not receive coaching implemented the new skill following a professional development session. Further, noncoached teachers delayed initial use of the target skill and could not use the new skill six months after they had learned it.

Figure 9.3   Impact of the Elements of High-Quality Professional Development Upon Implementation Rate

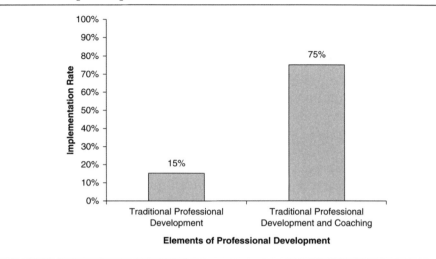

SOURCE: Sanders & Rivers (1996).

The early work in the field conducted on peer coaching by Joyce, Showers, and colleagues (Baker, 1983; Bush, 1984; Joyce & Showers, 1982; Showers, 1982, 1984) laid a sound foundation for future coaching research.

Cognitive Coaching

Since it was first developed in the 1980s, Cognitive Coaching has been the subject of numerous research studies. For this chapter, we reviewed 29 dissertations, 38 articles, 7 books or book chapters, 11 research reports, 19 presentations, and 19 other documents discussing Cognitive Coaching. "The mission of Cognitive Coaching," described in detail in Chapter 4, "is to produce self-directed persons with the cognitive capacity for high performance, both independently and as members of a community" (Costa & Garmston, 2002, p. 16).

In *Cognitive Coaching: A Synthesis of the Research,* Edwards (2008, p. 1) identified nine outcomes that can be expected from Cognitive Coaching: (1) increase in student test scores and "other benefits to students," (2) growth in teacher efficacy, (3) increase in reflective and complex thinking among teachers, (4) increase in teacher satisfaction with career and position, (5) increase in professional climate at schools, (6) increase in teacher collaboration, (7) increase in professional assistance to teachers, (8) increase in personal benefits to teachers, and (9) benefit to people in fields other than teaching. For the purposes of this chapter, Edwards's nine outcomes can be collapsed into impact on students (outcome number 1) and impact on teachers (outcome numbers 2 through 8). Research on the benefits to people in fields other than teaching is not discussed here (outcome number 9). Also, benefits to students that are not academically related is not discussed in this chapter. What follows is a detailed examination of those other benefits expected from Cognitive Coaching.

Impact on Student Achievement

The research examining effects of Cognitive Coaching on students can roughly be split into two categories. First, we discuss research examining the effect of Cognitive Coaching on teacher-student interactions, and second, we discuss research examining how Cognitive Coaching affects student achievement. "The ultimate goal of teacher education projects is to facilitate student learning. The effect, however, is indirect, amenable to multiple influences, and likely to be seen over time rather than immediately" (Hull, Edwards, Rogers, & Swords, 1998, p. 268). Teachers who volunteered to participate in the Pleasant View Project received training on nonverbal classroom management and Cognitive Coaching over a three-year period. A matched control group of teachers did not receive training on either. Examining change in student achievement scores on the Iowa Test of Basic Skills (ITBS) over the three-year period, Edwards and colleagues (Hull et al., 1998) found growth in mathematics, writing, and total ITBS scores in both groups. They reported that the growth of students whose teachers received Cognitive Coaching and nonverbal classroom management training was larger than that of the students of matched control group teachers. These findings do not represent statistically significant differences.

Rennick (2002) examined literacy achievement of kindergarteners whose teachers participated in one of three professional development programs. The district staff developer provided (1) balanced literacy training utilizing Cognitive Coaching to 21 kindergarten teachers, (2) two-week long orientations on balanced literacy to 12 teachers, or (3) no training at all to 40 kindergarten teachers. In this quasi-experimental design, Rennick did not randomly assign or randomly select participants. Rennick used a battery of assessments to examine student reading and writing. When comparing results of students, he found significant increases in academic achievement among students whose teachers were coached when compared to students of teachers from either of the other two groups. Due to the nonrandomized quasi-experimental design of this dissertation study and the differences in the amount of time devoted to the two types of professional development, we cannot infer that these differences were due entirely to Cognitive Coaching.

Slinger (2004), in her dissertation, examined the impact of Cognitive Coaching on student literacy scores among first graders whose teachers had been coached or not. Slinger used a concurrent nested model research design to collect both qualitative and quantitative data simultaneously. Five teachers responsible for 73 students volunteered to be coached. Slinger matched five teachers to act as a control group based upon three hierarchical criteria: (1) similar student academic profiles, (2) years of teaching experience, and (3) gender. Teachers in the control group were responsible for slightly fewer students. Teachers reported general growth as a result of Cognitive Coaching. Yet, upon analysis of data from students taught by both groups of teachers, Cognitive Coaching did not result in any statistically significant difference. However, Slinger did report findings of "overwhelmingly positive qualitative data" from teachers that participated in Cognitive Coaching (Slinger, 2004, p. 173). Specifically, three outcomes were suggested: (1) change in focus from procedural to instructional, (2) increase in communication of teachers toward the specific, and (3) positive reaction to Cognitive Coaching as a form of professional development.

In another study, Hull et al. (1998) reported the impact of Cognitive Coaching on students with special education needs. Although finding the effects of Cognitive Coaching on students in need of a special education was an incidental result discovered through interviews, the researchers reported statistically significant reductions in the number of students referred to special education by teachers who received three years of training in Cognitive Coaching and nonverbal classroom management. The cause of the reduction in referrals is unclear. It may be due to (a) changes in cognitive processes and perception as a result of Cognitive Coaching, (b) better classroom management for difficult students therefore decreasing the number of erroneous referrals, or (c) some combination of the two previous reasons. However, this finding is promising and merits more research.

As with other models of coaching, randomized, experimental studies of the impact of Cognitive Coaching on student achievement are needed to show a clear link between the two. We offer this observation not criticizing past research but suggesting a direction for future methodological decision making.

Impact on Teachers

Researchers (Alseike, 1997; Edwards & Newton, 1995; Hull et al., 1998; Krpan, 1997; Smith, 1997) examining the impact of Cognitive Coaching have reported increases in teacher efficacy as a result of coaching, being coached, and reciprocal coaching. Edwards and Newton (1995) and Edwards, Green, Lyons, Rogers, and Swords (1998) used the Teacher Efficacy Scale developed by Gibson and Dembo (1984) as the primary measure of increased efficacy of the teacher. Various researchers have proposed alternative meanings for what the two subscales of the Teacher Efficacy Scale measure, and there is considerable debate over the construct dimensions of the scale (Coladarci & Breton, 1997; Guskey & Passaro, 1994; Rich, Lev, & Fisher, 1996; Saklofske, Michayluk, & Randhawa, 1988; Woolfolk & Hoy, 1990). This problematic measure may not actually have measured teacher efficacy. Although this debate is outside the scope of this chapter, we turn to more recent research using a researcher-developed survey.

Alseike (1997) developed a survey to assess teacher efficacy, among other things. Comparing 121 teachers who received Cognitive Coaching to 136 teachers who did not, Alseike reported that those teachers who participated in coaching scored significantly above average on the dimension of efficacy. In discussing the findings, Alseike suggested that "cognitively coached teachers are more efficacious and interdependent than teachers who have not had Cognitive Coaching" (p. 124). The survey response rate was low at only 56% on the questionnaire portion.

Edwards and colleagues have found that teachers self-report increases in their job and career satisfaction following training in and use of Cognitive Coaching (Edwards, Green, Lyons, et al., 1998; Edwards & Newton, 1995). Further, teachers who were supervised using Cognitive Coaching judged their experience significantly more positively than teachers supervised through traditional supervision techniques (Edwards, 1993; Mackie, 1998).

Working in a Jewish day school in New Jersey, Moche compared three forms of professional development on teachers' reflective thinking (1999, 2000/2001). Teacher reflective thinking was measured using the Reflective Pedagogical Thinking Instrument (Simmons, Sparks, Starko, Pasch, & Colton, 1989). Eleven teachers received the traditional form of professional development in addition to Cognitive Coaching; 10 teachers served as a time control group, thus receiving traditional professional development along with informal discussions about their teaching; the third control group of 11 teachers received traditional professional development, which consisted of supervision and traditional workshops. Moche found that members of the treatment group who received Cognitive Coaching showed significant growth (gain of 1.64) in reflective thinking over the traditional supervision group (gain of .64) and traditional plus discussion group (gain of .30).

Moche's findings suggest that Cognitive Coaching increases teacher reflection. Yet, when Edwards (1993) examined reflective thinking and conceptual development of first-year teachers, she did not find a significant difference between first-year teachers who received Cognitive Coaching and those who did not. Other researchers have found increased teacher reflection in connection with participating in Cognitive Coaching (Alseike, 1997; Edwards & Green, 1999a; Edwards & Newton, 1995; Krpan, 1997; Slinger, 2004; Smith, 1997). More research on this aspect of Cognitive Coaching would be very helpful. For example, does Cognitive Coaching have more impact on experienced teachers than first-year teachers? Also, if Cognitive Coaching increases reflective thought, does this change in cognitive process translate into consistent and reliable changes in teaching practice that benefit students academically or otherwise? Does it increase the efficaciousness of teachers?

Recently, Aldrich (2005) examined Cognitive Coaching in online environments, concluding that quality Cognitive Coaching occurring online is both feasible and sometimes advantageous. Noting value in text-based communication, Aldrich reported that meaning is often more transparent when using tools such as chat and e-mail. Further, the ability to archive past communications and refer back at a later date was very valuable for some teachers. Using this process may reduce time demands and distance barriers and overall may be a new direction for Cognitive Coaching.

Conclusions on the Cognitive Coaching Research

After carefully studying the Cognitive Coaching literature, we believe that the studies included in this review offer evidence of positive outcomes and experiences as a result of Cognitive Coaching. Yet, rigorous means of investigation are largely missing. Few findings rest on experimental methodologies; too many rely on self-reported data or measures that have not been adequately validated. We are well aware of the difficulty of conducting scientific research in schools; each school has a unique culture, competing initiative, and its own idiosyncrasies. Although rich descriptions of experiences had by those involved in Cognitive Coaching are repeatedly documented through qualitative research, further studies determining when Cognitive Coaching is most effective and what impact Cognitive Coaching has on student achievement, teacher knowledge, and student and teacher behavior will significantly extend our understanding of Cognitive Coaching. This could be said for all of the various models of coaching.

Literacy Coaching

In 2004, the International Reading Association adopted Dole's (2004) definition of a literacy coach as anyone who "supports teachers in their daily work" (p. 462). Using this definition, coaching could involve an array of behaviors and practices, including modeling, book studies, informal conversations, examination of high-stakes exam data, material orders for classroom libraries, and so forth. Thus, one major difference between literacy coaching and other approaches to coaching discussed in this chapter is that it is not defined by a set of common core duties, a theory, or the manner in which coaches perform their jobs. Rather, the term *literacy coach* is used loosely to describe anyone who supports teachers with the goal of increasing literacy.

This all-encompassing definition means that literacy coaching may look vastly different from one location to another. In 2007, the Northwest Regional Education Lab published a report on Reading First literacy coaches. The same conclusions were reached: "Simply knowing that literacy coaches are in schools does not imply anything about how those individuals spend their time—there is a difference between being a coach and *doing coaching*" (Duessen, Coskie, Robinson, & Autio, 2007, p. iii). The authors added that, "Not only do coaches have many responsibilities, but the term 'coach' is used to describe many different configurations: full-time coaches to a single building, full-time coaches responsible for two or more buildings, part time coaches (especially in small schools), and teachers who provide part-time peer coaching to their colleagues" (Duessen et al., 2007, p. 6). These findings are very important given that an estimated 5,600 literacy coaches have been hired through the Reading First funding (Deussen & Buly, 2006).

The research cited in support of literacy coaching heavily relies on the research conducted on other models of coaching, namely, Cognitive Coaching, peer coaching, and instructional coaching (Buly, Coskie, Robinson, & Egawa, 2006; Duessen & Buly, 2006; Duessen et al., 2007). More research on literacy coaching is needed (Buly et al., 2006; Duessen et al., 2007; Greene, 2004; International Reading Association, 2004; Lewis et al., 2007; Poglinco, Bach, Hovde, Rosenblum, Saunders, & Supovitz, 2003).We did not find published, randomized-control-style studies of the effectiveness of literacy coaching on teacher behavior or student academic achievement, but several promising reports on the effectiveness of literacy coaching have been published and several studies are under way. For example, The Learning Network (2006) reported findings from Battle Creek, Michigan. The Learning Network training program includes "teacher leaders" who act in much the same way as literacy coaches. Although no control group was present, there is continual growth over a five-year period, as measured by fourth-grade reading scores on the Michigan Educational Assessment Program Test (MEAP). The number of students in fourth grade exceeding or meeting expectations (Level 1 and 2 on the MEAP) increased from 29% in 1999 to 86% in 2004 (see Figure 9.4). Due to the methodologies used, we cannot be sure this change was due in part, or at all, to literacy coaching activities.

The *Reading First Impact Study: Interim Report* (Gamse, Bloom, Kemple, & Jacob, 2008) was commissioned by Congress to evaluate the effectiveness of

Figure 9.4   Fourth Graders Exceeding or Meeting Michigan Educational Assessment Program Test Reading Score Goals

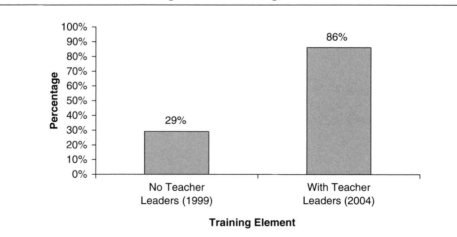

SOURCE: The Learning Network (2006).

the Reading First program. Reading First funding could be used for reading curricula and materials, professional development and coaching, and diagnosis and prevention. Gamse et al. (2008) employed a regression discontinuity design that relied on the process by which school districts allocated Reading First funding to select participating schools for this evaluation. The authors describe this research design as "the strongest quasi-experimental method that exists for estimating program impact" and state that this design can "produce unbiased estimates of program impacts" (p. x). Examining 238 schools in 17 districts and one state Reading First program, the authors report findings from three primary outcomes. Since literacy coaches are commonly hired using Reading First funding, we report some of the findings from this report. Gamse et al. reported increases in "highly explicit instruction" in Grade 1 (3.56%) and Grade 2 (6.98%) as well as increases in time spent teaching reading by first-grade teachers (8.56%) and second-grade teachers (12.09%). Although time spent by teachers in "high quality student practice" increased by 3.67%, the percentage of "students engaged with print" decreased by 8.42%. All of these estimated changes were significant. However, we must note that this report has been criticized heavily by leaders in literacy education such as Reid Lyon (Shaughnessy, 2008), and the results reported are not due entirely to literacy coaching, as this is only one possible way for schools to use Reading First funding.

Further study of the effects of literacy coaching is needed. Especially needed is investigation of these effects using research design and methodology that can infer causal relationships between receiving literacy coaching and changes in teacher practices and student academic achievement.

Instructional Coaching

The instructional coaching model developed at the University of Kansas Center for Research on Learning, by one of the authors of this chapter (Knight, 2007), was derived from several activities, including (a) the development and study of the theoretical framework for this approach to instructional coaching, (b) a teacher survey on modeling, (c) teacher interviews, (d) a study of teacher implementation, and (e) the iterative development of the instructional coaching model over seven years.

This work provides a point of departure for the development of instructional coaching; however, the informal and quasi-experimental methodologies employed in these studies, though appropriate during the development of a new model, have limitations with respect to generalization of the results to practices in schools. Thus, we are at the starting point for research on instructional coaching, not the end. The results for each study are described in the following section.

Development and Study of the Theoretical Framework

The "partnership approach" (Knight, 2007), which is the theoretical framework for the instructional coaching model discussed here, is grounded in the work of authors in many disciplines (including adult education, business, psychology, philosophy of science, and cultural anthropology) who write about knowledge transfer, knowledge development, and human interaction. The ideas of Paulo Freire (1970), Riane Eisler (1988), Michael Fullan (1993), Peter Block (1993), Peter Senge (1990), Richard J. Bernstein (1983), William Isaacs (1999), and others were synthesized into seven principles: equality, choice, voice, dialogue, reflection, praxis, and reciprocity.

For the initial study of this theoretical framework (Knight, 1998), 73 teachers were trained in visual imagery and self-questioning reading strategies, through two different approaches to professional development: a partnership approach and a traditional approach. Each teacher received training on both reading strategies (visual imagery and self-questioning), and each teacher was trained using both approaches (partnership and traditional). Using a counterbalanced research design, one half of the teachers learned self-questioning via the partnership approach and visual imagery via the traditional approach, while the second group learned self-questioning via the traditional approach and visual imagery via the partnership approach.

Knight (1998) used a 7-point Likert-type scale to measure engagement, feelings toward the training session, and expected implementation. Knowledge of content presented in the training was assessed using a researcher-developed knowledge test of critical information presented during the professional development. The results showed statistically significant differences between the partnership and traditional approaches when compared. These results suggested that when teachers participated in training that employed the partnership approach, they were more likely to be engaged, enjoy the session, remember the content of the training, and plan to implement the content they learned.

Impacts on Teachers

Modeling is one critical element of instructional coaching. To assess the affects of modeling, in the fall of 2003–2004, we surveyed 107 secondary teachers from the Topeka, Kansas, school district, who had viewed a model lesson from an instructional coach the previous year. The survey was an informal measure, containing 10 items addressing five questions, with a Likert-type scale from 1 signifying *strongly disagree* to 7 signifying *strongly agree*. The results, summarized in Table 9.1, suggest that the teachers believed they benefited from observing an instructional coach model in their classroom.

During academic year 2003–2004, 13 ethnographic interviews (Fontana & Frey, 1994) were conducted with teachers who had collaborated with an instructional coach at a middle school. In each of the 13 interviews, teachers stated that the model lessons were an essential part of the coaching process. One teacher in the study said, "I think it was very important

Table 9.1   Teacher Survey on Modeling Results

Question	Mean Score
Do teachers perceive that model lessons provided by instructional coaches have increased their fidelity to research-based teaching practices?	6.40
Do teachers perceive that instructional coaches have enough content knowledge to teach all lessons in the collaborating teachers' class?	3.18
Do teachers perceive that model lessons provided by instructional coaches have increased their confidence with respect to implementing teaching practices?	6.22
Do teachers perceive that model lessons provided by instructional coaches have made it easier for them to implement teaching practices?	6.51
Do teachers perceive that model lessons provided by instructional coaches have enabled them to learn additional teaching practices?	6.13

SOURCE: Knight (2007), p. 118.

for her to come in and model it. I think the value of actually seeing it happen is you get to see how it works and how she interacts with certain kids that are real problems. . . . It also instills confidence in myself. If we had just sat down and talked, I might have understood that, but seeing it in practice is a whole different thing. I think her value to me has been immense. I probably would have sunk without her" (Knight, 2007, p. 117).

During the summer of 2004, 82 teachers in the Topeka, Kansas, school district attended summer workshops on teaching practices developed at the University of Kansas Center for Research on Learning. Each of these teachers had instructional coaches in their schools to provide additional support for implementation of the newly learned teaching practices. In October 2004, instructional coaches conducted classroom visits to assess if the 82 teachers who attended the summer professional development session and received instructional coaching continued to use the new teaching practices. The coaches reported that 70 out of the 82 teachers who received coaching were implementing practices they had learned during the summer professional development session. Although there was no control group present for this study, 85% of teachers were implementing the new teaching practices into their classroom use. If we compare the 85% (Knight, 2007) to the rate of implementation that Showers (1983) reported following high-quality professional development without coaching, this represents a 70% increase in teacher implementation (see Figure 9.5).

Figure 9.5   Percent of New Teachers Implementing New Skills

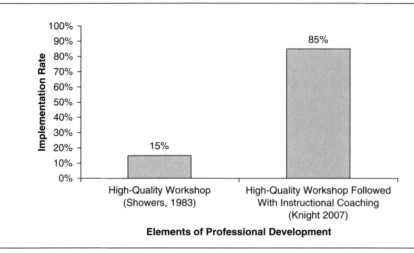

SOURCE: Knight (2007), p. 3.

Conclusions on the Instructional Coaching Research

Several activities have been conducted each year between 1999 and 2008 with the instructional coaches in the Topeka school district. First, all coaches have participated in frequent, extended, ethnographic interviews. Second, the project director conducted an ongoing literature search in areas relevant to coaching, including theory of change (Hall & Hord, 2005; Prochaska, Norcross, & DiClemente, 1994), interpersonal communication (Gottman, 2001; Scott, 2002; Stone, Patton, & Heen, 1999), nonverbal communication (Ekman, 2003), and negotiation (Fisher & Shapiro, 2005; Fisher, Ury, & Patton, 1991). Third, data gathered from the interviews and the literature search were used to modify and improve the instructional coaching model. Finally, the modified coaching methods were presented to coaches who in turn integrated them into their teaching practices. The approach to instructional coaching that grew out of this process was ultimately described in *Instructional Coaching: A Partnership Approach to Improving Instruction* (Knight, 2007).

The research conducted on instructional coaching, in particular the studies of implementation and teacher attitudes toward coaching, need further study. The implementation study, for example, contains only self-reported data, and there is no externally obtained reliable data to show whether teachers were actually doing what they reported. Also, the 10-item survey was informal, and thus not validated. As with most of the approaches to coaching discussed in this chapter, randomized experimental studies on instructional coaching will greatly enhance our understanding of the impact of the instructional coaching approach. Perhaps most importantly, more research on the impact of instructional coaching on student achievement is needed; this is a question currently being investigated.

CONCLUSIONS AND FUTURE DIRECTIONS FOR RESEARCH

Many approaches to coaching are relatively new. Consequently, much of the research conducted to date has been exploratory process and development, lacking the rigor of true scientific study. This is understandable. Since the various coaching models were in the early stages of development, their creators were mostly concerned with improving coaching methods through (a) coach and teacher feedback (e.g., through interviews and surveys), (b) quick informal data gathering, and (c) integration and testing of ideas presented in the literature on coaching and related fields.

This means that we must be cautious when we generalize from the research that has been conducted to date. What we know about coaching (like much of what we know about education) is much less than what we need to learn. For that reason, this chapter concludes with a discussion of topics we think researchers should consider.

What We Know

Coaching Impacts Teacher Attitudes

Research conducted by Edwards and colleagues shows increases in teachers' attitudes toward their job satisfaction over time (Edwards, Green, Lyons, et al., 1998) and in comparison to teachers who did not receive Cognitive Coaching (Edwards & Newton, 1995; Hull et al., 1998). It is unclear, however, if these impacts are unique to Cognitive Coaching, generalizable to other types of coaching, or even more broadly a response to receiving professional support taking any form.

Coaching Impacts Teaching Practices

The findings of Bush, Showers, Joyce, and others (Bush, 1984; Joyce & Showers, 1982; Showers, 1982, 1984; Showers, Joyce, & Bennett, 1987), combined with the findings from instructional coaches' reports on implementation rates (Knight, 2007), suggest that coaching increases implementation, or as it is known in the literature, skill transfer. A second conclusion to be drawn from the studies reviewed is that one-shot professional development without coaching follow-up does not lead to wide implementation. There may be approaches to professional development that are more effective than coaching, but a workshop without follow-up, the research clearly shows, is not one of them.

Coaching Impacts Teacher Efficacy

The many studies of Cognitive Coaching, and in particular the efforts of Edwards and colleagues (Edwards & Green, 1999a, 1999b; Edwards, Green, & Lyons, 1998; Edwards, Green, Lyons, et al., 1998; Edwards &

Newton, 1995; Hull et al., 1998), suggest that Cognitive Coaching positively increases teacher efficacy, although some have debated the construct dimension of the primary assessment tool employed during Cognitive Coaching research that examined teacher efficacy (Coladarci & Breton, 1997; Guskey & Passaro, 1994; Rich et al., 1996; Saklofske et al., 1988; Soodak & Podell, 1993; Woolfolk & Hoy, 1990). However, the sheer volume of studies showing an impact on teacher efficacy is impressive and persuasive.

Coaching Impacts Student Achievement

Wenglinsky's (2000) and Sanders and Rivers' (1996) research suggests that teacher quality is one of the most important variables (if not *the* most important variable) affecting student achievement. Also, several of the studies discussed in this chapter suggest that coaches do increase teachers' transfer of skills. In coaching research, the "missing link" is the studies that clearly show that coaching improves the specific teaching practices that increase student achievement.

What We Need to Know

Taking note of the numerous topics researchers could study in the field of coaching, and after reviewing more than 250 documents for this chapter, we have identified four major questions that seem to be particularly important for further study. We suspect that many of the answers to these questions are different, depending on which approach to coaching is being studied.

What Support Systems Should Be in Place for Coaching to Flourish?

The experiences of educators across the nation provide ample evidence that all educational systems are not created equal when it comes to supporting coaching. Researchers can provide a great service by identifying the systemic supports that are most important. In particular, we need to learn more about how administrators support coaches. Answers to the following questions would be especially helpful: What are the benefits when principals (a) meet and collaboratively plan with coaches, (b) participate in professional development, (c) attend and ideally cofacilitate workshops? Which approaches to instructional leadership are most effective for supporting coaches, and what specific actions can principals take to accelerate instructional learning in schools? What can superintendents do to support coaching?

We also need to know more about the specific professional learning that supports coaching, for both coaches and administrators. What kinds of professional learning do coaches need and how frequently do they need it? Who coaches the coaches? What professional learning do principals and other administrators need? Who coaches administrators? Simply put, what do coaches, administrators, and others in an educational system need to know, and what is the best way for them to learn it?

Researchers can also move the field forward by identifying ways in which organizations can support or impede the growth of professional learning. Rosenholtz (1991) has written about the importance of "learning-enriched cultures," but what can leaders do to encourage the development of such cultures in support of professional learning? Researchers should also identify specific accelerators or decelerators for professional learning. For example, when does the number of innovations being introduced into a system inhibit overall growth in the system? How can educational systems and teachers' unions work together to support coaching? What types of scheduling best facilitate opportunities for collaboration? How do professional learning communities support coaching, and how can coaches support professional learning communities?

Finally, there are a number of important questions related to evaluation and development of coaches. Coaches are a unique species in most schools, and appropriate methods of evaluation need to be developed, validated, and used. We believe any evaluation method must be valid and reliable. Some factors researchers might consider for evaluation could be whether coaches know (a) the practices they are sharing, (b) how to enact the approach to coaching they are employing, and (c) how to organize and use their time for maximum efficiency.

What Are Best Practices for Coaches?

A great deal has been written about the process of coaching, and indeed, about the entire process of relationship building. Cognitive Coaching and content coaching, for example, include excellent questioning strategies, and differentiated coaching provides coaches with a methodology for understanding and responding appropriately to others' learning styles. Researchers such as Gottman (2001) and Ekman (2003) describe excellent strategies that coaches can use to communicate better. Nevertheless, we can learn a great deal more if other aspects of coaching receive further study. A primary goal of research should be to identify the most effective *and* efficient ways to promote high-quality learning among professionals. Thus, we need to determine which kinds of learning require one-to-one interaction, and which kinds of learning can occur in small or large groups. Similarly, we need to determine when it is essential that coaches model in teachers' classrooms and what effective modeling looks like.

Additionally, researchers can promote growth among the coaching literature by identifying best practices for enrolling teachers in the coaching process and how frequently teachers and coaches should meet once coaching has begun. Researchers can also provide an excellent service by describing how coaches and teachers should identify starting points for coaching and how frequently and how often coaches and teachers should meet. The development and validation of tools coaches can use for gathering data, communicating with teachers, and accelerating professional learning would be very beneficial.

On Which Teaching Practices Should Coaches Focus?

When educators consider the teaching practices coaches could share, they should be forgiven if they are overwhelmed. Among practices coaches might share are literacy strategies; reading strategies; differentiation techniques; The Big Four of classroom management, content, instruction, and assessment for learning; curriculum, lesson planning, and mapping; questioning techniques; hands-on teaching; inclusive teaching practices; cooperative learning; project-based learning; colleague collaboration tools; rapport building; and communication techniques—the possibilities are endless.

Researchers can provide an important service by helping educators sort through this jungle of interventions and identify which teaching practices are most likely to improve student achievement in which situations. Coaches cannot do everything, and teachers cannot learn everything. For that reason, we need educational scientists to help us identify which practices are best bets for improving student achievement in which situations.

What Impact Does Coaching Have on Student Achievement?

For some, this is the only research question that matters. We understand, and applaud, the primacy of student achievement as *the* goal for professional learning—if this doesn't improve student learning, why would we do it?—but we would also offer some cautions. Coaching is one component of professional learning as it occurs in a system, and any evaluation of the impact coaching has on students also needs to evaluate other integral aspects of professional learning.

Guskey (2000) provides a model for evaluating five levels of professional learning. Level 1 assesses teachers' responses to all professional development activities. Level 2 assess teachers' knowledge of interventions. Level 3 assesses each school's capacity to support professional development. Level 4 assesses whether teachers are implementing teaching practices. Level 5 assesses the impact on student achievement.

Guskey's (2000) model highlights an important consideration for those who are intent on evaluating coaching. Undeniably, student achievement should be the most important concern of any assessment model. However, if program evaluation is based solely on achievement without considering the other levels of evaluation, teachers run the risk of abandoning programs that are exactly what their students need. If student achievement does not go up when a new approach is introduced, the reason may be that teachers didn't implement the program, that school structures stood in the way of implementation, or that the teachers did not have enough time or support to thoroughly learn or implement the program. Only when all five levels are attended to can evaluators know precisely which aspects of a program are working or are in need of improvement.

Researchers, then, can help educators in at least two ways. First, they can develop program evaluation tools that can be used to monitor growth and development in the five dimensions. Additionally, by highlighting coaching programs that are successful in all five dimensions, researchers can point the way for all educators and researchers as we continue the challenging and important work of providing all students with learning experiences that help them identify and achieve meaningful goals in their lives.

FINAL THOUGHTS

Like much in education, and life for that matter, what we know for certain about coaching is much less than what we would like to know. However, a great deal of preliminary work has been completed. This body of preliminary work suggests that coaching is a promising approach for accelerating professional learning in schools. The work of researchers mentioned here has laid a foundation for our understanding of what coaching can be, and it has provided a road map for future research on coaching.

Few tasks are more challenging than trying to lead professional learning across an educational system, whether a school, a district, a state, or a nation. Change is almost always unpredictable, and frequently educators are frustrated by the slow pace of school improvement efforts. There are no silver bullets in education, and we feel confident in predicting that there never will be. However, research that gives coaches and other educational leaders more proven tools for moving schools forward renders an extremely important service. We are grateful to the researchers we have mentioned in this chapter for the pioneering work they have conducted. Thanks to their work, we can be better informed as we tackle the very challenging and important work of leading professional learning in schools.

REFERENCES

Aldrich, R. S. (2005). Cognitive coaching practice in online environments. *Dissertations Abstracts International, 66*(12), 4358A. (University Microfilms No. 3197394)

Alseike, B. U. (1997). Cognitive coaching: Its influence on teachers. *Dissertations Abstracts International, 58*(8), 2911. (University Microfilms No. 9804083)

Baker, R. G. (1983). The contribution of coaching to transfer of training: An extension study. *Dissertation Abstracts International, 44*(11), 3260. (University Microfilms No. 8403713)

Bernstein, R. J. (1983). *Beyond objectivism and relativism: Science, hermeneutics, and praxis.* Philadelphia: University of Pennsylvania Press.

Block, P. (1993). *Stewardship: Choosing service over self-interest.* San Francisco: Berrett-Koehler.

Buly, M. R., Coskie, T., Robinson, L., & Egawa, K. (2006). Literacy coaching: Coming out of the corner. *Voices from the Middle, 13,* 24–28.

Bush, R. N. (1984). *Effective staff development. In making our schools more effective: Proceedings of three state conferences.* San Francisco: Far West Laboratories.

Coladarci, T., & Breton, W. A. (1997). Teacher efficacy, supervision and the special education resource-room teacher. *Journal of Educational Research, 90,* 230–239.

Costa, A., & Garmston, R. (2002). *Cognitive coaching: A foundation for renaissance schools.* Norwood, MA: Christopher-Gordon Publishers.

Dole, J. A. (2004). The changing role of the reading specialist in school reform. *The Reading Teacher, 57,* 462–471.

Duessen, T., & Buly, M. R. (2006). Connecting coaching and improved literacy. *Northwest Education, 12,* 43–45.

Duessen, T., Coskie, T., Robinson, L., & Autio, E. (2007). *"Coach" can mean many things: Five categories of literacy coaches in Reading First* (Issues & Answers Report, REL 2007-No. 005). Washington, DC: U.S. Department of Education, Institute of Education Sciences, National Center for Education Evaluation and Regional Assistance, Regional Educational Laboratory Northwest.

Ekman, P. (2003). *Emotions revealed: Recognizing faces and feelings to improve communication and emotional life.* New York: Times Books.

Edwards, J. L. (1993). The effect of cognitive coaching on the conceptual development and reflective thinking of first-year teachers. *Dissertation Abstracts International, 54*(3), 895. (University Microfilms No. 9320751)

Edwards, J. L. (2008). *Cognitive coaching: A synthesis of the research.* Highlands Ranch, CO: Center for Cognitive Coaching.

Edwards, J. L., & Green, K. E. (1999a, April). *Growth in coaching skills over a three-year period: Progress toward mastery.* Paper presented at the annual meeting of the American Educational Research Association, Montreal, Canada.

Edwards, J. L., & Green, K. E. (1999b, April). *Persisters versus nonpersisters: Characteristics of teachers who stay in a professional development program.* Paper presented at the annual meeting of the American Educational Research Association, Montreal, Canada.

Edwards, J. L., Green, K. E., & Lyons, C. A. (1998, April). *Personal empowerment, efficacy, and environmental characteristics.* Paper presented at the annual meeting of the American Educational Research Association, San Diego, CA.

Edwards, J. L., Green, K. E., Lyons, C. A., Rogers, M. S., & Swords, M. E. (1998, April). *The effects of cognitive coaching and nonverbal classroom management on teacher efficacy and perceptions of school culture.* Paper presented at the annual meeting of the American Educational Research Association, San Diego, CA.

Edwards, J. L., & Newton, R. R. (1995, April). *The effect of cognitive coaching on teacher efficacy and empowerment.* Paper presented at the annual meeting of the American Educational Research Association, San Francisco.

Eisler, R. (1988). *Chalice and the blade: Our history, our future.* New York: HarperCollins.

Ekman, P. (2003). *Emotions revealed: Recognizing faces and feelings to improve communication and emotional life.* New York: Henry Holt.

Fisher, R., & Shapiro, D. (2005). *Beyond reason: Using emotions as you negotiate.* New York: Viking Press.

Fisher, R., Ury, W., & Patton, B. (1991). *Getting to yes: Negotiating agreement without giving in* (2nd ed.). New York: Penguin.

Freire, P. (1970). *Pedagogy of the oppressed.* New York: Continuum.

Fontana, A., & Frey, J. H. (1994). Interviewing: The art of science. In N. Denzin & Y. Lincoln (Eds.), *Handbook of qualitative research* (pp. 361–377). London: Sage.

Fullan, M. (1993). *Change forces: Probing the depths of educational reform.* New York: Falmer Press.

Gamse, B. C., Bloom, H. S., Kemple, J. J., & Jacob, R. T. (2008). *Reading First Impact Study: Interim report* (NCEE 2008–4016). Washington, DC: National Center for Education Evaluation and Regional Assistance, Institute of Education Sciences, U.S. Department of Education.

Gibson, S., & Dembo, M. H. (1984). Teacher efficacy: A construct validation. *Journal of Educational Psychology, 76,* 569–582.

Gottman, J. M. (2001). *The relationship cure: A five-step guide for building better connections with family, friends, and lovers.* New York: Crown.

Greene, T. (2004). *Literature review for school-based staff developers and coaches.* Oxford, OH: National Staff Development Council.

Guskey, T. R. (2000). *Evaluating professional development.* Thousand Oaks, CA: Corwin Press.

Guskey, T. R., & Passaro, P. D. (1994). Teacher efficacy: A study of construct dimensions. *American Educational Research Journal, 31,* 627–643.

Hall, G. E., & Hord, S. M. (2005). *Implementing change: Patterns, principles, and potholes.* Boston: Allyn & Bacon.

Hull, J., Edwards, J. L., Rogers, M. S., & Swords, M. E. (1998). *The Pleasant View experience.* Golden, CO: Jefferson County Schools.

International Reading Association. (2004). *The role and qualifications of the reading coach in the United States.* Newark, DE: Author.

Isaacs, W. (1999). *Dialogue and the art of thinking together.* New York: Doubleday.

Joyce, B., & Showers, B. (1982). The coaching of teaching. *Educational Leadership, 40,* 4–10.

Knight, J. (1998). *The effectiveness of partnership learning: A dialogical methodology for staff development.* Lawrence: University of Kansas Center for Research on Learning.

Knight, J. (2007). *Instructional coaching: A partnership approach to improving instruction.* Thousand Oaks, CA: Corwin Press.

Krpan, M. M. (1997). Cognitive coaching and efficacy, growth, and change for second-, third-, and fourth-year elementary school educators. *Dissertation Abstracts International, 35*(4), 93. (University Microfilms No. 1384152)

Lewis, K., McCloskey, W., Anderson, K., Bowling, T., Dufford-Melendez, K., & Wynn, L. (2007). *Evidence-based decision-making: Assessing reading across the curriculum interventions* (Issues & Answers Report, REL 2007-No. 003). Washington, DC: U.S. Department of Education, Institute of Education Sciences, National Center for Education Evaluation and Regional Assistance, Regional Educational Laboratory Southeast.

Mackie, D. J. (1998). Collegial observation: An alternative teacher evaluation strategy using cognitive coaching to promote professional growth and development. *Dissertation Abstracts International, 59*(3), 678. (University Microfilms No. 9826689)

Moche, R. (1999). Cognitive coaching and reflective thinking of Jewish day school teachers. *Dissertation Abstracts International, 60*(2), 300. (University Microfilms No. 9919383)

Moche, R. (2000/2001). Coaching teachers' thinking. *Journal of Jewish Education, 66,* 20–29.

Poglinco, S. M., Bach, A. J., Hovde, K., Rosenblum, S., Saunders, M., & Supovitz, J. A. (2003). *The heart of the matter: The coaching model in America's Choice Schools.* Philadelphia: University of Pennsylvania, Consortium for Policy Research in Education.

Prochaska, J. O., Norcross, J. C., & DiClemente, C. C. (1994). *Changing for good.* New York: Avon Books.

Rennick, L. W. (2002). The relationship between staff development in balanced literacy instruction for kindergarten teachers and student literacy achievement. *Dissertation Abstracts International, 63*(5), 1769. (University Microfilms No. 3051831)

Rich, Y., Lev, S., & Fisher, S. (1996). Extending the concept and assessment of teacher efficacy. *Educational and Psychological Measurement, 56,* 1015–1025.

Rosenholtz, S. J. (1991). *Teacher's workplace: The social organization of schools.* New York: Teachers College Press.

Saklofske, D., Michayluk, J., & Randhawa, B. (1988). Teachers' efficacy and teaching behaviors. *Psychological Reports, 63,* 407–414.

Sanders, W. L., & Rivers, J. C. (1996). *Cumulative and residual effects of teachers on future student academic achievement.* Knoxville: University of Tennessee.

Scott, W. R. (2002). *Organizations: Rational, natural and open systems* (5th ed.). Upper Saddle River, NJ: Prentice Hall.

Senge, P. M. (1990). *The fifth discipline: The art and practice of the learning organization.* London: Random House.

Shaughnessy, M. F. (2008). *Interview with Reid Lyon: Reading First is the largest concerted reading intervention program in the history of the civilized world.* Retrieved May 8, 2008, from http://ednews.org/articles/25335/1/Interview-with-Reid-Lyon-Reading-First-is-the-largest-concerted-reading-intervention-program-in-the-history-of-the-civilized-world/Page1.html

Showers, B. (1982). *Transfer of training: The contribution of coaching.* Eugene, OR: Centre for Educational Policy and Management.

Showers, B. (1983, April). *Transfer of training.* Paper presented at the annual meeting of the American Education Research Association, Montreal, Canada.

Showers, B. (1984). *Peer coaching: A strategy for facilitating transfer of training.* Eugene, OR: Centre for Educational Policy and Management.

Showers, B., Joyce, B., & Bennett, B. (1987). Synthesis of research on staff development: A framework for future study and a state of the art analysis. *Educational Leadership, 45,* 77–87.

Simmons, J. M., Sparks, G. M., Starko, A., Pasch, M., & Colton, A. (1989). *Pedagogical language acquisition and conceptual development taxonomy of teacher reflective thought: Interview and questions format.* Ypsilanti, MI: Collaboration for the Improvement of Teacher Education, Eastern Michigan University.

Slinger, J. L. (2004). Cognitive coaching: Impact on student and influence on teachers. *Dissertation Abstracts International, 65*(7), 2567. (University Microfilms No. 3138974)

Smith, M. C. (1997). Self-reflection as a means of increasing teacher efficacy through cognitive coaching. *Dissertation Abstracts International, 35*(4), 935. (University Microfilms No. 1384304)

Soodak, L. C., & Podell, D. M. (1993). Teacher efficacy and student problem as factors in special education referral. *Journal of Special Education, 27,* 66–81.

Stone, D., Patton, P. M., & Heen, S. (1999). *Difficult conversations.* New York: Penguin-Putnam.

The Learning Network. (2006). *Data sheet: The Learning Network in Battle Creek, Michigan.* Katonah, NY: Richard C. Owen Publishers.

Truesdale, W. T. (2003). The implementation of peer coaching on the transferability of staff development to classroom practice in two selected Chicago public elementary schools. *Dissertation Abstracts International, 64*(11), 3923. (University Microfilms No. 3112185)

Wenglinsky, H. (2000). *How teaching matters: Bringing the classroom back into discussions of teacher quality.* Princeton, NJ: Policy Information Center.

Woolfolk, A. E., & Hoy, W. K. (1990). Prospective teachers' sense of efficacy and beliefs about control. *Journal of Educational Psychology, 82,* 81–91.

Index

CORWIN PRESS

The Corwin Press logo—a raven striding across an open book—represents the union of courage and learning. Corwin Press is committed to improving education for all learners by publishing books and other professional development resources for those serving the field of PreK–12 education. By providing practical, hands-on materials, Corwin Press continues to carry out the promise of its motto: **"Helping Educators Do Their Work Better."**